Andrew Geddes 1783–1844

SPONSORED BY

D0884894

HELEN SMAILES

with contributions from Peter Black
and Lesley A. Stevenson

ANDREW
GEDDES
1783–1844

PAINTER-PRINTMAKER

'A MAN
OF PURE
TASTE'

National Gallery of Scotland
EDINBURGH · MMI

Published by the Trustees
of the National Galleries of Scotland for the exhibition
Andrew Geddes 1783–1844 · Painter-printmaker · 'A Man of Pure Taste'
held at the National Gallery of Scotland, Edinburgh
from 15 February to 29 April 2001

© The Trustees of the National Galleries of Scotland 2001
ISBN 1 903278 16 3

Designed and typeset in Miller by Dalrymple
Printed by BAS Printers
Over Wallop

Front cover:
Andrew Geddes *Self-portrait*
[Scottish National Portrait Gallery]

Back cover:
Andrew Geddes *Agnes Geddes, The Artist's Mother*
[National Gallery of Scotland]

Contents

Foreword

In 1821 Sir David Wilkie's closest artist friend and protégé, Andrew Geddes, held his one and only promotional retrospective exhibition in his native Edinburgh. The occasion was the launch of Geddes's most ambitious history painting, *The Discovery of the Regalia of Scotland*, which had been carefully timed to coincide with the year of the coronation of George IV, the former Prince Regent. Remarkably, there has been no second exhibition devoted exclusively to Geddes, one of the most versatile and underrated Scottish artists of the first half of the nineteenth century. The rich holdings of Geddes's work in the permanent collections of the National Galleries of Scotland, which encompass his achievements as a figure painter and as a pioneer original etcher, have provided the essential catalyst for and the nucleus of the present exhibition. The exhibition and its companion publication will also afford the first opportunity to re-assess Geddes's relative importance as one of the most elusive and neglected dealer-collectors of Northern European Old Master paintings, prints and drawings. This connoisseurship was to earn him both the respect and the friendship of Sir Thomas Lawrence, the greatest artist collector of Old Master drawings of his time, and the epithet 'A Man of Pure Taste', awarded posthumously to Geddes by the history painter, Benjamin Robert Haydon. We are indebted to all our lenders, both private and institutional, for enabling us to represent selectively the full range of Geddes's achievements as painter, printmaker and collector.

The exhibition has been conceived, organised and researched by Helen Smailes, Curator of British Art at the National Gallery of Scotland. Throughout the final stages of preparation, she has worked very closely with Lesley Stevenson of the Conservation Department of the National Galleries of Scotland. Their joint contribution is to be welcomed as a substantial long-term investment in the Galleries' permanent collections. We are delighted to welcome as an external contributor to this collaborative project Peter Black, Curator of the Hunterian Art Gallery, University of Glasgow, and one of the few museum-based specialists in the history of printmaking now resident in Scotland. The collective research of our exhibition team could not have been published in the present form without the financial support of The Paul Mellon Centre for Studies in British Art. We are indebted to Dr Brian Allen, Director of Studies at the Centre, for facilitating this support and for his personal encouragement offered to the exhibition curator. In addition, we should like to acknowledge the generous donation volunteered by a private benefactor whose ancestor was directly associated with the family of Andrew Geddes.

Lastly, we are privileged to be associated once again with Baillie Gifford, the prestigious Edinburgh-based investment managers, who have sponsored *Andrew Geddes*. We hope that Baillie Gifford's confidence will be justified by the reception of this pioneering exhibition and will inspire the company to co-operate again with us in the future.

TIMOTHY CLIFFORD
Director-General, National Galleries of Scotland

MICHAEL CLARKE
Director, National Gallery of Scotland

Sponsor's Preface

Baillie Gifford is one of the largest investment management firms in the UK and although it has offices in London and the USA, its principal office remains firmly in Edinburgh.

It has always felt a strong commitment towards the city of Edinburgh and its activities and is a committed sponsor of the Edinburgh International Festival, Scottish Opera and the Scottish Chamber Orchestra. It has also, for a number of years, worked closely with the National Galleries of Scotland and has supported a number of recent exhibitions including *Turner and Sir Walter Scott, The Provincial Antiquities of Scotland, David Livingstone and the Victorian Encounter with Africa* and *The Winter Queen*.

Baillie Gifford is particularly pleased to be associated with the exhibition *Andrew Geddes (1783–1844) Painter-Printmaker 'A Man of Pure Taste'*, displaying as it does some wonderful portraits, etchings and Geddes's small collection of works by other important artists such as Van Dyck and Frans Hals.

BRIAN MALCOLM
Partner, Baillie Gifford

Acknowledgements

Any special exhibition is essentially the product of collaborative research, enterprise, and creativity. In the case of an artist as neglected as Andrew Geddes, this is especially true. Over the last two years, many people have provided invaluable assistance with the development of the exhibition project and the companion publication. For their personal as well as academic support, I am extremely grateful to my co-authors, Peter Black of the Hunterian Art Gallery in Glasgow and Lesley Stevenson of the Conservation Department of the National Galleries of Scotland. Among others who have shared their own research unconditionally or volunteered academic advice we are particularly indebted to Selby Whittingham, author of the revised entry on Geddes for the forthcoming *New Dictionary of National Biography*, Hamish Miles, Martin Hopkinson and David Alexander. Siobhan Watts, Conservation Scientist of the Conservation Centre, National Museums and Galleries on Merseyside, and Suzanne Lomax, Conservation Scientist at the National Gallery of Art, Washington DC, undertook technical analysis on behalf of, and in collaboration with, Lesley Stevenson. For the substantiation of the exhibition itself our greatest debt is to the generosity of our many private and institutional lenders. The collective contribution of the curatorial and administrative staff of the Department of Prints and Drawings at the British Museum has been outstanding and we extend our warmest thanks to Lucy Dixon, Antony Griffiths, Joanna Laurie, Sheila O'Connell, Janice Reading, Angela Roche and Kim Sloan.

We should also like to thank the following who have helped towards the preparation of the exhibition and the publication in numerous ways: Brian Allen, The Paul Mellon Centre for Studies in British Art, London; Elizabeth Binny; Jamie Hunter Blair; Melanie Blake, Witt Photo Survey, Courtauld Institute of Art, London; Patrick Bourne, Bourne Fine Art, Edinburgh; Xanthe Brooke, Nicola Christie, Alex Kidson and Julian Treuherz, National Museums and Galleries on Merseyside; Iain Gordon Brown, Ian Maciver, Brian Hillyard, Graham Hogg and Murray Simpson, National Library of Scotland, Edinburgh; Robert Brown, Hugh Hagan and Alison Rosie, National Archives of Scotland, Edinburgh; Michael Campbell, Campbell Fine Art, Tunbridge Wells; Mungo Campbell and Anne Dulau, Hunterian Art Gallery, University of Glasgow; Christopher Clarke; Timothy Clifford, Director-General, National Galleries of Scotland, Edinburgh; Jenny Cooksey, Leeds University Library; Susan Corrigall and John McClintock, National Register of Archives of Scotland, Edinburgh; Pat Crichton, Archivist, Hopetoun House, South Queensferry; Duncan Davidson; the late Principessa Orietta Doria Pamphilj Landi and Principe Jonathan Doria; Jeff Dunn, Mark O'Neill and Jean Walsh, Glasgow Museums; Eric Forster; J.R.C. Foster, Alastair Masson and Marianne Smith, The Royal College of Surgeons of Edinburgh; Burton Fredericksen, Getty Provenance Index; Pam Gilchrist, former Librarian, New College, University of Edinburgh; Estelle Gittins and Jeremy Rex-Parkes, Christie's Archives, London; Tony and Susan Gray; John Greenacombe, Survey of London and Jean Irving, National Monuments Record, London; Martin Greenwood; The Earl of Haddington; Robin Hamlyn, Chloë Johnson and Anne Lyles, Tate Britain, London; Malcolm Hay, Parliamentary Works Directorate, London; Gillian and Richard Holliday; Lord and Lady Irvine of Lairg; David Jaffé and Axel Rüger, National Gallery, London; Andrea Kusel,

Paisley Museum and Art Galleries; David Landau, *Print Quarterly*, London; Lowell Libson and Anthony Spink, Spink-Leger, London; Walter Liedtke, The Metropolitan Museum of Art, New York; Camilla and Corbett Macadam; Jack Mackenzie, AIC Photographic Services, Edinburgh; Nicholas Mackenzie; Duncan Macmillan, University of Edinburgh; Dallas Mechan, Kirkcaldy Museum and Art Gallery; Jennifer Melville and Lisa O'Connor, Aberdeen Art Gallery; Jacky Miller, Paxton House, Berwick-upon-Tweed; Lizzie and James Montgomery; Tim Moreton, National Portrait Gallery, London; Jane Munro, Fitzwilliam Museum, Cambridge; Andrew Norman and J.R. Webster, Belvoir Castle, Grantham; Richard Ovenden and the staff of the Department of Special Collections, Edinburgh University Library; Harry S. Parker, M.H. de Young Memorial Museum, San Francisco; Andrew McIntosh Patrick, The Fine Art Society plc, London; Revd J.W. Paul, St James's Garlickhythe, London; Dottoressa Paola Pavan and the staff of the Biblioteca Romana dell'Archivio sto Capitolino, Rome; Major Paul Payne; Annette Peach, *New Dictionary of National Biography*, Oxford; Mark Pomeroy, Nick Savage,Angela Summerfield and Helen Valentine, Royal Academy of Arts, London; Estelle Quick, Tain Through Time; John Raymond, University of Edinburgh; Antonia Reeve; Alan and Ellen Reid; Nevile Reid; Robert-Jan te Rijdt, Rijksmuseum, Amsterdam; Robin Rodger, Perth Museum & Art Gallery; Peregrine Sabin, Sabin Galleries Ltd, London; Alison Saynor; Charles Sebag-Montefiore; Daniel Shackleton; Janet Skidmore and the staff of the Registrar's Department, Victoria and Albert Museum, London; Richard Smith; Joanna Soden, Royal Scottish Academy, Edinburgh; Bridget Spurgin; Dianne Stein, Corporate Arts Planning, Edinburgh; John Stuart; Christopher and Ann Thompson; Hildegaard van de Velde, Stichting Nicolaas Rockox, Antwerp; Malcolm Warner and Scott Wilcox, Yale Center for British Art; Arthur Wheelock, National Gallery of Art, Washington DC; Hilary Williamson, Fine Art Library, and the staff of the Edinburgh Room, Edinburgh Libraries and Information Services; Arnott Wilson, University of Edinburgh; Andrew Wishart; Martha Wolff, The Art Institute of Chicago, Chicago; Mrs Mark Wrey.

I am grateful to my colleagues in the National Galleries of Scotland who have made vital contributions, in particular Suzanne Trevethan for her impeccable typing and her unfailing kindness and moral support.

Finally, a personal tribute is offered to those without whose commitment neither the exhibition nor the publication would have been realised: Chris Blagdon, Jake Chazan, Dr Garth Dyson and Dr Kathryn Sutherland; George and Helen Outram, who provided emergency living accomodation at a critical juncture, and those close friends and relatives who sustained me throughout my involuntary exile while writing.

HELEN SMAILES
Curator of British Art, National Gallery of Scotland

Lenders to the Exhibition

British Museum, London

Fine Art Library, Edinburgh City Libraries and Information Services

Glasgow Museums, Art Gallery and Museum, Kelvingrove

National Archives of Scotland, Edinburgh

National Gallery, London

National Gallery of Scotland, Edinburgh

National Library of Scotland, Edinburgh

National Museums and Galleries on Merseyside, Walker Art Gallery

Perth Museum & Art Gallery

Royal College of Surgeons of Edinburgh

Royal Scottish Academy, Edinburgh

Scottish National Portrait Gallery, Edinburgh

Society of Antiquaries of Scotland, Edinburgh

The Duke of Sutherland

Victoria and Albert Museum, London

*and other lenders who wish to
remain anonymous*

CHAPTER ONE

Edinburgh 1783–1803: Rembrandt and the Excise

In October 1793 David Geddes, Deputy-Auditor to the Scottish Board of Excise, completed the catalogue of his art collection and his private library which he had begun to form in Edinburgh over thirty years previously. This catalogue, compiled with the same rigorous attention to detail which characterised all of his records of domestic expenditure, listed title by title the contents of his library, his paintings, and his prints, both individual framed impressions, bound volumes and portfolios, all with their current market valuations and, when of special significance, their provenance. The concluding entry in the itemised bound volumes of prints was 'Temple of the Muses a most Splendid Copy a present to Andrew from Mr. Thomas Philipe, Folio', valued at £3.3s. David Geddes himself had been engaged in regular transactions with the London print and picture dealer and auctioneer since the late 1770s, if not considerably earlier. This important business relationship had developed into a friendship which the dealer extended to his client's only son, Andrew, born in 1783. Philipe's gift was, even by contemporary standards, an esoteric choice for a ten-year-old (or conceivably even younger) boy. The *Temple des Muses* was a seventeenth-century anthology of classical mythology, first published in 1665 and reprinted in a folio edition in Paris in 1768 and illustrated with engravings after Abraham van Diepenbeeck or Pierre Brébiette.[1] Philipe had recognised in the younger Geddes the makings of a connoisseur collector and the particular aptitude of the creative artist who, in 1844, would earn from his fellow painter Benjamin Robert Haydon (1786–1846), the epithet of 'A Man of pure Taste'.

Andrew Geddes was the second child of the second marriage of the Deputy-Auditor of Excise whose origins,

beyond the 1760s, have remained obscure. The elder Geddes's employment in the Scottish Excise is thought to have dated from 1763 when he was allegedly appointed clerk in the Auditor's office in Edinburgh. A decade later he was still employed in this capacity as one of three clerks to the Auditor and at an annual salary of £100. His colleagues at this time included two fellow collectors, John Caw (died 1784), Deputy Secretary, and John McGowan or McGouan (died 1803), Assistant to the Deputy Solicitor.[2] On 16 February 1766 David Geddes contracted his first marriage to Anne Proven or Provand (born 1736), younger daughter of the Revd Patrick Provand (died 1755), the Presbyterian Minister of Trinity Gask, a Strathearn parish of Perthshire. Of the three children of this marriage, Mary (born 1767), George (born 1768) and David (born 1770), only the daughter appears to have survived beyond infancy, both of the boys having succumbed to 'chin cough' in 1770. Anne Provand herself probably died by 1778 when her husband noted in his ledger of domestic expenditure or *Book of Disbursements* a payment to a Mrs Provand 'for family' – either in reference to a charitable donation, repeated in 1779, or more plausibly, to the temporary engagement as housekeeper of his sister-in-law whose husband sailed for Jamaica in November 1778.[3]

In 1778 Geddes was promoted to Deputy-Auditor, a position which he was to hold continuously until his death in 1803. From 1780 his connections with the Excise were strengthened by his second marriage on 3 January to Agnes Boyd (died 1828), daughter of 'the deceased James Boyd late Custom House Officer at Kirkcudbright' [fig.1].[4] Five children were born in rapid succession: Charlotte (1781–1806), Andrew (1783–1844), Anne (1785–1843), Katherine

(1787–1843), later Mrs Robert Paul, and Grizzel or Grace (1790–1855). David Geddes's second family was completed in 1799 by the birth of Margaret (died 1884), who married Alexander Scott in 1828 and whose descendants were later to inherit much of the Geddes family memorabilia.[5] In 1782, presumably in anticipation of the ensuing expansion of his household, Geddes moved from Niddry's Wynd in the Cowgate to St Patrick's Street in Crosscauseway. Finally, over the summer of 1788, he relocated again to the newly built tenement on the south side of Buccleuch Place, the grandest street on the South Side of Edinburgh, laid out as a continuation of the development of George Square, which he was to occupy until his death in 1803.[6]

Andrew Geddes's formal education was evidently in progress by 1789 when his father meticulously recorded a payment for school fees and coals in his *Book of Disbursements*.[7] At the age of eight or nine he was despatched to the celebrated Royal High School then located in Infirmary Street and where, as the artist's widow was to testify in her published *Memoir* of 1844, 'at that time any boy of any respectability, as well as many of the sons of the aristocracy, were educated.' A reluctant classical scholar under the tutelage of the Rector, Alexander Adam, young Geddes 'was a great favourite with his masters, notwithstanding the striking likenesses, or rather caricatures, he drew of them

on the margin of his books.' This aptitude was not only discouraged but actively and consistently frustrated by David Geddes who refused to countenance any form of instruction conducive to a precarious professional career as a painter. Some concessions and a measure of tolerance were, however, extended to the younger Geddes's related childhood fascination with the collecting of prints.

The aspiring artist's first independent purchases of prints, generally inferior impressions of engravings after Reynolds, were effected with the collaboration or connivance of William 'Bibles' Martin (1744–1820), antiquarian bookseller, print and picture dealer, and auctioneer.[8] The former shoemaker from Airdrie had occupied since 1774 a small shop in the High Street of Edinburgh near the head of the West Bow where he plied his original trade in conjunction with bookselling. As his alternative business prospered, shoemaking was abandoned in favour of dealing. By the year of Geddes's birth, Martin was already operating as a specialist print auctioneer at a variety of hired venues in the Old Town before he established his own saleroom in Old Bank Close off the Lawnmarket in or about 1789 and gradually diversified his stock-in-trade to encompass oil paintings [fig.2].[9] Late in life, in 1813, Martin was prevailed upon by the Edinburgh publisher Archibald Constable, himself an influential patron of Andrew Geddes, to sit for

Fig.1 · Andrew Geddes
*Agnes Geddes, The Artist's
Mother*, 1812
[Scottish Private Collection]

Fig.2 · John Kay
William Martin Auctioneering
from *A Series of Original Portraits*, 1837
[Scottish National Portrait Gallery]

exactly twenty minutes for a portrait sketch which Geddes reproduced as an etching, probably during the initial phase of his experimentation with the print medium.[10]

The commissioning of this portrait drawing commemorated Martin's longstanding business connections with both father and son. In his dual capacity as book and print dealer Martin had been one of the principal contributors to the development of David Geddes's private library and print collection, as confirmed by the annual record of their transactions in the *Book of Disbursements* from 1785. Geddes's other favoured agent was Thomas Philipe, the only London business contact whose every change of commercial address was logged by his client, accompanied by an annual chronicle of purchases of books and prints from 1779 to 1790 in the same ledger. By 1791, when he discussed with Geddes his requirement for a compilation of etched portraits by Wenceslaus Hollar, Philipe was clearly engaged in speculative collaboration with William Martin – an important extension of the London-Scottish print trade which undoubtedly benefited David Geddes and probably his son too.[11] The results of this collective enterprise and of forty years' accumulated and discerning connoisseurship – which, in turn, laid the foundations of Andrew Geddes's own connoisseurship of Old Master prints and prepared the ground for his experimentation from 1812 with 'original' etching – were to become fully manifest in 1804 when the artist entrusted the six-day posthumous sale of his father's choice collection of prints to Thomas Philipe.

The elder Geddes's print collection was predominantly, although by no means exclusively, Northern European in emphasis. The second day's sale on 1 May 1804, dedicated to the Flemish School, exemplified by Jordaens, Van Dyck and Rubens, was the prelude to the disposal on 2 May of eighty-four lots of Rembrandt etchings, many of these being India proofs or first impressions. Among the bound volumes dispersed on the concluding day, the rarest item was lot 116, 'A volume in Turkey, containing a capital work of Adam Aelsheimer, his portrait by Hollar; a work of Count Goudt, complete, extra fine.' In his maturity and, most probably after the death of his father and the disposal of his father's collections, Andrew Geddes was to regard as his own supreme mentors Rubens, Van Dyck and Rembrandt, the latter two as painter-etchers, conjoined with Titian in an artistic equivalent of the Holy Trinity. He

was likewise to follow the unusual precedent established by his father in according a special place to the work of Elsheimer in his own private collection.[12]

From the 1750s Rembrandt's etchings and drypoints were avidly collected south of the Border to the extent that, by 1778, 'It was a Madness to have his Prints, the prints of no Master have been more eagerly desired or purchased at greater prices.' Rembrandt mania was fuelled by connoisseurship and not by pedagogical ideals, virtuoso collectors vying with each other in pursuit of rare impressions prized as independent works of art. On a more modest scale and with limited means at his disposal, David Geddes was self-evidently one of a fraternity of middle-class Edinburgh devotees of Rembrandt's etchings about whom, as yet, relatively little is known, but whose collections were actually or potentially at his young son's disposal.[13] Among these other acolytes was Geddes's colleague from the Excise Office, the lawyer John McGowan or McGouan (died 1803), a friend of Prince Charles Edward Stewart's secretary Andrew Lumisden and a friend and patron of Lumisden's brother-in-law, the outstanding Scottish Old Master engraver Robert Strange. Such was the priority given to Rembrandt in McGowan's 'great Collection of Prints and etchings of all the Masters' that David Wilkie would later claim from personal recollection that, 'Johnny M'Gowan has given the artists of Edinburgh a bias, in their treatment of subjects, that will not easily be eradicated.'[14]

In February 1790, another maverick member of this circle, the Honble Andrew Erskine (died 1793), youngest son of the musical 5th Earl of Kellie, pawned to David Geddes a magnificent calf-bound copy of the so-called 'Luxembourg Gallery'. This volume of engravings, which was never redeemed, passed through Geddes's posthumous sale in 1804. In 1814, following the abdication of Napoleon I, Andrew Geddes, who also owned a copy of the same compilation published in 1710, visited Paris where he would have been able to view at close quarters Rubens's epic cycle of narrative paintings in honour of Marie de' Medici, known to him, vicariously, since childhood through the pawned volume of first impressions of the related engravings. As a print collector in his own right, Erskine was of sufficient calibre to be nominated specialist Scottish advisor for the ten-day London auction in 1796 of the collections formed by Colin Macfarquhar (*c*.1745–1793), the outstanding Rembrandt collector of David Geddes's acquaintance and his near neighbour in Buccleuch Place.

Macfarquhar had founded jointly with the Edinburgh engraver Andrew Bell the *Encyclopaedia Britannica*, of which the first edition had appeared between 1768 and 1771 in response to the perceived shortcomings of the *Encyclopédie* of Diderot and D'Alembert. The profits accruing from this hugely influential publishing venture enabled Macfarquhar to amass a collection of Rembrandt's etchings which, in local terms, was unrivalled and which, as packing-case after packing-case arrived from London, was eagerly inspected by the young Andrew Geddes 'before he was tall enough to reach the table'. In his will, of which David Geddes was appointed a co-executor, Macfarquhar specified a London venue for his posthumous sale, 'which would not probable [sic] turn out to proper Account ... in Edinr.' Philipe and Martin acted as London and Edinburgh agents for the sale under the jurisdiction of the auctioneer Mr King of Covent Garden. The core of the print collection was uncompromisingly Northern European – Rembrandt, Rubens, Lievens, Hollar, Van Dyck (including the *Iconography*), Cornelius Visscher, Berchem, Wouwermans, a complete edition of the work of Ostade and 'the Work of Adam Elsheimer, by Count Goudt', conceivably the copy in David Geddes's ownership in 1803.[15]

In the year of the Macfarquhar sale, Andrew Geddes was obliged to matriculate as a student of Classics at the University of Edinburgh where, during his inaugural academic session, he coincided with the fourteen-year-old James Wardrop (1782–1869), later a distinguished ophthalmic surgeon and patron of Geddes and who claimed to have studied with the artist as a pupil of John Graham at the Trustees' Academy in Edinburgh. After approximately two years, Geddes left the University without graduating, having acceded, out of his 'very great veneration' for his father, to the latter's pre-emptive decision to place him with the Excise without further consultation.[16] In the absence of Macfarquhar, a sustained and sustaining counter-influence

to the exigencies of the Excise Office was provided by another notable Scottish collector of Rembrandt prints, John Clerk, Lord Eldin (1757–1832), who refused to comply with the elder Geddes's request to desist from encouraging his son's artistic aspirations.

John Clerk – styled Lord Eldin from 1823 on his appointment as a senator of the College of Justice – was the eldest son of John Clerk of Eldin (1728–1812), amateur geologist, topographical draughtsman, writer on naval tactics and younger brother of Sir George Clerk of Penicuik. Himself a zealous collector of Rembrandt etchings, John Clerk senior had profited from their close study in the production of his own amateur etchings of which sets were marketed in London by Thomas Philipe.[17] Clerk's son, who rose to become one of the most successful advocates in Scotland, earned Sandby's praise for his draughtsmanship and was above all a passionate collector whose distinguished collection of Dutch and Flemish paintings would justify his selection as a founder-director of the Institution for the Encouragement of the Fine Arts in Scotland in 1819. On his death, unmarried, in 1832, his collections were sold at auction over a period of twenty-four days in January and March 1833. The fourth day of this sale was entirely given over to Eldin's collection of Rembrandt etchings which reflected his guiding principles of comprehensiveness and quality. These etchings were complemented by his Rembrandt drawings, accounting for thirty-eight lots on the eighth day of the sale. From this collection, the twelve-year-old Andrew Geddes had regularly been lent drawings to copy – a remarkable expression of trust and commitment to which he later paid tribute in a small cabinet portrait of his patron [fig.3], and perhaps also through the presentation of India proof impressions of his own etchings.[18]

Fig.3 · Andrew Geddes
John Clerk, Lord Eldin
[Scottish National Portrait Gallery, Edinburgh]

Fig.4
Andrew Geddes
Alexander Nasmyth
c.1820–5
[Royal Scottish Academy,
Edinburgh]

CHAPTER TWO

The Order of Release, 1803: The Trustees' Academy, Alexander Nasmyth's Academy and the Royal Academy Schools

The death of David Geddes on 15 March 1803 delivered the long-awaited order of release. By June, his twenty-year-old son, sole heir to the property in Buccleuch Place occupied by the Geddes family since 1788,[19] was engaged in close consultation with Thomas Philipe who offered judicious support for the younger Geddes's resolve to embark definitively on an alternative career as a professional painter. In an extended letter of 20 June 1803, Philipe counselled his protégé that, although

> *your prospects in the Excise Office are not cheering ...*
> *I much commend your prudence in continuing in the*
> *Office in your present Station; until you can better*
> *yourself with Certainty. Your Duty is not laborious,*
> *and you will have plenty of time to improve yourself in*
> *the profession in which your friends encourage you to*
> *look forward to for support and Independence ... I need*
> *not tell you that portrait is the most profitable Branch*
> *of the Art, provided a good Likeness is given – to excell,*
> *however, even in a Head, much patience and observa-*
> *tion is requisite.*

In the course of that year Geddes had apparently secured a junior clerkship and in 1804 was to receive a modest promotion to second clerk to the new Auditor, James McDowall. The sale of David Geddes's collections having already been instigated – occasioned, no doubt, by a combination of financial exigency and the anticipated need to underwrite, at least partially, a more formalised course of artistic instruction – Philipe was invited to estimate the market potential of the prints.[20] Following the precedent of Colin Macfarquhar, who had specified a London venue for the auction of his own choice collections, Andrew Geddes employed Philipe as the agent for the six-day auction

from 30 April to 5 May 1804. For the modest sale of the complementary collection of Dutch, Flemish and Scottish paintings on 24 February 1804, Geddes resorted, very revealingly, to a local venue and to his late father's long-established business associate and his own early mentor, William Martin.[21]

Geddes followed Philipe's cautionary advice until 1805. On 2 April, John Clerk wrote from London to Messrs Thomson & Pearson of the Edinburgh Excise Office as trustees for David Geddes's family, endorsing Andrew's imminent resignation and departure for London 'in order to improve himself in the art, as well as to procure greater Eclat to his professional name as having studied here ... I have some considerable time past regretted that he remained in the Excise Office instead of devoting his whole time to the profession on which he ultimately relies for his success in life.' Geddes set his sights upon the Royal Academy Schools, a strategy which was neither wholly predictable nor readily reconcilable with his supposed status as a self-taught artist since demonstrable proficiency in figure drawing was a pre-requisite of admission.[22] Years later the expatriate London-based Scottish ophthalmic surgeon James Wardrop (1782–1869), an almost exact contemporary of Geddes as a student of classics at Edinburgh University and, in his maturity, both a connoisseur-collector and a patron of the artist, recalled in an unpublished memoir that, while serving an apprenticeship with his uncle the Edinburgh surgeon Andrew Wardrop, 'I had excellent lessons in drawing from Graham the teacher of Wilkie, Burnet, Fraser & Geddes all well known Artists about this period.'[23] Wardrop's otherwise unprecedented assertion concerning Geddes cannot be substantiated from any of the extant records of the Trustees' Academy during the critical period of its reorganisation under the Mastership of John Graham (1798–1817) and, being retrospective, may have been insecurely based on personal knowledge. Indirectly, however, Wardrop's problematic testimony serves to elucidate Geddes's decision to bypass the Trustees' Academy and also to strengthen the credibility of another tradition linking him with the portrait and landscape painter, Alexander Nasmyth (1758–1840).

In 1805, when Geddes finalised his resignation from the Excise Office, the Trustees' Academy still comprised the only structured training facility for the intending professional artist in Edinburgh and the principal alternative or complement to studio-based instruction with an established practitioner. This was despite the cramped accommodation allocated to the Academy in David Martin's former studio in St James's Square and, from 1806, in a tenement garret in Picardy Place. Peripatetic drawing masters and private academies, such as those managed by Nasmyth at the custom-built studio-cum-residence at 47 York Place which he occupied from 1799 or by George Walker at Hunter's Square from (or by) 1804, catered primarily, although by no means exclusively, for the relatively affluent (and predominantly female) amateur.[24]

A pioneering venture which preceded the institution of the Royal Academy in London and its attendant Schools by some eight years, the Trustees' Academy was the first publicly subsidised art school in Britain. It owed its inauguration in 1760 to the Board of Trustees for the Improvement of Fisheries and Manufactures in Scotland, a quango constituted in 1727 following the Act of Union of 1707 and invested with limited devolved responsibilities towards the compensatory promotion of the woollen and linen manufactures and fisheries as the staple industries of Scotland. The ostensible aims of the Board's school in its earliest phase were strictly utilitarian and confined to the improvement of applied design, and the curriculum was correspondingly elementary, excluding both life drawing and painting in oils. Most of the Academy's students were apprentice tradesmen – carvers, gilders, house-painters, weavers and embroiderers. Yet, in 1786, when reviewing the case for the continuation of their school, the Trustees noted with gratification that 'several *artists* of very considerable merit received the Rudiments of their education at the academy', notably the neoclassical landscape painter Jacob More, internationally acclaimed as 'More of Rome', and Alexander Nasmyth whom Wilkie was later to honour as 'the father of the landscape painting school of Scotland.' This duality of purpose was equally discernible in the pattern of appointments to the Mastership of the Academy from its inaugural years, the majority of the successful candidates being figure painters of proven reputation or even some distinction.

In 1799 the *Edinburgh Evening Courant* carried an advertisement addressed specifically to aspiring professional artists. The Trustees' reformed Academy, headed by the London-Scottish portrait painter John Graham, was to be 'furnished with copies of the finest Statues and busts from the Antique in which it is proposed, as far as may be practicable, to conduct the studies of those attending it, upon the plan of the Royal Academy in London.' The long-term importance of Graham's initiative – which, however, did not extend to life drawing – was enhanced by his two major innovations, both of which were initially resisted by the Trustees as a radical departure from their original remit. These innovations comprised the introduction of oil painting in 1802 and a complementary system of annual premiums for history painting, modelled on that of the London-based Society of Arts.[25] But for the intransigence of David Geddes, the reconstituted Trustees' Academy would have provided – and perhaps did provide since Wardrop's testimony cannot be entirely discounted – through its facility for part time attendance, the obvious recourse for his only son during his reluctant employment as a junior excise officer.[26] Apart from the apprentice surgeon James Wardrop, among the first respondents to the press campaign of 1799 were the fourteen-year-old David Wilkie (1785–1841), John Burnet (1784–1868), then apprenticed to the Edinburgh engraver Robert Scott and ultimately one of the most successful engravers of Wilkie's subject pictures, and William Allan (1782–1850), subsequently a highly influential Scottish history painter and Master of the Trustees' Academy from 1826 to 1843. Of these three, all of whom concurred in Allan's hero-worship of Graham as 'the first to give an impulse to art and to move the enthusiasm of the rising class of artists of that period,' both Wilkie and Burnet were to become associated with Geddes on terms of intimate friendship as was, to a lesser extent, Allan.

In 1805 the Academy was in a state of transition. Graham's opportunistic advocacy and attempted implementation of radical reform were compromised by his own limitations as a practising artist, by financial stringency, and by the Trustees' self-perpetuating ambivalence towards the utilitarian ideology which had justified the existence and the methodology of their drawing school since 1760. The foundation course remained essentially unchanged, comprising copying from 'the flat', that is, from engravings or from drawings by the Old Masters or by previous Masters of the Academy. This corresponded, with fewer resources and closer regulation, to the type of instruction which Geddes had already devised for himself. The projected collection of casts after the Antique, an essential prerequisite for the development of proficiency in figure drawing in the continuing absence of a life class, was as yet at an embryonic stage of development. The diaspora of the inaugural generation of Graham's ablest and most committed students began in 1805.

In 1806, echoing Clerk of Eldin's testimonial to the trustees of David Geddes, Wilkie wrote to his own father of his determination to meet the challenges and rigours of a new professional life in London: 'When I was in Scotland I considered that every thing depended on my success in London; for this is the place of encouragement for people of our profession, and if we fail here we never can be great anywhere.' Later that year he was joined by Burnet, who had been preceded in 1805 by Allan. In May 1805 Wilkie himself had moved permanently to London, bearing with him his newly completed and first major subject picture, *Pitlessie Fair* (painted in 1804, National Gallery of Scotland), as his showpiece and prospectus.[27] His immediate objective was to secure admission to the Royal Academy Schools with their superior facilities for art education and to which applicants were required to submit a finished drawing from the Antique (the elementary stage of drawing 'from the flat' was omitted, students beginning their studies in the cast gallery).[28] On 15 January 1807 Geddes's name was entered in the ledger of recent admissions to the Schools. His co-entrants included William Etty, John Seguier and Cornelius Varley and his contemporaries in

the painting school, both Wilkie and Benjamin Robert Haydon. No details of Geddes's age or the circumstances of his admission were recorded. If the usual stipulation was applied and if Wardrop's recollections were indeed unreliable, then how did Geddes qualify for admission?[29]

In her *Memoir* of 1844 Adela Geddes referred to an exploratory visit to London undertaken by her future husband during the late 1790s or early 1800s. His mentor and *cicerone* on this occasion was the expatriate miniature painter Anthony Stewart (1773–1846) from Crieff in Perthshire [fig.5], a friend of the artist's father and a friend of the artist himself in succession. Geddes was later to acknowledge this association, which extended to a collaboration in dealing, in the form of a friendship portrait or conversation piece depicting himself discussing a picture with Burnet and Stewart.[30] In 1794 when the artist-diarist Joseph Farington had been introduced to Stewart at Boydell's Shakespeare Gallery in Pall Mall, he had noted that the young miniature painter was 'bred … under

Fig.5 · Andrew Geddes
Anthony Stewart, 1812
[Scottish National Portrait Gallery, Edinburgh]

Nasmith'. Stewart, who was a decade older than Geddes, and his fellow expatriate and miniature painter, Andrew Robertson, were the precursors of a distinguished generation of professional Scottish artists who sought private instruction from Alexander Nasmyth as 'the first landscape painter in Edinburgh'. Many years later his son ventured an impressive roll-call of these 'young students' to whom his father had offered encouragement and/or formal tuition: 'Amongst these young men were David Wilkie, Francis Grant, David Roberts, Clarkson Stanfield, William Allan, Andrew Geddes, "Grecian" Williams, Lizars the engraver, and the Rev. John Thomson of Duddingston.' Geddes's connection with Nasmyth's academy, which, by inference, predated his departure for London in 1806, almost certainly facilitated his admission to the Royal Academy Schools and was to remain one of the most important formative influences on his early career as an independent artist [fig.4].[31]

By 1800 the usual duration of a studentship of the Academy Schools had increased to ten years, a prolonged commitment which Geddes, as a mature student, had presumably neither the means nor the intention of fulfilling. His contribution to the Royal Academy annual exhibitions during his inaugural year as a student, *St John in the Wilderness*, ushered in a period of experimentation encompassing both portraiture – as Philipe had advised in 1803 – and subject pictures. At the same exhibition *The Village Politicians*, painted by Wilkie for Lord Mansfield (now displayed at Scone Palace in Perthshire) drew prodigious crowds and elicited a commission from Sir George Beaumont for *The Blind Fiddler* (Tate Britain). In 1808 Wilkie's *Card Players* (Lord Denham), commissioned by the Duke of Gloucester in 1807, was also launched at the Academy and in 1809, at the exceptionally young age of twenty-four, he was elected an Associate. The spectacle of his compatriot's meteoric rise to metropolitan fame and the experience of intensive exposure to his early subject pictures evidently held a particular fascination for Geddes, although, unlike many of his Scottish and English contemporaries, he neither achieved nor apparently aspired to an independent reputation as a genre painter in the Wilkie tradition. In 1810 Geddes's unique exhibit at the Academy was *Draught Players* which, in subject matter and composition, invited comparison with *The Card Players* of 1808. Of Wilkie's other major genre paintings of this period *The Village Festival* (Tate Britain, transferred from the Angerstein collection at the National Gallery) had been commissioned by John Julius Angerstein in 1808 and was completed in time for the artist's one-man retrospective exhibition in 1812. It clearly provided the general inspiration for an unrealised subject picture by Geddes for which an elaborate compositional drawing is preserved in the Paul Mellon Collection at the Yale Center for British Art [fig.6] and which is one of a small corpus of surviving drawings indicative of a sustained private dialogue with the work of Wilkie without known manifestation in the form of finished oil paintings.[32]

Fig.6 · Andrew Geddes
Outdoor Meeting
[Paul Mellon Collection, Yale Center for British Art]

CHAPTER THREE

The Return to Edinburgh 1810–14
and the Incorporated Society of Artists

Wilkie had welcomed Burnet to London in 1806 with the declaration, 'I am glad you are come for London is the proper place for artists' – a conviction to which Geddes did not wholly subscribe. In 1810 Geddes and his sisters took possession of a two-storey apartment in the tenement at 55 York Place in the New Town of Edinburgh a few doors away from Alexander Nasmyth's residence and studio at Number 47 and within several minutes' walk of Raeburn's studio at Number 32 on the opposite side of the street. Within two years Geddes's Edinburgh studio was operational and publicly advertised as his professional address in Scotland with effect from 1811. The establishment of this alternative northern studio, opportunistically timed in anticipation of increased localised potential for patronage, was to be the most conspicuous expression of his dual London-Scottish artistic identity.[33]

In March 1810, the year following his election as an Associate of the Royal Academy, Wilkie noted in his journal that Raeburn had taken a lease of the late John Hoppner's house in London with a view to settling there permanently. On 4 June Wilkie escorted Raeburn to the Crown and Anchor to meet members of the Academy including the President Benjamin West. Two years earlier Raeburn had petitioned for sequestration following the catastrophic failure of the firm in which his son Henry and his stepson-in-law were business partners. The redemption of his own related debts had obliged Raeburn to sell the house on the north side of York Place, which he had partially redesigned to incorporate a gallery for the display of portraits and a studio equipped with a complex arrangement of shutters facilitating precision control of the flow of light into the room. Although he retained a tenancy in the property, the irony of this turn of events was considerable, Raeburn having moved to York Place in 1799 in order to accommodate his expanding business as the heir apparent to the late David Martin and at a time when Alexander Nasmyth had virtually abandoned portraiture for landscape painting. The principal outcome of Raeburn's reconnoitre visit to London was a decision not to transfer his portrait practice to the south. Yet the prospective departure of the doyen of portrait painters in Edinburgh and, effectively, in the whole of Scotland cannot have escaped the attention of Andrew Geddes.[34]

The paradox of this financial crisis as the incentive for Raeburn's abortive experiment in the southern capital was further highlighted by the fact that, in 1809, he had sublet his private gallery in York Place to the newly constituted Incorporated Society of Artists under the presidency of the portrait painter George Watson. Raeburn's motivation was ideological as well as financial. At the initial meeting of the Society – also commonly termed the Associated Artists – in April 1808, it was resolved to establish an annual 'Exhibition in Edinburgh similar to the Royal Academy'. This market-oriented palliative measure was intended to diminish the increasing exodus of Scottish painters to London by intensifying the stimulus of internal competition and improving chances of patronage in Edinburgh through the relatively autonomous structure of an academy regulated by artists for artists. Among those who responded with alacrity to the prospect of a guaranteed facility for public exhibition were the English miniature painter Nathaniel Plimer (1757–c.1822) in 1808 and, in 1809, Andrew Geddes.[35]

The Shropshire-born expatriate had arrived in London

in 1781 where he was employed as a servant to the enameller Henry Bone before joining his brother Andrew Plimer (1763–1837) – subsequently a far more prolific and successful miniature painter than Nathaniel – as a pupil of Richard Cosway. The elder Plimer exhibited at the Royal Academy from 1787 to 1812 and at the Society of Artists in 1790 and 1791 and, until very recently, was believed to have remained in London throughout his career. From 1804 to 1813/14, however, he featured in the Edinburgh street directories as a portrait or miniature painter of 1 St James's Square with a variety of nomenclatures from 'Nicol Plimer' to 'N. Plummer'. After attending the foundation meeting of the Associated Artists, Plimer participated in their opening exhibition at Core's Lyceum before quarrelling with the executive committee over its refusal to accede to his request for his share of the profits from the 1808 exhibition. In October Plimer was paid off and tendered his resignation –

the first manifestation of the factiousness in which Raeburn himself, a Committee member from 1809, was implicated and which would precipitate the untimely demise of the society in 1813.

Nathaniel's continuing presence in Edinburgh, despite the rift with the Associated Artists, was commemorated in two successive years by his future son-in-law. In private memoranda of pictures completed in Scotland in 1812, 1813 and 1814, Geddes listed 'Mr. Plimer. Small whole-length', 'Fancy Portrait of Mr. Plimer sleeping', and 'Miss Plimer ¾ size of life', the latter almost certainly being a reference to Adela Plimer (1791–1881) whom Geddes was eventually to marry in London in 1827 after a courtship reputedly begun in his twentieth year.[36] A number of tributary portraits were to follow. After taking up etching in or about 1812, Geddes executed a drypoint of Nathaniel Plimer, probably from a now unrecorded drawing, which his daughter Adela later dismissed with vehemence as 'quite a caricature … [although] no doubt Mr. Geddes was going to try some Rembrandtish effect' [fig.7]. Rembrandt – and, quite specifically and appropriately, his side-lit etched *Self-Portrait at the Window, Drawing on an Etching Plate* of 1648 – was also to be the guiding inspiration for Geddes's half-length portrait of Andrew Plimer of 1815 [fig.8], one of an important group of artists' portraits executed on Geddes's return to London and amongst his most accomplished and characteristic portraiture in oils.[37]

From 1809 to 1812 Geddes exhibited annually with the Associated Artists, being extensively represented as a portrait and landscape painter in 1809, and, again, as a portraitist in 1812. For the first three years, pending the establishment of his own Edinburgh studio, he lodged with Nasmyth who, together with his son and fellow-landscape painter Patrick, was admitted to full membership of the Associated Artists following the annual exhibition of 1809. Geddes's high-profile commitment to the Edinburgh Association during this period in preference to the Royal Acad-

Fig.7 · left · Andrew Geddes
Nathaniel Plimer
[The British Museum, London]

Fig.8 · right · Andrew Geddes
Andrew Plimer, 1815
[National Gallery of Scotland, Edinburgh]

Fig.9 · right · Alexander Nasmyth
Andrew Geddes Sketching in the Kent Countryside
[National Gallery of Scotland, Edinburgh]

Fig.10 · above · Andrew Geddes
A Storm Coming On or *The Approaching Storm*,
probably 1810
[Scottish Private Collection]

emy – with the exception of *The Draught Players* in 1810, he did not contribute again to the Academy until 1813 when he despatched four portraits from 55 York Place in Edinburgh – was rewarded in 1811 when he was proposed for election to membership. While his primary motive was undoubtedly the consolidation and development of patronage for his portraiture from a basis of relative security, he may have entertained additional expectations, as did the proponents of the scheme, of the Society's short-lived attempt in 1809 to found a life academy for the use of established as well as aspiring professional artists.[38]

Interestingly, in view of his putative training and enduring friendship with Nasmyth, Geddes chose to advertise his own secondary pursuit of landscape painting in both the 1809 and the 1810 Edinburgh exhibitions. James Nasmyth recalled how his father 'diligently impressed upon his pupils ... the felicity and the happiness attendant upon pencil drawing. He was a master of the pencil ... it was his Graphic Language.' Nasmyth senior was to illustrate his success in inculcating this love of drawing from nature in Geddes in an engagingly informal sketch of his former pupil observing the Kent countryside [fig.9]. Throughout his career Geddes indulged this shared passion through his preferred medium of black chalk heightened with white in a multiplicity of pure landscape drawings, occasionally and selectively re-interpreted as etchings or drypoints and, in their individual motifs or compositional structure, referring explicitly to the landscape etchings of Rembrandt. For his freshly handled little landscape painting of 1810 *A Storm Coming On* or *The Approaching Storm* [fig.10], he drew upon his long-standing connoisseurship of Rembrandt and Rubens and, specifically, upon his recollection of the celebrated etching of *The Three Trees* of which Geddes and his father both owned fine impressions.[39]

Geddes's strategy in returning to Edinburgh after a brief interlude at the Royal Academy Schools was to be rewarded, by his own testimony, with a bonanza of portrait commissions. Many were executed as small full-lengths, either on mahogany panel or on canvas in the cabinet format which he refined to a specialism and which, despite his apparent lack of aptitude for consistent self-promotion as an original artist and his critically detrimental predilection for Old Master 'pasticcio compositions', were to earn him occasional public plaudits as the latter-day equivalent of Netscher and Metsu. Geddes's aspirations towards local pre-eminence in his native Edinburgh found their most focused expression through his self-presentation in Van Dyckian dress – or, more probably, in the persona of Van Dyck – in a small cabinet portrait commissioned by the 11th Earl of Buchan in 1812 [fig.11] and exactly contemporary with Geddes's half-length portrait of the Earl himself. This self-portrait was undoubtedly dedicatory, as well as self-promotional, in intention, since Geddes shared Reynolds's and Wilkie's estimation of the supremacy of Van Dyck in British portraiture, strengthened by a personal empathy with the painter-etcher of the *Iconography*, his compilation of etched portraits. From the late 1780s Buchan, founder of the Society of Antiquaries of Scotland and a self-appointed cultural plenipotentiary for Enlightenment Scotland, assembled a dynastic-cum-national portrait gallery in his

Fig.11 · Andrew Geddes
Self-portrait in Van Dyck Dress, 1812
[The Society of Antiquaries of Scotland on loan to the
Scottish National Portrait Gallery, Edinburgh]

Fig.12 · left · Andrew Geddes
Archibald Constable, 1813
[Scottish National Portrait Gallery, Edinburgh]

Fig.13 · right · Andrew Geddes
George Chalmers, 1812
[Scottish National Portrait Gallery, Edinburgh]

private residence at Dryburgh Abbey. The dimensions of the 1812 self-portrait of an artistic celebrity in the making corresponded exactly to Buchan's specifications for portraits destined for his Caledonian Temple of Fame.[40]

Of Geddes's new Edinburgh patrons, the most committed and influential was indubitably the bookseller and publisher Archibald Constable (1774–1827). From humble beginnings as a bookseller's apprentice he had progressed to publishing on his purchase of the long-established and widely circulated *Scots Magazine*, and had come to prominence in 1802 with the launch of the Whig *Edinburgh Review* under the editorship of Sydney Smith. By 1812,

when he acquired in partnership with Robert Cadell the copyright and stock of the *Encyclopaedia Britannica* – the creation of Geddes's mentor Colin Macfarquhar – Constable had begun his long association with Sir Walter Scott. From 1813, when he sat to Geddes for a small full-length cabinet portrait [fig.12] until his death in 1827, he was to publish most of the Waverley Novels. Ironically, it was this prestigious association which was to destroy his own publishing empire by insolvency in 1826, Scott then transferring his allegiance to Constable's erstwhile business partner, Robert Cadell.

Constable's patronage of Geddes had been initiated in 1812 when he painted in Craigcrook, Constable's country residence in Corstorphine on the outskirts of Edinburgh, a conversation piece in small full-length format of the publisher's mother Mrs Thomas Constable and his daughter Anne.[41] That same year Geddes completed for Constable in London a full-scale half-length portrait [fig.13] of the expatriate Scottish antiquary and historian George Chalmers

(1742–1825) whose contemporary literary celebrity rested essentially upon *Caledonia; or an Account, Historical and Topographical of North Britain ... Chorographical and Philological* of which the first two volumes had appeared in 1807 and 1810. As Constable confirmed in a letter of 16 July 1812 to Chalmers, this commission was conceived as Geddes's passport to success in his native city:

> *Allow me to express my thankfulness for your obliging acquiescence in my request sent by Mr Geddes – bringing your portrait to Scotland with him will be of no small use to him in his Proffession – and it shall be by & bye placed with one or two others in the best appartment in my Chateau [i.e. Craigcrook Castle] there to remain as a memorial of your friendship & of my respect.*

It was this commission, and the expectations attendant upon it, which appears to have prompted Geddes's experimentation with the art of etching [fig.76].[42] Finally, and presumably with the same objective, Constable issued two collateral commissions for portrait drawings of two further literary luminaries with whom he had business dealings in Edinburgh. In 1812, the year of his appointment as Professor of Oriental Languages at Edinburgh University, Alexander Murray (1775–1813) sat to Geddes for a pencil portrait [fig.14] which was later reproduced by John Burnet as a soft-ground etching. The following year the geographer Hugh Murray (1779–1846), one-time editor of the *Scots Magazine* and a contributor to Constable's *Edinburgh Gazetteer*, was to become the subject of a similar chalk and pencil drawing.[43]

The priority invariably accorded to portraiture by the Incorporated Society of Artists – and which caused some contemporary reviewers to classify the genre as the only distinctive contribution of an identifiably Scottish school – was exploited to the full by Geddes in the fifth annual exhibition in 1812. In its exhaustive critique of the exhibition, the *Scots Magazine* paid him the compliment of reviewing all of his five portraits and identifying as the most promising, his full-scale 'excellent likeness' of his fellow portrait painter, the pastellist Archibald Skirving (1749–1819).[44] This was among the most ambitious of a series of artists' portraits, a subsidiary specialism which Geddes continued to explore on his return to London in 1814 [fig.16]. Apart from Skirving, Nathaniel Plimer (see p.24) and the self-taught landscape painter the Revd John Thomson of Duddingston (1778–1840) both sat to Geddes in 1812, followed in 1813 by the London-based expatriate Scottish landscape painter and drawing master, Andrew Wilson (1780–1848). A former pupil of Nasmyth and a friend of Wilkie since 1806, Wilson had already demonstrated his flair for dealing as the co-adjutor in Italy of the Scottish artist-dealer James Irvine, himself the agent of the great Scottish entrepreneur and speculator William Buchanan. Wilson's cumulative experience of the trade was to prove of

Fig.14 · left · Andrew Geddes
Professor Alexander Murray, 1812
[Scottish National Portrait Gallery, Edinburgh]

Fig.15 · Andrew Geddes
Captain Robert Skirving of Croys, 1813
[Scottish National Portrait Gallery, Edinburgh]

seminal importance for his later collaborative transactions with, and tutelage of, Geddes.[45] The latter's acquaintance with Skirving, of uncertain origin and duration, initiated further experimentation with the process of etching in co-operation with his sitter whose proficiency in the technique is not otherwise recorded. At a late stage of development, Skirving washed with aquatint Geddes's etching after his oil portrait of 1812 [fig.17]. Then, in 1813, the pastellist's younger brother, Captain Robert Skirving of Croys in Kirkcudbrightshire, was induced to extend his patronage to Geddes for a characteristic small full-length now in the Scottish National Portrait Gallery [fig.15].[46]

Geddes's energetic pursuit of re-integration into the artistic milieu of his native Edinburgh found more convivial expression in his membership of the Dilettanti Club to which Nasmyth showed a particular attachment. The Club, which convened in a tavern on the High Street, numbered among its quota of artist members Raeburn, Hugh William 'Grecian' Williams, William Allan, the Revd John Thomson of Duddingston and, during return excursions from London, Wilkie. The non-practising *cognoscenti* included Walter Scott, Henry Cockburn, Francis Jeffrey, Professor John Wilson alias Christopher North, James Hogg 'the Ettrick Shepherd' and, as secretary, David Bridges the younger (1776–1840). During the early 1820s Allan was to execute a virtuosic conversation piece of the Club in full session in which Nasmyth was placed centre stage as the artistic elder statesman. In the background, half obscured by the dominant group comprising Hogg, Scott, Nasmyth and Professor Wilson, is a bystander who may be tentatively identified as Geddes [fig.18].

Fig.16 · Andrew Geddes
Archibald Skirving, 1812
[National Gallery of Scotland, Edinburgh]

Fig.17 · Andrew Geddes and Archibald Skirving
Archibald Skirving
[Scottish National Portrait Gallery, Edinburgh]

Fig.18 · Sir William Allan
The Celebration of the Birthday of James Hogg (?), 1823 or 1825
[Scottish National Portrait Gallery, Edinburgh]

By profession a draper and by inclination a bibliophile like his father and namesake David Bridges senior (died 1830), the Club Secretary maintained a shop in the Parliament Close in proximity to Allan's studio and which merited a lively description as the '*Sanctum Sanctorum* of the Fine Arts' in John Gibson Lockhart's *Peter's Letters to his Kinsfolk*. Dubbed by the wits of *Blackwood's Edinburgh Magazine* 'the Director-General of the Fine Arts for Scotland', Bridges indulged himself with art criticism and the patronage and/or promotion of Allan, Wilson, Thomson of Duddingston, John Watson Gordon and, from 1812,

Geddes. Apart from a half-length portrait of himself – etched by Geddes in head and shoulders format in 1816 – the 'Director-General' commissioned or instigated the commissioning of companion small whole-length portraits of his parents, painted at Duddingston in 1812 in Geddes's best early manner [figs.19 & 20].[47]

From 1813 – despite the productivity recorded in his *aide-mémoire* of twenty-four pictures including twenty original portraits and a conversation piece in the style of Watteau – Geddes ceased forthwith to exhibit with the Incorporated Society of Artists. The reasons for this sudden disengagement can only be inferred, speculatively, from circumstantial evidence. Although the Society's exhibitions had proved to be popular public amusements, they had failed to compensate for the paucity of patronage in real terms. Then, in 1812, George Watson, whom Geddes's youngest sister Margaret described as a friend of the artist, was manoeuvred into resigning the Presidency of the Society in favour of Raeburn following the latter's objections to the precedence allocated to Watson's portraits in the hanging of the annual exhibition. The most disruptive and protracted dispute, of which Nathaniel Plimer had been the first casualty, concerned the financial management of the Society. In 1811, the year of Geddes's nomination for membership, it had been agreed to divide the accumulated income from successive annual exhibitions amongst the membership and to distribute future proceeds similarly on an equal basis. A sum of £500 was retained as a sinking fund, to be enhanced by annual additions of £100, with the aim of underwriting permanent exhibition premises and a related academy incorporating the projected life class. This scheme, which assured the less established members – such as Geddes – of a regular, although modest income, was opposed by Nasmyth and Raeburn in the name of the Society's

longer-term aspirations. The division of the sinking fund itself in 1813 led to the resignation of prominent members of the Raeburn faction, including Alexander and Patrick Nasmyth successively, and the dissolution of the Society. An alternative association, to which Geddes did not subscribe, continued to exhibit for a further three years under the leadership of Raeburn at 32 York Place.[48]

Ironically, it was in this year of schism that Geddes executed one of his most refined and engaging cabinet portraits, a commission in which he paid an allusive tribute to Raeburn. The young lawyer and future Chief Magistrate of Calcutta, Charles Knowles Robison (died 1846), was the son of John Robison (1739–1805), Professor of Natural Philosophy in the University of Edinburgh, who had sat to Raeburn for one of his most imposing and virtuosic portraits painted at the turn of the eighteenth century and later gifted to the University by Robison's widow.[49] In 1813 the younger Robison held the post of Secretary to the Edinburgh Skating Club which enjoyed unrivalled prestige as the oldest established club in Britain. Although not avowedly socially exclusive, its membership was dominated by the landed gentry and the legal surrogate aristocracy. The club, which normally convened at Lochend or Duddingston, was distinguished by its commitment to figure skating of the most sophisticated order. The pictorial potential of 'the poetry of motion', in the memorable phrase of the judge Lord Cockburn, had captivated Raeburn who, during the early to mid-1790s, had painted an iconic like-

Fig.19 · left · Andrew Geddes
David Bridges Senior, 1812
[Scottish Private Collection]

Fig.20 · centre · Andrew Geddes
Euphemia Cargill Macduff, Mrs David Bridges, 1812
[Scottish Private Collection]

Fig.21 · right · Sir Henry Raeburn
The Revd Robert Walker, c.1792–4
[National Gallery of Scotland, Edinburgh]

Fig.22 · Andrew Geddes
*Charles Knowles Robison Skating
on Duddingston Loch*, 1813
[Private Collection]

ness of the Minister of the Canongate Kirk, a long established member of the Club, demonstrating the balletic
grace of the so-called 'travelling position'. Raeburn's small
full-length of the Revd Robert Walker [fig.21], which was
presented by the artist to the sitter's eldest daughter in 1808
some four years after Robison joined the Club, but whose
early history is otherwise elusive, was evidently known to
Geddes and/or his sitter at first hand, either prior to,
or as a consequence of, the 1813 commission. Whereas
Raeburn focused with exquisite precision upon the profiled
form of his skater against a generalised background,
Geddes indulged his own preoccupation with landscape
by elaborating the distinctive topography of Arthur's Seat
and Duddingston Loch and, in the middle distance,
Duddingston Kirk which accommodated the safety equip-
ment belonging to the Club. Robison himself [fig.22]
proudly displays the Club insignia suspended from a scarlet
ribbon, an oval medal bearing the Horatian motto 'Ocior
Euro' ('Swifter than the East Wind').[50]

Geddes's other notable contribution of the year 1813 was
one of his most inventive and well-integrated pictorial
experiments in the manner of Rembrandt, to whom he was

to offer the ultimate tribute of purchasing *The Toilet of
Bathsheba* on returning to London in 1814. Having first
completed a characteristic small full-length of his mother
the previous year [fig.23], Geddes adopted for a definitive likeness the compositional and conceptual model of a
Rembrandt which had had a particular resonance since the
late eighteenth century when imitative Rembrandtesque
heads had proliferated in British portraiture. This particular Rembrandt had entered the Royal Collection through
the gift of the 1st Earl of Ancram to Charles I as a portrait
of the artist's mother [fig.24], a tradition which persisted
despite a confusing conflation with the legendary Countess
of Desmond in the course of the eighteenth century. In his
related drypoint of 1822 [fig.78], executed after his own
portrait of 1813, Geddes was to pursue still further, through
the intrinsic qualities of this print medium, his exploration
of tonal contrasts and intensity of shadow as a powerfully
expressive vehicle for conveying the mood and personality
of his sitters. Finally, by way of personal homage to the
supreme exponent of the art of self-portraiture and as an
advertisement of his own artistic affiliation, Geddes portrayed himself in the guise of his mentor [fig.25].[51]

Fig.23 · right · Andrew Geddes
*Agnes Geddes,
The Artist's Mother*, 1813
[National Gallery of Scotland,
Edinburgh]

Fig.24 · far left · Rembrandt
Portrait of an Old Woman
[The Royal Collection
© HM Queen Elizabeth II]

Fig.25 · left · Andrew Geddes
Self-portrait, 181[?]
[Scottish Private Collection]

Fig.26 · Rembrandt
The Toilet of Bathsheba, 1643
[The Metropolitan Museum, New York]

CHAPTER FOUR

The Parisian Interlude of 1814, the Artist as Dealer and the Alternative Lure of London

On returning to London in 1814 after the collapse of the Incorporated Society of Artists, Geddes embarked on his first documented purchase of an outstanding Old Master painting. In its 1818 review of the contemporary exhibition of Old Master painting at the British Institution in London, the *Annals of the Fine Arts* contextualised the Institution's exhibition programme and reformative cultural policy with a revealing commentary on their socio-economic implications for the expansion of the international art market: 'England has of late become *the mart* [author's italics] for the sale of fine pictures; and though many of the highest quality have appeared at sales on the continent, it has been with the view of attracting the English purchaser that they have been brought from their sanctuaries.' A related phenomenon was the rise of the British artist-dealer of whom Andrew Geddes is arguably one of the most underrated representatives.[52]

In June 1814 the dealer Alexandre Delahante having decided to return to Paris, his entire stock-in-trade of Italian, Flemish and Dutch Old Masters was auctioned in London. His return had been prompted by the enforced abdication of Napoleon I that April and the temporary restoration of the Bourbon monarchy arising from the Allied invasion of France. At the first day's sale on 3 June Geddes secured *The Trial of the Faith and Fortitude of Saint Anthony*, reputedly by Annibale Carracci, for £21 and, for £105 or 100 guineas, *The Toilet of Bathsheba* [fig.26] by Rembrandt. How Geddes raised the capital to secure this prized investment – which he believed to have been painted for Rembrandt's friend the Burgomaster Jan Six of Amsterdam – has not been ascertained. The picture was to remain in his possession until 1828 when, with reluctance and through necessity, he sold it to a highly esteemed fellow collector, Sir Thomas Lawrence.[53] In 1815 Geddes commemorated this supremely important acquisition by commissioning John Burnet to execute an engraving for publication in London by Josiah Boydell & Company [fig.27]. The letterpress on the finished engraving, of which an impression was proudly despatched to Geddes's mentor and patron, Lord Eldin, in July 1815, bore a joint dedication from Geddes and Burnet to the advocate, Alexander Oswald of Changue (1777–1821). Oswald, who sat to Geddes for a half-length oil portrait exhibited in 1821 [fig.28], periodically engaged Geddes's services as a dealer to develop his own private collection and was to become a founder-director of the Institution for the Encouragement of the Fine Arts in Scotland in 1819. Their joint plans for an extended tour of the Continent were unexpectedly frustrated by Oswald's death in 1821.[54]

Within a month of the abdication of Napoleon, Wilkie and Benjamin Robert Haydon left for France, followed – presumably after the Delahante sale in early June – by Burnet, Geddes and two unnamed companions. The second party, for whom Geddes, as an accomplished linguist and Francophile, acted as spokesman, travelled through Flanders to Paris and the artistic Mecca of the Musée Napoléon. Re-named in 1803 in honour of the First Consul and future Emperor, the former Louvre was still resplendent with a prodigious wealth of treasures looted from the aristocratic, royal and even papal collections of the conquered territories of Europe during a systematic programme of spoliation which was masterminded for Napoleon I by his director-general of the Fine Arts, Baron Doménique Vivant Denon. Burnet reputedly spent five months studying intensively in the Louvre. For Geddes the cummulative experience proved so profound that he would leave for Italy in 1828 with the aim of renewing acquaintance in Naples with some of the confiscated works first encountered in 1814. (Of these, quite a substantial number were grudgingly repatriated during the Restoration after a diplomatic campaign by Canova, supported by the international artists' colony in Rome, and despite a predatory counter-initiative on the part of the Prince Regent, the future George IV.) In the interim, seven of Geddes's copies in oils after Veronese, Titian, Giorgione, Correggio, Jordaens and Rubens would be included in his one-man retrospective exhibition in Edinburgh in 1821, both as a didactic exercise and as a manifesto for his own connoisseurship.[55]

At the Palais du Luxembourg Geddes would have viewed at first hand – as Wilkie most certainly did – Rubens's epic cycle of paintings on the life of Marie de'Medici, known to him, vicariously, since childhood through the bound volume of engravings acquired by his father from the Honble Andrew Erskine in 1790. Of the magnificent collection of works by Rubens then adorning the Musée Napoléon and including the *Descent from the Cross* from Antwerp Cathedral, the huge *Assumption of the Virgin* [fig.29] removed from the Austrian Imperial collections in Vienna on Denon's instructions in or shortly after 1809. This was to furnish the compositional prototype for Geddes's unique recorded public commission as a religious painter, a commission which he owed to the intermediary of John Burnet.[56]

By 1815, the beautiful Wren church of St James's Garlickhythe in the City of London was in a parlous state of repair. The great east window having been identified as the cause of a dangerous structural weakness, the Vestry decided to block up the aperture and to substitute an altarpiece in the form of a large easel painting. The donor was Burnet's brother, the Revd Dr Thomas Burnet, then Curate of St James's, who was to spend his entire ministry in the parish and, by 1853, had been appointed rector. By 26 July 1815, when Geddes wrote to Lord Eldin about the presentation impression of Burnet's engraving after *The Toilet of Bathsheba*, he was 'busily employed on a large picture of the ascension of Christ which I fear will keep me in London all year …' On 14 January 1816 the church was reopened for worship, both the renovations and Geddes's exertions having been successfully completed [fig.30].[57]

The choice of an Ascension, although relatively unorthodox, must have obtained the consensus of the Vestry and the donor, conceivably in endorsement of an initiative on the part of the artist himself in direct response to his experience at the Louvre. Recent cleaning of the altarpiece, whose tonal range had been distorted by fire damage, has revealed the rich painterliness and sonorous colourism of which Geddes was capable at his best, even when working on a scale totally outwith his natural range as a figure painter. For the actual design, he adopted the two registers of the Vienna *Assumption* with the Apostles gesticulating animatedly below and the figure of Christ above in a dynamic upward movement recalling that of the flight of cherubim in the Rubens original.[58]

In May 1815 Andrew Wilson wrote to David Bridges junior from Sandhurst with news of recent transactions on be-

Fig.27 · John Burnet
Engraving of Rembrandt's
The Toilet of Bathsheba, 1815
[The British Museum, London]

Fig.28 · Andrew Geddes
Alexander Oswald of Changue
[Glasgow Museums: Art Gallery &
Museum, Kelvingrove]

half of Bridges and a fellow Edinburgh collector and patron of Geddes, Gilbert Laing Meason. Concerning Geddes, Wilson, another regular correspondent of Bridges, declared himself 'satisfied that good fortune will attend his endeavours in London; he appears on the right road and may the good qualities of the man triumph with his Art.' Wilson's optimism may well have been grounded in the favourable reception of Geddes's recently completed altarpiece by two of their most distinguished contemporaries, J.M.W. Turner and Sir Thomas Lawrence,[59] and certainly in the progress of his cabinet portraiture. That progress was most convincingly charted through Geddes's resumption of the sequence of artists' portraits begun in Edinburgh three years previously. In *Peter's Letters to his Kinsfolk*, John Gibson Lockhart's alter ego Peter Morris, while claiming for Raeburn as Edinburgh's premier portrait painter a European stature on a par with that of Lawrence, noted further that 'the splendid example of his career has raised about him several, that seem destined to tread in his steps with gracefulness scarcely less than his own. Such, in particular, are Mr. Geddes, whose fine portrait of Mr. Wilkie has lately been engraved in London – Mr. John Watson, a very young artist, but (I prophesy) not far from very splendid reputation … and, lastly, Mr. Nicholson.'[60] This very focused

Fig.29 · above · Sir Peter Paul Rubens
The Assumption of the Virgin, 1620
[Kunsthistorisches Museum, Vienna]

Fig.30 · right · Andrew Geddes
The Ascension, 1815
in St James's Garlickhythe, London
[Photograph courtesy of the
National Monuments Record]

speculation concerning Geddes's potential succession to Raeburn was to be reactivated in 1823 by the latter's death.

In 1816 Geddes exhibited a portrait of Haydon, his former contemporary at the Royal Academy Schools. The following year he launched a trio of artists' portraits at the Academy's annual exhibition which, both individually and collectively, earned Geddes one of his extremely rare reviews in the London press, and contributed in 1817 to the first of his three abortive nominations for election to Associate membership. Both George Sanders (1774–1846) [fig.31] – the Fife-born miniature and portrait painter who, like Geddes, retained a clientele in Edinburgh as well as in his adoptive London – and Wilkie were presented as the cultured gentleman artist, Wilkie's profession being evoked through the marginal inclusion of a mahlstick and a decorative still-life arrangement of studio properties, including a high-backed sitter's chair [fig.32]. A commission from Alexander Oswald, the dedicatee of Burnet's engraving after *The Toilet of Bathsheba*, Wilkie's portrait was engraved in mezzotint within the year by William Ward. The choice of cabinet format for the original oil was of itself, whether premeditated or not, a compliment to Geddes's most dedicated champion and intimate friend who adopted the small full-length for his own portraiture of this period.[61]

Fig.31 · left · Andrew Geddes
George Sanders, 1816
[National Gallery of Scotland,
Edinburgh]

Fig.32 · right · Andrew Geddes
Sir David Wilkie, 1816
[Scottish National Portrait Gallery,
Edinburgh]

The third member of the triumvirate, William Allan, provided the perfect pretext for a topical essay in Orientalism in conjunction with Rembrandtism, and for the exotic indulgence of Geddes's preference for the so-called 'fancy portrait' of which Wilkie was to declare that, 'If Mr. Geddes could once get the public applause on his side, he would never lose it, his works are so far above what is called the fashion; and in this style of art, it is my decided opinion, he has more taste than any artist in Britain.'[62] The critical reception of Geddes's fancy portrait, now known only from his own tenebrist etching retouched with drypoint and dated 18 June 1815 [fig.81], was enhanced by the presence in the same Academy exhibition of Allan's *Sale of Circassian Captives to a Turkish Bashaw*. In 1805, after the briefest interlude in London, where he rejoined his friend and contemporary from the Trustees' Academy, David Wilkie, Allan had sailed for St Petersburg. He was to spend the next decade travelling in the Russian interior, making expeditions to Turkey, Tartary and the shores of the Black Sea and gathering the raw material, including studio properties of costume, arms and armour, for the Orientalist

subject pictures which he was to evolve as a specialism from 1814, prior to his 'conversion' to the regeneration of Scottish history painting. Geddes's portrait of Allan in character, with its Byronic self-dramatisation and admixture of reality and fantasy (the costume being faithfully observed from an original in his sitter's possession) epitomised Allan's approach to Circassian narrative painting and the persona which he cultivated through the elaborately 'Orientalised' environment of his Parliament Close studio in the Old Town of Edinburgh. This was memorably evoked by Lockhart in *Peter's Letters to His Kinsfolk* as

> *a complete fac-simile of the barbaric magnificence of the interior decorations of an eastern palace. The exterior of the artist himself harmonized a good deal with his furniture; for he was arrayed, by way of a* robe-de-chambre, *in a dark Circassian vest, the breast of which was loaded with innumerable quilted lurking-places, originally, no doubt, intended for weapons of warfare, but now occupied with the harmless shafts of hair-pencils; while he held in his hand the smooth cherrywood stalk of a Turkish tobacco-pipe, apparently converted very happily into a pallet-guard.*[63]

In 1817 the Gordon Cumming family were to extend their patronage to Geddes for one of his most accomplished essays in modish Oriental fancy portraiture. That year Charles Lennox Cumming-Bruce (1790–1875), younger son of Sir Alexander Penrose Gordon Cumming, first baronet, sat to Geddes for an elaborate cabinet portrait which, by 1824, graced the family seat at Altyre near Elgin, inherited by the sitter's elder brother the second baronet. The rationale for Cumming-Bruce's flamboyant portrayal in Turkish or Syriac dress against a backdrop of the ruined Roman temples at Baalbek [fig.33] remains open to speculation, nothing being known of his early career or presumed travels prior to his marriage in 1822 to the granddaughter of James Bruce, the Abyssinian explorer, and his election as MP for Inverness Burghs in 1831.[64] During the same period Cumming-Bruce's sister Amelia Penrose Cumming, later Mrs B. Yeaman, posed for Geddes in the guise of a sibyl [fig.34], being identified as such by her attributes of scrolls or Sibylline Books in which her prophecies are about to be

Fig.33 · Andrew Geddes
Charles Lennox Cumming-Bruce, 1817
[Yale Center for British Art]

Fig.34 · Andrew Geddes
Amelia Penrose Cumming of Altyre,
c.1817
[Private Collection]

recorded . This conceit had recently been exploited by Sir Thomas Lawrence in the rather mannered portrait of his intimate friend, Mrs Jens Wolff, as the Erythraean Sibyl, exhibited at the Royal Academy in 1815, and whose immediate influence was clearly discernible in Raeburn's commissioned portrait of Eliza Maria Campbell, married in that same year to Amelia's brother, the second baronet. In Geddes's case, however, any passing homage to Lawrence was overlaid with a more discerning compliment to the Old Master connoisseurship of his patrons by allusion to the *Cumaean Sibyl with a Putto* of Guercino (now in the collection of Sir Denis Mahon) or, less convincingly, to the *Persian Sibyl* of Domenichino (The Wallace Collection, London) which had been imported into London from the Orléans collection in 1798.[65]

Commissions such as these seemed to substantiate John Gibson Lockhart's and Andrew Wilson's optimistic predictions of Geddes's concurrent prospects in London and in Edinburgh respectively. It was conceivably to the Gordon Cummings that Geddes owed an introduction to their relative by marriage, the legal *littérateur* and erst-while Attorney for the Crown in Scotland, Henry Mackenzie (1745–1831). (Equally, depending on the exact chronology of the related portrait commissions, Mackenzie may have acted as the intermediary with his northern kinsmen). In 1776 Mackenzie had married a daughter of Sir Ludovic Grant of Grant, Penuel Grant, whose sister Helen had allied herself to Sir Alexander Penrose Cumming, first baronet, three years earlier. Born at the time of the Forty-Five Jacobite Rising, Mackenzie was a remarkable exemplar of the Enlightenment intellectual of the generation of David Hume, John Home and Principal Robertson, through whose friendship he became, in the estimation of Sir Walter Scott, a living link between the literature of the previous and the present generation, and, as such, a worthy dedicatee of *Waverley* in 1814. Even as late as the second decade of the nineteenth century, as Lord Cockburn observed in his *Memorials*, Mackenzie's literary reputation remained virtually synonymous with his authorship of *The Man of Feeling*, his novel in the manner of Lawrence Sterne whose publication in 1771 had elicited comparisons with the fame of Rousseau's *La Nouvelle Héloïse*. Cockburn's pen portrait of the ageing Mackenzie in his *Memorials* as 'thin, shrivelled and yellow, kiln-dried, with something when seen in profile

of the clever wicked look of Voltaire' provides a fascinating gloss, through its passing reference to the French *philosophe* and dramatist, upon the calculatedly anachronistic subtlety of Geddes's portrayal of a displaced eighteenth-century luminary in his natural habitat [fig.35].

Mackenzie's self-perpetuating celebrity made his portrait a strategic choice for the artist's own self-advertisement by means of an engraving published in 1822.[66] Similar considerations of existing and vicarious celebrity motivated one of Wilkie's most sustained altruistic initiatives on behalf of a fellow Scottish artist. In 1817, while Wilkie was travelling round the West of Scotland collecting material for subject pictures, he renewed contact in Glasgow with the Evangelical theologian and social reformer Dr Thomas Chalmers (1780–1847)who would become one of the intellectual and spiritual leaders of the Free Church during the Disruption of 1843. Grace Chalmers's acquaintance with Wilkie dated from their school days in Cupar in Fife, while her husband's friendship had been consolidated by the artist's quest for a London publisher for Chalmers following the theologian's first visit to the southern capital in 1807. On returning to London from his West of Scotland excursion, Wilkie was approached by the Glasgow bookseller and publisher John Smith for the use of one of his recent sketches of Chalmers as the frontispiece to an edition of sermons delivered at the Tron, the prestigious Glaswegian charge to which Chalmers had been presented in 1815.[67] These sketches having proved too slight, and further sittings to Wilkie impractical, both Raeburn and Lawrence, despite expressions of strong interest in principle, declined the immediate commission on the grounds of inconvenience.

In December 1818 Wilkie opportunistically urged upon Chalmers, who had initially refused to countenance any portraitist other than Wilkie, the merits of 'Mr Geddes a very worthy friend and old acquaintance of mine who [I] consider a very rising Artist in the line of Portrait painting … He has been much employed and very successful in Edinburgh and is now painting there a very large picture of the great personages finding the regalia of Scotland.' Geddes himself pressed his case diplomatically in the follow-up letter to Chalmers on 29 April 1819 in which he notified him of the despatch to Glasgow of a presentation impression of Ward's mezzotint after his 1816 portrait of Wilkie. He offered to 'accede to any arrangements agreeable to you for

Fig.35 · Andrew Geddes
Henry Mackenzie
[Scottish Private Collection]

painting the Portrait' in accordance with his own current practice of wintering in Edinburgh. Final arrangements were deferred until the autumn of 1821 – Wilkie again acting as intermediary – which necessitated the rapid completion of the portrait in time for the opening on 10 December of Geddes's retrospective exhibition at Bruce's Great Room in Waterloo Place, Edinburgh. The progress of Geddes's three-quarter length portrait of the theologian and author seated in an interior, and that of the companion portrait of his wife, was ultimately followed with the closest interest by Chalmers who had not previously sat for his likeness in oils. Wilkie advocated a metropolitan re-launch for the picture at the forthcoming Royal Academy annual exhibition.[68] However, Geddes chose to exploit its topicality by vigorously promoting in the Edinburgh press, at his own exhibition, and through agents in Edinburgh, Glasgow and London the subscription for a mezzotint to be executed by William Ward and published in December 1822 [fig.36]. In the meantime Geddes himself had possibly experimented unsuccessfully with the production of a print of which, according to his later testimony in the letter to the antiquary and print collector Edward Vernon Utterson, 'only 4 Trial proofs were taken the *Steel* plate having corroded before being finished.'[69]

Fig.36 · William Ward after Andrew Geddes
The Revd Dr Thomas Chalmers, 1822
[Scottish National Portrait Gallery, Edinburgh]

CHAPTER FIVE

Edinburgh 1819: the Founding of the Royal Institution, Geddes and the Hopetoun and Ellesmere Van Dycks

In petitioning Thomas Chalmers in December 1818, Wilkie had emphasised among Geddes's credentials both the extent of Scottish patronage for his portraiture and the fact that he was currently engaged upon a contemporary history painting of the rediscovery of the Honours of Scotland (see page 54). Wilkie did not mention another momentous development which might induce Geddes to retain a part-time commitment to his native Edinburgh, despite the recent re-adjustment of his professional priorities in favour of London. Earlier that year their mutual friend Andrew Wilson had relinquished his Professorship of Drawing at Sandhurst Military Academy to take up appointment as Master of the Trustees' Academy. In 1831 he recalled the circumstances of his arrival in Edinburgh in a trenchant letter to James Skene of Rubislaw, then Secretary of the Royal Institution for the Encouragement of the Fine Arts in Scotland:

> *When I went down to Edinr in 1818 I was for a twelvemonth employed at Hopetoun House as a cleaner of pictures and as a teacher of drawing. I had no hope of being employed to paint a picture; Mr Nasmyths business had declined entirely in that way; the Institution was established the year following and I left off my private teaching and continued to enjoy a reasonable degree of encouragement in painting: and look to what has been done since by Mr Thomson of Duddingston* [the Revd John Thomson of Duddingston] *and of all the varieties of talent among the young men. This has been all much owing to the Influence of the efforts of the Institution on the public the very existence of the Artists Academy has sprung from this impulse and there has been a corresponding increase in portrait painting.*

Wilson's letter, an eloquent if partial justification of the enlightened founding objectives of the Institution, was written five years after the formation of the secessionist Scottish Academy (incorporated by Royal Charter in 1838) by a group of his contemporaries disaffected with the elitist and non-consultative management of the parent body. Nasmyth, Wilson and, to a lesser degree, Geddes, were all to remain affiliated to the Institution.[70]

A privately funded and predominantly aristocratic organisation, the Institution was explicitly modelled, with correspondingly high expectations, upon the British Institution in London which had been one of the newest and most compelling attractions in the southern capital at the time of Geddes's arrival in 1806. The founding members were the Earl of Elgin, James Russell, Professor of Clinical Surgery in the University of Edinburgh, Gilbert Laing Meason of Lindertis, an Old Master collector serviced by Wilson, and Sir John James Steuart of Allanbank (1779–1849). The latter, who had inherited the baronetcy of Allanbank in Berwickshire in 1817, became a personal friend of Geddes, whom he patronised both for his original portraiture [fig.70] and, most especially, for his expertise in Northern European Old Master painting. Steuart was also a tolerably gifted amateur practitioner of watercolour and oil painting and, most significantly, of etching.[71] Membership of the Institution burgeoned and by 1827 it had already been granted a Royal Charter. In 1824 the Directors admitted eleven of the most prominent Scottish artists to Associate membership, but their continuing exclusion from participation in the administration of the Institution or its financial management was to precipitate the schismatic establishment of the Scottish Academy two years later.

In 1822 William Henry Playfair, one of the principal architects of the New Town of Edinburgh, was engaged by the Board of Manufactures to erect a Doric temple to the arts on Princes Street, whose grandeur was to be commensurate with the cultural optimism generated by the founding of the Institution. The same optimism would be celebrated by Nasmyth in a commemorative painting of the construction of the building in 1825 [fig.37]. The Board contained this expenditure by entering into leases with the Institution and the Royal Society of Edinburgh and a tenancy agreement with the Society of Antiquaries of Scotland and, ironically, with the Royal Scottish Academy from 1835.[72]

The provision of accommodation for the Institution had been necessitated by its pro-active exhibition policy. In 1826 the fifth exhibition of modern Scottish painting was mounted in Playfair's newly-opened temple, previous exhibitions having been staged in Mr Bruce's Gallery at 24 Waterloo Place in 1821, 1822, 1824 and 1825. The Institution's diversification into contemporary art in response to

lobbying from its practitioners was at least partially occasioned by the diminishing availability in Scotland of loans of privately owned Old Master paintings and the absence, as yet, of any permanent public collection. The first two exhibitions in 1819 and 1820 were held in Raeburn's gallery at 32 York Place and organised by Wilson who, in 1826, would become the prime mover of the Institution's decision to form such a collection. In December 1829, when his proffered sale of Van Dyck's *Lomellini Family* (National Gallery of Scotland) was under consideration, he would urge the directors to envisage 'a Gallery of National importance.'[73]

Through the agency of Wilson, Geddes signalled his availability as an artist-dealer by joining the land-owning oligarchy in supporting the inaugural Old Master exhibition in 1819. Recent elections to the directorate included Alexander Oswald, John Clerk (Lord Eldin) and the 4th Earl of Hopetoun. Geddes's sole contribution was a three-quarter length portrait of the Infanta Isabella Clara Eugenia, Archduchess of Austria and Regent of the Netherlands, dressed in the habit of the Third Order Regular of St Francis which she had entered in 1621 [fig.39]. Then regarded as a fully autograph work by Van Dyck, the picture had been purchased, according to Geddes's own statement in 1821, 'by Mr Phillipe [i.e. Thomas Philipe] a consider-

Fig.37 · Alexander Nasmyth
The Commencement of the Building of the Royal Institution, 1825
[National Gallery of Scotland, Edinburgh]

Fig.38 · Follower of Rembrandt
Old Woman Plucking a Fowl
[National Gallery of Art, Washington DC]

Fig.39 · Studio of Sir Anthony van Dyck
The Infanta Isabella Clara Eugenia
[Walker Art Gallery, National Museums
on Merseyside]

Fig.40 · Attributed to Sir Anthony van Dyck
Portrait of a Young Man
[Duke of Sutherland Loan to the
National Gallery of Scotland, Edinburgh]

able print dealer in London who went frequently to Holland in the prosecution of his business, from the Family to whom the picture had been presented by Isabella the sum paid for it by Mr Phillipe now more than twenty years ago was Three hundred pounds, since his death Mr. Geddes purchased the picture from Mrs. Phillipe.'[74]

Since 1818, as he was to remind James Skene in 1831, Wilson had been employed by the 4th Earl of Hopetoun as drawing master, picture restorer and consultant-cum-executive curator of the Earl's collection of Old Masters at Hopetoun House near South Queensferry. By 1819 Wilson had embarked on the authorised transformation of this collection, disposing of inherited Grand Tour investments which could no longer bear the scrutiny of a new generation. In the course of these transactions Lord Hopetoun, also a patron of contemporary Scottish art, was persuaded to commission five large original landscapes by Wilson, including *Evening in the Bay of Genoa* (1821, National

Gallery of Scotland). In 1820 Wilson exploited his position to secure an entrée for Geddes as dealer. That December Geddes offered the Earl a package of pictures comprising one landscape by Richard Wilson and six Dutch and Flemish Old Masters, followed in the New Year by a Van der Helst portrait group of a lady and child.

The first group was dominated by the *Infanta Isabella* for which the transaction was successfully concluded at 350 guineas by February 1821[75] and by the so-called Rembrandt, *Old Woman Plucking a Fowl* [fig.38]. The

'Rembrandt', then predictably identified as a portrait of the artist's mother, already had a distinguished Scottish provenance through the former ownership of the 7th Earl of Wemyss. It had been sold on to Geddes by his friend, the London-Scottish miniature painter Anthony Stewart following an auction at Christie's in April 1819. Ironically, Lord Hopetoun appears to have declined the offer (at 250 guineas) in favour of a rival *Rembrandt's Mother* whose purchase from the London dealer Bernard Pinney had been negotiated by Wilson in 1819. On departing for Italy in 1828, Geddes was to submit both of his prized Rembrandts – the other being, of course, *The Toilet of Bathsheba* – for the consideration of Sir Thomas Lawrence at a total asking price of 700 guineas.[76] In the meantime, he commemorated his ownership of *Infanta Isabella* by executing an etching of a head and shoulders detail.

As an authority on Van Dyck, Wilson played a dual role as the agent of a pre-existing market and as an arbiter of evolving taste in contradistinction to his co-adjutor Andrew Geddes, the impetus of whose collecting was aesthetic rather than entrepreneurial. Geddes later exalted Van Dyck to his personal equivalent of the Holy Trinity in a fancy picture uniting the Flemish master with Rembrandt and Titian.[77] By 1826, when Geddes's own commemorative etching of the picture was available for inclusion in the variable portfolios of his etchings issued privately that year, he had secured, from an unknown source, a half-length 'Van Dyck' portrait of a young man, possibly on account of the sitter's supposed lineal relationship to the Infanta Isabella. In memoranda supplied to the antiquary David Laing, in preparation for his critical catalogue of Wilkie and Geddes etchings in 1874 or 1875, Adela Geddes described the sitter as 'Philip the Second Mary Queen of England's husband', father of the Infanta [fig.40]. She added that the Van Dyck 'was bought by Lord Francis Egerton from Mr. Geddes & is I believe in the Bridgewater collection.'

The likeliest conjectural date for this transaction is around or after 1832 when Geddes executed a much-admired copy of Titian's *Diana and Actaeon* (Duke of Sutherland Loan to the National Gallery of Scotland).[78] Lord Francis Egerton, created 1st Earl of Ellesmere in 1846, was the second son of Earl Gower, 2nd Marquess of Stafford and 1st Duke of Sutherland, who had married the richest heiress in Britain, Elizabeth, Countess of Sutherland in her own right. In 1798 the fabulous corpus of Italian and French Old Master paintings from the collection of the Duc d'Orléans ('Philippe Egalité'), which had first been offered for sale in 1791, was shipped to London where the majority were reserved by the dealer Bryan for a family consortium consisting of the 3rd and last Duke of Bridgewater, his nephew Earl Gower and Gower's brother-in-law, the Earl of Carlisle. The Duke's share of the Orléans heritage was added to his existing collection, noted for its Dutch pictures, in a spacious gallery at his London residence, Cleveland House. On the death of the bachelor Duke in 1803, Earl Gower, who was bequeathed liferent possession of the pictures with entail to Lord Egerton, transferred most of his own collection to Cleveland House. Re-named 'the Stafford Gallery', Cleveland House was opened to the public weekly in the summer season and frequented by, amongst others, Wilkie, 'everywhere peering into the works of the Dutch and Flemish Schools.' Lord Egerton having duly inherited his great-uncle's property and pictures at Earl Gower's death in 1833, Geddes's Van Dyck and his own reputation for expertise in the Northern European Schools thus became associated with the most prestigious private collection of Old Master painting in Britain outside the Royal Collection.[79]

Fig.41 · Andrew Geddes
The Sceptre from the Regalia of Scotland, 1818
[Courtesy of the National Archives of Scotland, Edinburgh]

CHAPTER SIX

Retrospective and Royal: the Discovery of the Regalia and the Edinburgh Exhibitions of 1821 and 1822

Over the winter of 1818, as Wilkie notified Dr Thomas Chalmers, Geddes was preoccupied with 'a very large picture of the great personages finding the regalia of Scotland.' The sensational rediscovery of the Scottish Regalia in February of that year was the single most compelling inducement to a re-invigorated commitment to his native Edinburgh, apart from the inauguration in 1819 of the Institution for the Encouragement of the Fine Arts in Scotland.

In the absence from Scotland of the Scottish sovereign, the Regalia, or Honours, of Scotland – comprising the Crown, dating from the reign of Robert I or 'Robert the Bruce', the Sword of State, presented to James IV by Pope Julius II, and the Sceptre, fashioned during the reign of James V – had been invested with extraordinarily potent significance from 1603, the year of the Union of the Crowns and the rapid departure for London of James VI of Scotland and I of England. Following the Scottish coronations of Charles I and Charles II in 1633 and 1651, the Honours were used almost exclusively as a signifier of the King's presence at sittings of the Scottish Parliament. The ratification of the Treaty of Union in 1707 generated a heated debate concerning the prospective appropriation of the symbols of Scottish sovereignty by the English Parliament. At the adjournment of the Scottish Parliament, the Honours were locked away in the stone-vaulted Crown Room of Edinburgh Castle to await the eventual restoration of independence.

For over a century rumours abounded as to their theft or destruction in contravention of the Treaty of Union which had actually provided for their preservation. In 1817, an earlier campaign for a royal warrant to search the Crown Room was successfully reactivated through the tireless commitment of Sir Walter Scott. Scott's 'fat friend' the Prince Regent having granted authorisation, the designated Commissioners – including the Lord Provost of Edinburgh, Major-General John Hope, Earl of Hopetoun, Thomas Thomson, elder brother of the Revd John Thomson of Duddingston and Deputy Clerk-Register of Scotland, and Scott himself – assembled on 4 February 1818. To Scott's joy, the royal insignia were discovered intact at the bottom of the oak chest in which they had been secured in 1707.[80] In order to satisfy the Prince Regent of the authenticity of the insignia, the Commissioners compiled a detailed report of their proceedings, dated 21 February and accompanied by meticulous scale drawings of the individual components of the Regalia. Of the total complement of seven drawings, the Revd John Thomson (1778–1840) supplied a pencil 'perspective drawing' of the Crown, the Edinburgh engraver and genre painter William Home Lizars (1788–1859) executed Indian ink sketches of the Crown, the scabbard of the Sword of State, and the silver rod or Sceptre, William Allan produced a sketch of the Sword of State, and Geddes both an Indian ink drawing of the Sceptre [fig.41] and an oil sketch on cartridge paper of the Crown. The four artists, who appear to have been recruited through the intermediary of Thomson or his brother the Deputy Clerk-Register, were allowed preferential access to the Crown Room on 7 February and were required to deliver the results three days later. On 7 February the artists were accompanied by two other expert witnesses, the mineralogist Thomas Allan and Robert Jamieson, Professor of Natural History in the University of Edinburgh.[81]

The immediate rationale for the visual recording of the Regalia had been documentary rather than interpretative, but was rapidly transformed and superseded in the related ventures of Scott and Geddes, both independent and collaborative. Scott's project for a lavishly illustrated picture book dedicated to the topography and antiquities of Scotland was probably conceived over the winter of 1817–18, arguably in consultation with three of his friends, the Revd John Thomson, W.H. Lizars and the English architect and draughtsman Edward Blore. Scott and Thomson had been acquainted since the 1790s when the future incumbent of Duddingston was reading theology at Edinburgh University. His older brother, the jurist and legal antiquary Thomas Thomson (1768–1852), had trained for the Bar with Scott and became a lifelong and intimate friend. This close network of social relationships, which predetermined the choice of some of the Edinburgh illustrators for *The Provincial Antiquities and Picturesque Scenery of Scotland* (1819–26), undoubtedly also had some bearing upon the Royal Commissioners' nomination of artists in February 1818, Allan also being a friend and protégé of Scott and the illustrator of Archibald Constable's edition of the Waverley Novels published in 1820.

Scott's own role in the rediscovery of the Regalia and the ensuing public excitement induced him to propose that an historical account be incorporated in *The Provincial Antiquities*. An extended version of his preliminary essay on the Honours of Scotland, issued as a pamphlet to accompany the special exhibition in the Crown Room of the Castle in May 1819, appeared in 1820 in parts three and four of the new serial publication. The topicality of the Regalia and their centrality in Scott's publication were highlighted by their selection for the cover illustration in the form of a wood engraving after a drawing by Lizars. It was not until 1824, following the exposure of inaccuracies in Lizars's representation of the Regalia – and which clearly could not be condoned in a publication initiated by one of the Royal Commissioners – that Geddes became associated with Scott's project through the provision of a frontispiece for the ninth part of the *Provincial Antiquities* [fig.42]. The prototype for the frontispiece of 1824 was a small oil painting, known in several versions, and which was probably ceded to Scott under the terms of his contract as author of the letterpress. Scott, who held one of eight equal shares as a co-proprietor in the venture, chose to waive payment for his texts in exchange for the guaranteed presentation of the

Fig.42 · below left · E. Goodall after Andrew Geddes
Frontispiece to the Provincial Antiquities, part IX, 1824,
with wood engraving of the Regalia of Scotland
[National Gallery of Scotland, Edinburgh]

Fig.43 · right · Andrew Geddes
Sir Walter Scott, c.1818
[Scottish National Portrait Gallery, Edinburgh]

Fig.44 · below left · Andrew Geddes
Compositional sketch for
The Discovery of the Regalia of Scotland, c.1818
[The British Museum, London]

original drawings and paintings commissioned for illustration. Geddes, in common with the other associated artists and engravers, would have received his fee, stipulated in advance by contract, from the publishers Rodwell and Martin who defrayed the capital costs of the project.[82]

Even in its present state of deterioration, Geddes's small oil at Abbotsford retains a pictorial integrity independent of the history painting upon which he was engaged in Edinburgh in December 1818. The same quality of independence and integrity characterised Geddes's unique and strikingly sensitive portrait of 'The Wizard of the North' [fig.43] which served as a model for the pivotal figure in the centre of the finished picture and, according to the artist's own subsequent testimony, was one of a series of preparatory portrait studies of the Regalia Commissioners.[83] Geddes himself ventured in 1821 by way of an apologia that the compositional deficiencies of the *Discovery of the Regalia of Scotland* – which one London critic dismissed as an unintegrated assemblage of portraits – were partially attributable to 'the difficulty of getting anything like documents for many of the portraits, arising from distance and other causes.' On at least one occasion, he was assisted by Wilkie who, on 25 January 1819, made a special excursion to Ditton Park 'to make a sketch of the Duke of Buccleuch for Geddes'.[84]

The total effect of the completed picture can be gauged only by extrapolation from the schematic sketch in the British Museum, annotated by the artist with the identities of the chief protagonists [fig.44]. An extended eulogy in the *Edinburgh Evening Courant* on 15 December 1821 claimed for 'this NATIONAL WORK' a status comparable to the 'higher productions of the Venetian school' in its 'strength of chiaro-scuro and power of colouring.'[85] In December 1821, in a patriotically self-congratulatory review of Geddes's Regalia picture, *The Scotsman* opined that its very creation testified to 'the great advance the arts have made of late years in this country, and more particularly, when such a vast undertaking can be executed without any of that high patronage which such a work would seem to demand.' This paradoxical observation, which simultaneously endorsed and invalidated the role of the Institution for the Encouragement of the Fine Arts in Scotland in the name of free enterprise, belied the fact that Geddes's expectations were precisely those of 'high patronage'. If his project was con-

ceived as an independent speculation, then its public promotion was calculated at every stage.

By October 1820, the year of the accession of George IV, the former Prince Regent, Andrew Wilson was urging Lord Hopetoun to view the Regalia picture, then nearing completion in Geddes's London studio. The following spring, when Geddes was represented in the inaugural modern exhibition of the Edinburgh Institution by his portrait of Alexander Oswald, he reserved for the Royal Academy the first showing of his contemporary history painting whose topicality was highlighted by the preparations for the sumptuous coronation of George IV in Westminster Abbey on 21 July. Geddes's strategy earned him minimal coverage in the London press other than a chauvinistic one-line dismissal in Leigh Hunt's *The Examiner*: 'Much good painting is wasted on an insignificant subject, 293. The Discovery of the Regalia of Scotland by Mr. Geddes's – and no tangible proof of the alleged 'excitement' recorded retrospectively by the *Edinburgh Evening Courant*.[86]

Prospects in Edinburgh, where the topicality of the Regalia was seemingly undiminished, were self-evidently more promising. Apart from Geddes, both William Allan and 'Grecian' Williams were to explore the commercial advantages of the one-man exhibition, carefully timed, in Williams's case, to coincide with the opening of the Institution's new exhibition galleries in Playfair's Doric temple on the Mound. In 1821 the Institution's modern exhibition was mounted in Mr Bruce's Gallery in Waterloo Place which, in November, became the venue for Benjamin Robert Haydon's touring exhibition of his *Dentatus, Solomon, Agony of Christ,* and 'all his Drawings from Nature and the Elgin Marbles'. Geddes's major retrospective, totalling seventy exhibits, opened at the same venue on 10 December, coinciding with Haydon's own promotion. Pride of place was given to the Regalia picture as the raison d'être of the entire exhibition and to 'small whole-lengths' to which, according to the *Edinburgh Evening Courant*, 'no artist has so sedulously and successfully devoted himself as Mr. Geddes.' Apart from the cabinet portraits of Allan in Circassian costume, Wilkie, Sanders, and Robison as a skater, the full-scale portraits on canvas included, among the 'half-lengths' devoted to Scottish celebrities, the surgeon John Thomson (Royal College of Surgeons of Edinburgh). Subscriptions were solicited for engravings after the half-lengths of Dr Chalmers and the brilliant Whig advocate Francis Jeffrey (1773–1850), a pivotal figure in the intellectual life of Scotland during the first half of the nineteenth century. Jeffrey was literary editor and co-founder with Sydney Smith, Lord Brougham and Francis Horner of the *Edinburgh Review*, published by Geddes's early Edinburgh patron, Archibald Constable. The three-quarter-length portrait of Jeffrey, which Geddes himself reproduced as an etching, had been launched at the Royal Academy in 1820, the year of its execution [fig.45].[87]

Geddes's inclusion of the fancy portrait of Henry Broadwood (1793–1878) 'in the costume of Henri Quatre' to represent his London patronage may have concealed an alternative agenda. Francophile in taste and by education, Broadwood may well have cast himself as 'Le bon roi Henri' in response to the reinvigorated cult of Henri IV during the Bourbon Restoration [fig.46].[88] At the age of twenty-one he had inherited the country estate of Reeves Hall on Mersea Island in the Blackwater Estuary and a legacy of twenty thousand pounds from his father John (1723–1812), senior representative of the Broadwood dynasty of pianoforte manufacturers. Essentially a non-participant in the family business, Broadwood was eventually connected with the London brewers Messrs Broadwood, Mundell & Co. In his alternative persona as a high-living man-about-town, Gentleman of the Privy Chamber to George IV and MP for

Bridgewater, Broadwood was to invest part of his diminishing inheritance in a host of 'Watteaus' of questionable authenticity, of which several were shown at the British Institution in 1835 and 1839.

Broadwood's compulsive pursuit of Watteaus from the 1830s was to be matched, on a far more discerning basis, by Geddes's brother-in-law Andrew James. In 1813 Geddes had recorded in his private memorandum of completed pictures a 'Conversation piece style of Watteau', the earliest public manifestation of a lifelong preoccupation which was shared by Wilkie, Turner, Lawrence and most of the leading British painters of the time. In Geddes's case, his fascination with Watteau may be partially explained by a contemporary perception of the eighteenth-century French master as heir to the tradition of the great European colourists from Titian to Rubens and Van Dyck, the very tradition which Geddes himself espoused and championed. For his 1821 Edinburgh exhibition, which served a multiplicity of purposes – as a survey of his range of portraiture, a bid for patronage as a history painter and a display of connoisseurship in the form of his Old Master copies from the Louvre – Geddes selected no fewer than four of his own 'pasticcio' compositions in the style of Watteau. This was the context in which Broadwood's portrait was first presented to the public.[89]

Geddes's aspirations for the Regalia picture and the at-

Fig.45 · left · Andrew Geddes
Francis Jeffrey, Lord Jeffrey, 1820
[National Portrait Gallery, London]

Fig.46 · right · E.S. Lumsden
after Andrew Geddes
Henry Broadwood
[National Gallery of Scotland]

tendant exhibition motivated his third attempt to secure election to Associate membership of the Royal Academy in October 1821. Mortified by his failure – he and Allan, despite the successful Academy launch of the latter's *The Murder of Archbishop Sharpe*, secured precisely one vote each – Geddes is said to have abandoned any further attempt until 1832. His enormous history picture, which remained unsold, was entrusted to the custody of his sisters and eventually cut into fragments. After the artist's death, his enterprising widow retrieved a number of the portrait heads for sale to the relatives of the chief protagonists.[90] In the short term, however, Geddes's hopes were sustained by a momentous turn of events in Edinburgh in August 1822 and the passing accolade of royal favour. Early that month Geddes, Wilkie and William Collins travelled north by the mail coach from London – sustained by Geddes's supply of snuff! – to join the posse of artists, including J.M.W. Turner, who had flocked to the Scottish capital to witness the first State visit to Scotland by a reigning monarch since the return of Charles II in 1652, and the first visit by a senior representative of the house of Hanover since the invasion of Scotland by the Duke of Cumberland in the wake of the last Jacobite Rising. Having received exactly three weeks' advance notice of the King's intended arrival, the Lord Provost of Edinburgh appealed to Sir Walter Scott to devise and stage manage the civic welcome and celebratory pageantry. From his temporary headquarters at his town house in Castle Street, Scott masterminded a programme including four pageants centred on the Scottish Regalia which were intended to recall the King's authorisation, when Prince Regent, of the investigative search for the Scottish Crown Jewels in 1818, and

thereby to convince a sceptical populace of the Hanoverian monarch's respect for, and commitment to, the preservation of Scotland's distinctive identity. The most spectacular and politically charged pageant in the sequence was a symbolic re-enactment of the pre-Union ceremony of 'The Riding of the Parliaments' in the form of a State progress from Holyrood Palace to Edinburgh Castle, necessitating the demolition of several old buildings in the Royal Mile. Escorted by mounted troops, interspersed with the Highlanders of the Celtic Society, the royal carriage followed in the train of the Honours of Scotland borne by their traditional custodians and guarded by the Lord Lyon King of Arms [fig.47].[91]

Scott's skilful manipulation of these events for maximum pictorial effect was matched by the opportunism of the assembled artists and a corresponding bonanza of commemorative oils, drawings and watercolours. The King's last official engagement in Scotland, which took place at Hopetoun House on 29 August, was the conferment of a knighthood upon Scott's friend and neighbour at Abbotsford, Captain Adam Ferguson, Keeper of the Regalia of Scotland, and, with a timely sense of decorum, upon Henry Raeburn. Ten days before Raeburn's preferment, the King had peremptorily commanded the organisation at Holyrood House of a private exhibition which 'would enable His Majesty to judge of the state of the Art in this country', albeit with no promise of formalised patronage. Apart from Raeburn, the nominated participants in this representative exhibition of contemporary Scottish painting were Wilson, 'Grecian' Williams, the Revd John Thomson, Alexander Nasmyth, George Watson and, as the only invited expatriate, Andrew Geddes.[92]

Fig.47 · Denis Dighton
detail from
The Procession of George IV to Edinburgh Castle, 1822
[Scottish National Portrait Gallery,
Edinburgh]

CHAPTER SEVEN

The Later 1820s: the Ascendancy of Lawrence and Geddes's 'Chapeau de Paille'

At a time when Geddes was apparently threatened with litigation over his Ascension altarpiece, Sir Thomas Lawrence responded with an unqualified commitment of support: 'Having very often expressed in conversation with my Friends my sincere opinion of the Work in question, I of course shall not hesitate to offer the same opinion, on any occasion on which you may consider my testimony, as an Artist, of any service.'[93] Following the abdication of Napoleon in 1814, the Prince Regent (the future George IV) had been persuaded to commission from Lawrence a celebratory series of monumental portraits of the allied monarchs, statesmen and military commanders. The royal commission having confirmed Lawrence's stature as the leading portrait painter in Europe, he was elected President of the Royal Academy in 1820. By the 1820s, the influence of Lawrence, which is traceable as a leitmotif in Geddes's own portraiture from about 1812, had been extended through personal acquaintance to a dialogue of connoisseurship, based on mutual esteem and a shared passion for the collecting of Old Master drawings. By 1828, when he was evidently quite a regular visitor to Lawrence's residence, Geddes had deposited at Russell Square a number of his own drawings whose ownership was to be contested with Sir Thomas's executor after his death in 1830. Yet, in 1832, on his return from Italy Geddes was to participate, with missionary zeal, in the abortive crusade to have the Lawrence collection secured for the British nation – a crusade for which Lawrence himself had provided a precedent through his influential advocacy of the purchase of the Parthenon sculptures (the 'Elgin Marbles') for the British Museum and the Angerstein collection of paintings as the nucleus of the National Gallery.[94]

Through the agency of the *marchand amateur* William Young Ottley, the dealer Samuel Woodburn and Jean-Baptiste Wicar, Napoleon's commissioner responsible for the spoliation of works of art from Italy, and through direct purchasing at the sales of Sir Joshua Reynolds and Benjamin West, both his predecessors in the presidency of the Academy, Lawrence formed one of the most impressive cabinets of Old Master prints and drawings ever assembled in Britain. Although particularly rich in examples of the Italian High Renaissance, notably Raphael and Michelangelo, this cabinet included a number by Rubens and Rembrandt in which Geddes's interest was sufficiently intense to justify their commemorative acquisition during the eventual dispersal of the Lawrence estate. Amongst the Rembrandts was *Christ Among the Doctors* [fig.48], which was owned successively by Lawrence, W. Esdaile and the London corn merchant and connoisseur Andrew James (1791/2–1854). The latter was the husband of Ann Plimer and, from 1827, the brother-in-law of Andrew Geddes. James, whose own collection was auctioned in 1873, may well have acquired the drawing for its personal associations as well as for aesthetic reasons. At the third day's sale of Geddes's collections in 1845, which included the artist's purchases from the Lawrence and Esdaile collections, lot 339 was '*Christ among the Doctors – a fine spirited drawing, by Rembrandt*', provenance unstated. What is rather more certain is that Geddes had first-hand knowledge of the drawing once owned by Lawrence (and presumably of other representations of the subject by Rembrandt through the medium of etchings) and that it provided the inspirational model for one of his most elaborate original compositional drawings [fig.49].[95]

The fascination of Lawrence as a creative artist is first discernible in Geddes's surviving original work – and, coincidentally and contemporaneously, in the portraiture of Raeburn around the time of his election to full membership of the Royal Academy in 1815 – in a three-quarter length portrait of his second sister Anne (1785–1843) which

has recently been transformed by conservation [fig.50]. Geddes's own forte lay in his natural facility in the handling of paint and a distinctive and exquisite sensitivity to colour which, on occasion, was deployed with a panache and opulent sensuousness comparable to that of Lawrence. Appropriately, Geddes's affinity with Lawrence found its most compelling expression in an unfinished self-portrait [fig.51 and cover] which Adela Plimer assigned by recollection to the year of her marriage in 1827 but which, judging by the apparent age of the artist, may have been painted several years earlier.[96]

Geddes's prolific draughtsmanship encompassed during the 1820s, among a wide diversity of styles, delicately refined pencil portrait studies, frequently highlighted with chalks and strongly reminiscent of Lawrence's manner. Amongst these is a drawing of Alexander Nasmyth's daughter Charlotte (British Museum) a landscape painter in her

Fig.48 · above left · Rembrandt
Christ Among the Doctors
[Louvre, Paris]

Fig.49 · above right · Andrew Geddes
Christ Among the Doctors
[National Gallery of Scotland, Edinburgh]

Fig.50 · right · Andrew Geddes
Anne Geddes, The Artists's Sister, *c.*1812
[National Gallery of Scotland, Edinburgh]

Fig.51 · left · Andrew Geddes
Self-portrait
[Scottish National Portrait Gallery Edinburgh]

own right as well as a collaborator with her father. Executed in 1823, it was inherited by her niece Jane Terry, daughter of Elizabeth Nasmyth and her actor husband Daniel Terry. Terry posed for Geddes in a conversation piece variously entitled *Dry Reading* or *Dull Reading* which, as the *Art Journal* observed in 1853, 'has much of the character of the Dutch School in composition and colour.'[97] In 1949 the drawing of Charlotte was sold from the collection of the designer and illustrator Walford Graham Robertson together with two exactly contemporary Geddes drawings of a similar type depicting the vendor's grandmother Miss Walford as a youthful society beauty prior to her marriage to Jeremiah Greatorex. These drawings were the prelude to a sequence of commissioned full-scale portraits in oils of which the half-length of Greatorex [fig.52] and an unrelated three-quarter-length of his bride or bride-to-be were the

most distinguished, the latter constituting Geddes's most sophisticated response to the proximity and pre-eminence of Lawrence [fig.53].[98]

Despite the new exhibition facilities afforded by the Institution in Edinburgh, Geddes reserved for the Royal Academy exhibition of 1822 and its metropolitan audience his conversation piece of the family of the Peebleshire landowner Archibald Montgomery of Whim (1771–1844) in which he implicitly courted comparison with the group portraiture of Lawrence [fig.54].[99] Three years later the Academy was again the venue for the launch of Geddes's most prestigious commission of the 1820s, a massive three-quarter-length portrait of Frederick Augustus, Duke of York (Duke of Rutland, Belvoir Castle) whose imposing scale and general conception recalled the Prince Regent's commissions to Lawrence. (The completion of this great

Fig.52 · Andrew Geddes
Jeremiah Greatorex
[Glasgow Museums: Art Gallery & Museum, Kelvingrove]

Fig.53 · Andrew Geddes
Mrs Jeremiah Greatorex, possibly when Miss Walford
[Tate Britain, London]

Fig.54 · left
Andrew Geddes
*Archibald Montgomery of
Whim and his Family*
[Scottish Private Collection]

Fig.55 · right
Thomas Hodgetts after
Andrew Geddes
*Frederick Augustus, the
Duke of York*, 1826
[Scottish National Portrait
Gallery, Edinburgh]

series, now hung in the Waterloo Chamber at Windsor, was protracted. Lawrence's full lengths of the 1st Duke of Wellington, Prince von Blücher – amongst the finest – and Count Hetman Platoff were shown at the Academy in 1815.) Frederick Augustus, a personal friend of the Duke of Rutland at whose London residence in Arlington Street he was to die in 1827, probably sat at the behest of the Duchess, herself a talented amateur artist and architect, with whom Geddes appears to have enjoyed a particularly cordial relationship and upon whose death in 1825 Wilkie was to offer his condolences in a letter from Rome in 1826.[100] That New Year, J.M.W. Turner, another habitué of Belvoir, wrote to the watercolourist James Holworthy, 'Let me join you in concern for your loss at Belvoir has now faded away from me, and I think Geddes feels much the same way, tho' I hope not for his picture of the family.' By then Geddes was engaged on the sequel to the York commission, a conversation piece of the Rutland family whose completion was interrupted by the sudden death of his patron. In July Hugh William Williams offered his congratulations to Geddes on the publication of Thomas Hodgetts's mezzotint [fig.55] after the royal portrait, which 'is much admired among my friends though the most of them are Whiggs ... I could almost wish the Royal Duke would pop off that you might have an immediate and extensive sale.' The critical success of the print was matched by the approval of George IV who, by the testimony of Adela Geddes, deemed the Geddes 'the best likeness ever painted of his brother, and the Duke of Cambridge called personally at our residence in Brook-

street, to express his approbation.'[101]

In *Peter's Letters to His Kinsfolk*, published in 1819 within a year of the appearance of Ward's mezzotint after Geddes's portrait of Wilkie, John Gibson Lockhart had nominated Geddes as one of the most likely successors to the Scottish Lawrence, Henry Raeburn. Andrew Wilson, who shared with Raeburn and Geddes the honour of being selected by the King for his private exhibition of representative modern Scottish painting in August 1822, had indulged in a similar eulogy of Geddes in his correspondence with David Bridges junior in 1815 and 1816. On 8 July 1823 Wilson, Master of the Trustees' Academy, wrote post haste to his friend and co-adjutor announcing the death of Raeburn from 'a total failure of the system' earlier that same day:

> *I do not know Geddes if you can be induced to alter your determination as to remaining in London but who is now to fill the place of Sir H. as a portrait painter in Edinr? I suppose we must have an Englishman: the House in York Place did not belong to Raeburn it was purchased by a lady at the time of his failure and he has since paid for it the Interest of £2000 yearly it could not be converted into a House but at great expence & it could be had now on the same terms I suppose or it will be sold.*

Of the virtually instantaneous response in London to the loss of the recently appointed King's Limner for Scotland, the *Annual Biography and Obituary* testified that, 'though Sir Henry was comparatively much less known there, an equally strong sensation was produced.' At a meeting of the Royal Academy held on 14 July the President Sir Thomas Lawrence 'expressed his high admiration for the talents of the deceased ... His loss Sir Thomas conceived ... had left a blank in the Royal Academy, as well as in his own country, which could not be filled up.'[102]

This flurry of speculation did not dissuade Geddes from his primary allegiance to London. Three years later, when he was acting as intermediary in a sale of prints to his own patron John Sheepshanks by Hugh William Williams, Geddes was informed that 'Mr Colvin Smith, who fills Raeburn's *shoes* is about to go to Rome ...' A competent if somewhat unlikely occupant of this position, Colvin Smith (1796–1875) had recently purchased the house in York Place. He was soon to be displaced, although not marginalised, as Raeburn's chief successor by a far stronger contender and another of Lockhart's nominees, John Watson Gordon (1788–1864), nephew of Raeburn's true rival in Edinburgh, George Watson. In 1850 Watson Gordon would succeed Allan as President of the Royal Scottish Academy and receive a knighthood on his appointment as Queen's Limner for Scotland.[103] His London allegiance notwithstanding, Geddes continued to cultivate his affiliation to the Institution in Scotland in tandem with his support of its metropolitan counterpart. In 1824, despite his failure to participate in the Institution's exhibitions of 'Living Artists'

since the inaugural occasion in 1821, he was elected a non-resident Honorary Member. Having duly given his assurance that, 'it will at all times afford me the greatest pleasure to assist in forwarding the Views of the Institution by every means my local situation will permit', he did not transfer his loyalty to the secessionist Scottish Academy in 1826 and did not publicly support exhibitions until a decade later.[104]

In 1826, in emulation of a similar exploratory venture by Wilkie in 1824, Geddes published privately in London the first in a limited edition of portfolios with variable contents of ten etchings. In the accompanying prospectus he claimed, with a degree of disingenuousness and assumed dilettantism, that these were the productions of 'his hours of leisure from his more immediate Engagements' and that, in the event of public disapproval, he would 'more cheerfully descend from that most proverbially expensive of all

Fig.56 · right · Andrew Geddes
*Summer, c.*1826
[National Gallery of Scotland, Edinburgh]

Fig.57 · below left · Sir Peter Paul Rubens
'Le Chapeau de Paille', probably 1622–5
[National Gallery, London]

Figs.58 a & b · below · Andrew Geddes
*Study from Rubens and related study for Summer, c.*1823–6
[National Gallery of Scotland, Edinburgh]

animals – a Hobby.' Concurrently he executed a remarkable landscape etching which, apart from being indicative of a recent excursion to Scotland, may claim to be the earliest representation by a Scottish artist of the presumed site of the battle of Bannockburn in 1314 [fig.82].[105] While the general topography is sufficiently accurate to have been based on drawings made on the spot, the actual spatial relationships have been telescoped in order to focus symbolically on the connection between Stirling Castle (on the left), still garrisoned in June 1314 by the English forces of Edward I, and the large, flat, perforated stone in the foreground where Scotland's liberator Robert I ('Robert the Bruce') reputedly raised the Royal Standard prior to his decisive victory on 24 June. Whatever the precise circumstances of his own visit, Geddes would certainly have been aware of the most powerful of all existing literary traditions associated with the site. In 1787, when he sat to Nasmyth for the iconic likeness now in the Scottish National Portrait Gallery, Robert Burns paused at Bannockburn during his Highland tour. Six years later he composed the most enduring and inspirational celebration of William Wallace as folk hero, 'Scots Wha' Hae wi' Wallace Bled', or the address of Bruce to his troops before Bannockburn.

On 15 March 1827, following upon the publication of Geddes's 1826 portfolio, 'Grecian' Williams wrote to the Institution's Secretary, James Skene of Rubislaw, as already noted, an amateur etcher: 'I am really glad to find that you approve of my suggestion regarding Mr Geddes's Etchings I feel sure that it will gratify him exceedingly to learn that *through you* they will be taken for the collection of the Royal Institution. In writing to Mr Geddes I shall give him a hint to send a picture or two for next year's exhibition – he has a very beautiful one he calls his Chapeau which I shall particularly request him to send. It will really do honour to any Exhibition.'[106] Despite its eminent saleability, Geddes's 'Chapeau', an engaging fancy portrait entitled *Summer* [fig.56], had failed to secure a bidder at the British Institution exhibition of 1826. He was all the more inclined to oblige by re-submitting his 'Chapeau' to the Edinburgh Institution where it would be displayed to maximum advantage in 1828, its prototype by Rubens having been lent by the statesman Robert Peel to the Institution's complementary exhibition of Old Master paintings in the same year.

The sobriquet *'Le Chapeau de Paille'* ('The Straw Hat') had become attached to the Rubens original in the late eighteenth century and, despite its inappropriateness – the sitter wears a felt hat of the type adopted by both sexes in the Netherlands in the 1620s – remained integral to the picture's celebrity status. The sitter was then, and generally still is, thought to be Susanna Lunden, née Fourment, whose younger sister Hélène married Rubens in 1630 [fig.57]. Purchased in Antwerp in 1822 by a consortium of London and Brussels dealers, the picture was exported to London where the special exhibition in Old Bond Street in 1823 prompted a chauvinistically triumphalist eulogy in the local press: 'The chef d'oeuvre of Rubens as a portrait painter, the wonder of Flanders, the admired and inimitable Chapeau de Paille, has at last become the prize of British wealth and enterprise, and after feasting the eyes of the London amateurs, is to grace the Palace of a Monarch peculiarly qualified, by natural taste and elegant acquirements, to feel and to appreciate its beauties.' The said monarch, George IV, having withdrawn from the transaction, the 'Chapeau' was sold to Peel in 1824.[107]

The genesis of Geddes's 'Chapeau' can be traced through two pastel studies [figs.58a & 58b] of which the first was presumably executed on site in Old Bond Street. This experience must have encouraged him to seek for his own collection of Rubens drawings the 'Capital drawing, by Rubens, of Helena Forman', subsequently included in Geddes's posthumous sale at Christie's in 1845.[108] The finished composition of *Summer*, one of Geddes's more creative and thoroughly assimilated appropriations from an Old Master painting, was sold to the Royal Institution in 1828 for the foundation collection of the projected 'Gallery of National Importance' which Andrew Wilson, in his dual capacity as dealer and Master of the Trustees' Academy, was to advocate formally to the directorate in 1829. It was a purchase entirely in harmony with the Institution's simultaneous patronage and promotion of Old Masters and contemporary Scottish painting, and with the duality of the public image which Geddes himself sought to cultivate.[109]

CHAPTER EIGHT

London 1827: Marriage and 'Mr. Watteau'

In the course of 1823, the year of Raeburn's death and Wilson's exhortations to Geddes to return to Edinburgh, Geddes moved from his previous lodgings in Conduit Street and took the lease of a house at 58 Brook Street within the parish of St George's, Hanover Square. This property, which was renumbered 23 in 1867, lay on the border between the Conduit Mead Estate under the jurisdiction of the City of London and the prestigious Mayfair Estate owned since the seventeenth century by the Grosvenor family, the wealthiest urban landlords in the country, later elevated to the peerage in the dukedom of Westminster. Brook Street extends westward from Hanover Square, transecting Bond Street, and culminates in Grosvenor Square. Whereas the western section of Brook Street, intensively developed from the 1720s, was generally inhabited by titled residents in the 1820s, the commercialised eastern extremity between Davies Street and Bond Street – where Geddes settled – was 'of such a mixed Character of Houses as not to be thought an eligible situation for Persons of Rank' and was subject to colonisation by the hotel trade. The artist's new lodgings, which were immediately adjacent to the house at number 25, celebrated for its occupancy by George Frederick Handel from 1724 to 1759, had previously been leased by William Carpenter between 1819 and 1822 [fig.59].[110]

William Hookham Carpenter (1792–1866) was the son of James Carpenter, the prosperous bookseller of Old Bond Street who specialised in publications on the visual arts. The latter enjoyed a wide circle of acquaintances among contemporary artists and engravers through his related publishing enterprise, and was also known as a zealous dealer and collector. The younger Carpenter's tenancy in Lower Brook Street coincided with his attempt to establish an independent business in the same line following his marriage in 1817 to Margaret Sarah Geddes (1793–1872), younger daughter of Captain Alexander Geddes of Alderbury in Wiltshire. Andrew Geddes's enduring friendship with the Carpenters may well have evolved as a result of their successive tenancies in Lower Brook Street. This friendship assisted, quite fortuitously, in perpetuating a false tradition which has continued to associate in supposed kinship the two unrelated Geddes families, while claiming for the childless Scottish artist the status of father-in-law to the landscape and genre painter William Collins![111] Geddes's professional relationship with Mrs Carpenter as a fellow portrait painter – a remarkably prolific and successful practitioner who, when at her peak during the 1830s and 1840s, would be widely regarded as the natural successor to Lawrence – was sufficiently cordial to justify her inclusion in his gallery of artists' portraits and her selection for his 1821 retrospective exhibition in Edinburgh. In 1824 she reciprocated by painting a portrait of Geddes which passed upon his death into the collection of his wife's niece, Sarah Ann James. However, it was to William Carpenter that Geddes owed his first substantial public memorial. In the year following Geddes's death Carpenter was appointed Keeper of Prints and Drawings at the British Museum. Between 1847 and 1858 he systematically acquired for the Museum a significant number of rare proofs of his late friend's etchings which were added to the existing small corpus of choice impressions from the collection of Geddes's patron John Sheepshanks.[112]

Geddes's relocation to Brook Street in 1823 may not have been unrelated to its proximity to the Plimer household in Maddox Street within the immediate vicinity of the parish

church. On 5 May 1827 Andrew Geddes married Adela Plimer in St George's, Hanover Square, in the presence of John and Elizabeth James and the bride's sister or mother both of whom were named Ann. During Geddes's extended courtship, allegedly sustained despite adverse circumstances over twenty-four years, Adela Plimer was at one time engaged as governess to the children of Anne Napier, daughter of the 7th Lord Napier, who married Sir Thomas Gibson Carmichael in 1816. Years later, in her widowhood, Mrs Geddes was to be offered a similar position by the Reid family, amongst whom the orphaned Nevile Reid, Lady Carmichael's nephew, sat to Geddes for two portrait drawings in the penultimate year of the artist's life [fig.73]. As late as 1901 the Gibson Carmichael picture collection included an intimately scaled cabinet portrait by Geddes described as *The Artist's Wife and a Friend* whose published dimensions correspond almost exactly to those of the *Portrait of Two Women* in the National Gallery of Scotland [fig.60]. If these are indeed one and the same, then the Gallery possesses a very personal tribute to the artist's intended bride as she would have appeared during the 1820s.[113]

Adela Plimer's late marriage in the spring of 1827 was followed on 1 August by that of her older sister Ann to Andrew James (1791/2–1854), a London corn dealer. This dual connection by marriage was to cement an important association between James and his new brother-in-law in the latter's capacity as connoisseur-dealer as well as creative artist. Although James himself has remained an elusive

figure, he was known, according to the essayist and critic Edmond de Goncourt, as 'Mr. Watteau' on account of his dedication to collecting Watteau's works, most especially his drawings. It was this particular aspect of Watteau's activity which fascinated Geddes who, like Wilkie, sought to emulate the French draughtsman's animated three-colour drawing technique, both in exploratory studies from Watteau originals (as represented in the collection of the British Museum)[114] and in his own independent compositions in the chalk medium [fig.61]. The extent of James's collection – and, consequently, the range of material which became potentially accessible to his brother-in-law – may be estimated from the fact that Watteau drawings accounted for no fewer than eighty lots in the second of two successive sales from the inheritance of the collector's unmarried daughter Sarah Ann James in 1891.[115]

In addition to this remarkable group of Watteau drawings (of which four were purchased by the National Gallery of Ireland), Gustav Waagen, Director of the Royal Gallery of Pictures in Berlin, noted shortly after James's death during his exhaustive inspection of the principal private cabinets in Britain, that 'no collection, either public or private ... contains a series of admirable drawings by this master [Rembrandt] so illustrative of his various classes of subject – sacred, genre, portrait and landscape. Most of these proceed from the collections of Sir Joshua Reynolds and Thomas Lawrence. The latter are marked with the initials of Mr. Esdaile, who, as is well known, purchased all the

Fig.59 · right
Richard Buckler
Geddes's house and Handel's former house at nos 58 and 57 Lower Brook Street, 1839
[The British Library, London]

Fig.60 · left · Andrew Geddes
Portrait of Two Women, possibly the Artist's Wife and a Friend
[National Gallery of Scotland, Edinburgh]

Fig.61 · far right
Andrew Geddes
Three studies after Watteau
[The British Museum, London]

Rembrandt drawings of the Lawrence collection from Mr. Woodburn.' Most of these drawings were dispersed in fifty-one lots, together with a related group of etchings, in a partial sale from James's collection at Christie's in 1873. They included, as already noted, Lawrence's Rembrandt drawing of *Christ Among the Doctors* which Geddes used as the essential prototype for his own original composition. On 17 June 1840 Geddes had been one of the principal bidders at the Christie's sale of the Old Master drawings collection formed by the London banker William Esdaile (1758–1837). The highlight of this sale consisted of a group of one hundred Rembrandt drawings which Esdaile had acquired at the dispersal of Sir Thomas Lawrence's cabinet. Of Geddes's purchases in 1840, most were destined for his brother-in-law, Andrew James.[116]

The full extent of the commercial and creative interchange between James and his brother-in-law and their respective collections has yet to be ascertained. In 1835, the year in which Geddes exhibited a conversation piece of James's children at the Royal Academy, he entered in the mixed sale from his own Old Master collection, in collaboration with Sir John James Steuart of Allanbank, a Watteau *Garden Scene*, reputedly once owned by Reynolds. The same Watteau, whose purchase by Geddes in 1821 coincided with the exhibition of his own 'pasticcios' in Edinburgh, has been identified provisionally as a version of *La Cascade*. Then, in 1841, after rationalising his previous collection, Geddes acquired from the Marquess Camden sale in London a variant of *L'Occupation selon l'âge*, now in the National Gallery of Ireland. Both of these Watteaus subsequently entered the James collection.[117]

Geddes's immediate priorities following his marriage were, however, radically different. In 1825, after experiencing a nervous breakdown, his close friend Wilkie had embarked on three years' restorative travel in Europe. From Rome, where he spent the winters of 1826 and 1827, Wilkie wrote again to Geddes, reiterating with renewed urgency, his exhortations to study in Italy: 'Come before it be *too* inconvenient for you to leave London every year this will be

more difficult, and the time more precious. Let me advise you therefore to cut and run at once.' The expiry of the lease in Lower Brook Street in 1828 provided a natural incentive, as did conceivably the death on 11 January of Agnes Boyd Geddes which severed the artist's strongest personal link with his native Edinburgh. By August, in anticipation of financing an extended stay in Italy, Geddes had embarked on the selective disposal of his Old Master collection. The landscape painter the Revd John Thomson of Duddingston to whom, presumably in the absence in Rome of the arch entrepreneur Wilson, he had applied for assistance, offered letters of introduction but declined to collaborate in further sales ventures in Scotland after his initial failure due to 'the scarcity of money here ... as far as my personal experience goes ... I never had so unproductive a season.' At the same time, Geddes approached Lawrence with 'the first offer of the two Pictures by Rembrandt in my possession. I would part with them at present for 700 Gs. Believing such a price to be an advantageous investment of money to any person wishing such property.' Lawrence selected *The Toilet of Bathsheba*. In addition, he was offered, as a connoisseur of Michelangelo, 'the Picture by Jacomo da Pontormo from the Cartoon of Michelangelo ... done undoubtedly under the eye of Michelangelo', and described in Vasari's *Lives of the Painters*.[118]

Of his Italian Old Master pictures, *Christ Disputing with the Doctors*, 'a grand gallery picture of the life size' attributed to Titian's contemporary, Andrea Schiavone, was omitted from the reckoning. In 1830 Geddes was to purchase two further Schiavones in Venice, a *Holy Family with the Infant St John the Baptist and Saints* and *Christ and the Canaanitish woman interceding for her Daughter* which incorporated 'a most exquisite landscape, shewing his powers in that department.' In the meantime Geddes had already commemorated his ownership of the first Schiavone in one of his most elaborate and densely wrought reproductive etchings [fig.75]. The execution of Geddes's etching, published in its final state in 1826, formed a fitting prelude to a three-year sojourn in Italy.[119]

CHAPTER NINE

The Italian Sojourn 1828–30

After leaving London during the late autumn of 1828, the Geddeses travelled overland to Italy via Paris and Lyon, crossing Mont Cenis and pausing at Genoa and Florence before taking the Perugia road to Rome. While in Genoa Geddes renewed contact with Andrew Wilson who, as stated previously, had returned to Italy in 1826 to concentrate on dealing, with occasional forays into landscape painting, the official justification for his resignation from the Trustees' Academy in Edinburgh. From Genoa the Wilson family escorted their compatriots to Rome where Geddes was to be privileged with a 'second view of the works formerly congregated in the Louvre in 1814' and where, as Wilkie had registered in 1827, 'Wilson was the chief painter, and Campbell the chief sculptor' among the resident colony of Scottish artists.[120] On arrival Geddes secured lodgings at 49, Via della Croce off the Piazza di Spagna in the heart of the foreign artistic community. Within a short distance lay the Via Margutta, the locality favoured by visiting Dutch and Flemish painters in the seventeenth century, and where, in 1821, a British Academy of Arts had been established with the sanction and/or financial support of the diplomat William Richard Hamilton, the Royal Academy and its President Thomas Lawrence (who sent a personal donation), the Dukes of Bedford and Devonshire and, ultimately, the King.

Over the winter of 1828 Geddes fraternised with J.M.W. Turner of whose second visit to Italy in 1828–9 he observed to John Sheepshanks, that, 'The People here cannot understand his style at all.' Geddes's foremost priority was self-education by immersion in the study of the Venetian school. By April 1829 he was about to embark on a full-scale replica of one of the outstanding treasures of the Villa Borghese,

Titian's *Sacred and Profane Love*. This copy, despite its curiously unfinished state, was to be purchased by the Royal Academy in London as a posthumous tribute to Geddes in 1845. In conjunction with the copy, he was contemplating the desirability of a reproductive print, perhaps in the form of an etching, subject to the availability of English copper of the requisite quality and of a printing press. For advice on the prospective market for a print, he turned to John Sheepshanks. In the same letter Geddes urged him to exploit the opportunity of a new papal accession to despatch to Rome a batch of engravings after Lawrence's portrait of the late Pius VII, painted in Rome for the Prince Regent in 1819 (Royal Collection). Lawrence himself had shown Geddes a proof impression of the print immediately prior to the latter's departure from London.

Sheepshanks's confident patronage of Geddes, already a vital factor in sustaining his experimentation with 'original' etching, was to become a leitmotif of the artist's Roman sojourn. During the late 1820s Sheepshanks had retired from the inherited family cloth manufacturing business in order to dedicate himself to collecting. By 1826, when Geddes paid him the compliment of a presentation set of his own original etchings,[121] the affluent Sheepshanks was assiduously amassing an unrivalled collection of over seven thousand Old Master etchings and drawings of the Dutch and Flemish schools upon which, aided and abetted by the dealer Samuel Woodburn and possibly by Geddes's friend the engraver John Burnet, he ultimately lavished almost £13,000. Concurrently, Sheepshanks was patronising contemporary British etchers, including Geddes, Wilkie, and Edwin Landseer. From about 1830 and especially after the disposal of his main print collection in 1836, he began to concentrate on purchasing contemporary British paintings, either from the Royal Academy's summer exhibitions or direct from the artists. In 1857 he was persuaded by Richard Redgrave, one of the chief promoters of the South Kensington Museum (the embryonic Victoria and Albert Museum), to gift his private collection of contemporary painting as the nucleus of a National Gallery of British Art associated with the Government Schools of Art. Through this gift, supplemented by Sheepshanks's subsequent presentation of his etchings, including the collected oeuvre of Geddes, the Museum acquired *A Man Smoking*, Geddes's essay in the seventeenth-century Dutch 'guardroom' genre, and his small copy, painted in October 1830, of Giorgione's celebrated triple portrait in the Manfrini Palace in Venice.[122]

In the meantime, as Geddes enthused to Sheepshanks in April 1829, 'what is new to me is the Landscape of this Country it is indeed a Country for a Landscape painter & one cannot sufficiently appreciate the Works of R. Wilson till they [*sic*] come to Italy everything puts you in mind of

Fig.62 · Nicolas Poussin
Landscape with St John on Patmos
[The Art Institute of Chicago]

Fig.63 · Andrew Geddes
'Nellie Hepburn'?, 1830
[Scottish Private Collection]

him'. Accordingly, the summer was spent at the village of Subiaco, about forty miles from Rome, where Geddes executed a number of pure landscapes in oils, of which *Ruins of the Baths of Nero at Subiaco* and *Carrara* were launched at the British Institution in London in 1834 as the first in a succession culminating, in the year of his death, with the exhibition of *Subiaco – Early Morning* at the Royal Academy.[123]

The winter of 1829 witnessed the fulfilment, or more accurately, supposed fulfilment of another artistic pilgrimage when, according to Adela Geddes, the Geddeses transferred their lodgings to Poussin's former residence 'on the Monte Pinciano, overlooking the whole city of Rome, with the residences of Claude Lorraine and Salvator Rosa within view: it might be truly called classical ground'. The Pincio itself, which adjoins the Villa Borghese, had been laid out between 1809 and 1814 by Napoleon's architect Giuseppe Valadier as the largest public garden in the centre of Rome. It rapidly became the most fashionable Roman 'passeggiata', frequented, during the 1820s, by amongst others, Joseph Severn, John Keats, Princess Pauline Borghese and most of the resident artistic community. The Geddeses leased a house at the head of the Spanish Steps at number 11 on the Piazza of S. Trinità dei Monti, one of the principal French churches in Rome where, in 1682, Claude Lorrain had been buried, and it does indeed command

spectacular panoramic views over the city of Rome and the Vatican. In 1874 Adela Geddes described her second Rome lodging to the antiquary David Laing as 'Claude & Nichol Poussin's house.' In actuality, it was neither. From 1627 to 1650 Claude had lived continuously in the parish of S. Maria del Popolo in the Via Margutta, whereas Poussin, even after his marriage in 1630 to Anne-Marie Dughet, the sister of Gaspard Dughet, had occupied throughout his later residences in Rome a modest house in the Via del Babuino below the Pincio.

In making a symbolic choice for his new lodgings, Geddes had unwittingly subscribed to a contemporary myth integral to the early nineteenth-century personality cult of Poussin. According to this myth, the house adjoining the Trinità was identified as that of Poussin and the 'Tempietto' at the intersection of the Via Sistina and the Via Gregoriana, as the residence of Claude. Both Andrew Wilson and Geddes – whom Wilson was to commend for the selfsame reason to the Edinburgh collector Gilbert Laing Meason in 1830 – took pride in their respective connoisseurship of Poussin which, in 1840, would be crowned by Geddes's purchase of the magnificent *Landscape with St John on Patmos* [fig.62].[124]

Geddes's move to Poussin's reputed residence coincided, opportunely, with his participation in the formation on 24 November 1829 of a prestigious international society of artists and *cognoscenti* under the personal patronage of Cardinal Camerlengo. The principal objective of the Società degli Amatori e Cultori delle Belle Arti, which convened in Rome, was to organise an annual public exhibition through the agency of a multinational governing council comprising fifteen artist members and fifteen non-practising and predominantly aristocratic and/or ambassadorial members. The admission proceeds from the annual exhibitions were to be allocated to the purchase of exhibits which were then re-distributed by lottery. The artist members of the first council under the Presidency of the Duke of Corchiano included, according to a report in the *Diaro di Roma* of 14 April 1830, the painters Horace Vernet, Karl Adolf Senff, Joseph Severn, Penry Williams, Andrew Geddes and Vincenzo Cammuccini and, among the sculptors, Bertel Thorvaldsen, Pietro Tenerani and John Gibson.[125] Of the British contingent, Severn, Williams and Gibson were also members of the British Academy of Arts in Rome.

In December Wilkie wrote from London, urging Geddes not to capitulate to the 'disappointment' of his first winter's residence in Rome: 'May I hope to hear you are now full of work & if not with regular portraits do let it be with that you do so well – fancy pictures. Now that you are in Rome embue yourself with Italian Art, and let your fancy pictures have that character I saw in one or two of your works in the hall of the Edinbr Institution [i.e. *Summer*] that looked so famously full of tone & richness.' The Società's inaugural exhibition was staged, by special dispensation, on the Capitol in 1830. Unfortunately, it is not known whether plans to publish a catalogue were ever realised. To this exhibition Geddes reputedly lent an example of the specialism so much admired by Wilkie, rendered with captivating luminosity and redolent of Reynolds's portraits in the same genre [fig.63]. At a later stage in its history, following its acquisition for a Scottish private collection, Geddes's Italian fancy portrait assumed an alternative and implausible identity as a likeness of one Nellie Hepburn, variously described as the head gardener's or village carpenter's daughter![126]

It was almost certainly as a direct result of his membership of the Società that Geddes secured the most important commission of his Italian sojourn and one which provided the consummate pretext for an elaborate exercise in fancy portraiture. Among the British 'amatori' or patron members of the Società in 1830 was John Talbot, 16th Earl of Shrewsbury, an honorary member of the Academy of St Luke in Rome and senior lay representative of the Roman Catholic Church in England in succession to the (converted) Duke of Norfolk. During at least one of their periodic visits to Rome, the Italophile Talbots lodged in the Palazzo Doria Pamphilj. In 1835 the Earl's younger daughter Gwendoline Catherine (died 1840) was to marry Marcantonio Aldobrandini, later Prince Borghese, while, in 1839, her older sister Mary Alethea Beatrix (died 1858) became the bride of Prince Filippo Andrea Doria Pamphili-Landi.[127]

Lord Shrewsbury's commission for a fancy portrait of his two young daughters, masquerading as winsome *ciocare* or local peasant girls, was presumably begun in 1829 when Geddes made a series of preparatory studies in black chalk. From the outset, the most significant element of the composition, apart from the picturesque peasant costume, was the most exclusive accessory available, by special dispensation, to the daughters of England's senior Catholic layman – the Pope's pug dog [figs.64 & 65]. In the finished picture, dated 1830 and now in the Doria Pamphilj collection in Rome, Geddes exploited to maximum effect the vibrant colouristic possibilities of the peasant costume [fig.66].[128]

Of the celebrity artist members of the Società, two were induced to sit to Geddes in or about 1830. Vincenzo Cammuccini (1771–1844), doyen of the Roman history painters, was internationally renowned by 1810 when he had been received by Napoleon and Jacques-Louis David in Paris and had been selected in 1811 to collaborate in the redecoration of the Palazzo del Quirinale in Rome in anticipation of Bonaparte's arrival. Appointed Superintendent of the Apostolic Palaces by the Pope in 1814, Cammuccini remained pre-eminent in the cultural life of the city after the French occupation. In 1829 he joined Bertel Thorvaldsen and Cardinal Camerlengo in ratifying the founding constitution of the Società and the following year was created Baron by Pius VIII and entrusted with the reorganisation of the fine art collections of the Vatican Museums. Geddes's portrait of Cammuccini was eventually acquired by Sir Robert Peel (1788–1850) possibly during the early 1840s, the period of his premiership, for his private portrait gallery at his country residence, Drayton Manor in his Staffordshire constituency of Tamworth. A patron of Wilkie, William Collins and Clarkson Stanfield, Peel amassed a

distinguished collection of Dutch and Flemish pictures of which seventy-seven, notably Hobbema's *The Avenue, Middelharnis*, De Hooch's *The Courtyard of a House in Delft* and Rubens's '*Chapeau de Paille*' were purchased from Peel's heirs for the National Gallery in 1871, transforming the existing holdings.

In addition he purchased for Drayton Manor, presumably as a pendant for Cammuccini's portrait, one of three Geddes portraits of the sculptor John Gibson (1790–1866) from whom, in 1834, Peel had ordered a version of *Cupid Disguised as a Shepherd*, similarly destined for his Staffordshire residence.[129] In 1817, with the assistance of William Roscoe and the d'Aguilar, Lawrence and Robinson families in his adoptive Liverpool, Gibson had settled permanently in Rome. Two years later, after receiving instruction from the two leading sculptural exponents of European Neoclassicism, Antonio Canova and Bertel Thorvaldsen, successively, Gibson had secured the patronage of the 6th Duke of Devonshire for a marble group of *Mars and Cupid*. This was to be displayed in the sculpture gallery at Chatsworth, an influential precedent which was soon to establish Gibson as one of the most favoured sculptors among English collectors in Rome. Within a decade Gibson was the acknowledged leader of the expatriate colony of British sculptors, including Richard Wyatt and Joseph Gott and the Scots Laurence Macdonald and Thomas Campbell, and was vying with Pietro Tenerani for the status of premier

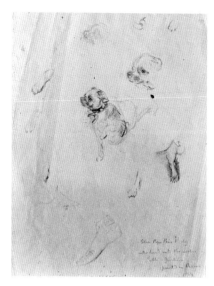

Fig.64 · far left · Andrew Geddes
Compositional study for 'The Ladies Talbot', c.1829
[National Gallery of Scotland, Edinburgh]

Fig.65 · left · Andrew Geddes
Studies of Pope Pius's Pug Dog for the 'The Ladies Talbot', c.1829
[National Gallery of Scotland, Edinburgh]

Fig.66 · right · Andrew Geddes
The Ladies Talbot, 1830
[Doria Pamphilj Collection, Rome]

sculptor in Rome following the death of Canova in 1821 and during the frequent absences in Denmark of the latter's rival, Thorvaldsen.

In 1829, when he participated with Geddes in the founding of the Società, Gibson was also elected Resident Academician of Merit of the Academy of St Luke through the concerted lobbying of Cammuccini and Thorvaldsen. The much-admired Peel portrait of Gibson – which the sculptor viewed again in Sir Robert's company at Drayton Manor while paying a return visit to Britain in 1847 to supervise the installation of the William Huskisson monument in Liverpool – is now known only from a mezzotint by Samuel Bellin of London, published in 1839 [fig.67]. The original was inaccurately described by the sitter himself by recollection as a 'repetition' replicating, on a reduced scale, a three-quarter length oil executed by Geddes in 1830 and amongst his most imposing full-scale portraits [fig.68]. The similarity in pose between the two portraits suggests that they were related but independent compositions, sharing a common origin in the same sittings.[130]

In the more elaborate of the two compositions, Gibson's Liverpudlian origins are emphatically recalled by means of the monument commemorating his early friend Mrs Emily Robinson on which he was engaged in 1829–30 and which was installed in St James the Less in Liverpool. In the background the Torso Belvedere from the Vatican serves as a reminder of the sculptor's contemporary status within and commitment to the city of Rome. Following its debut at the Academy in 1832, the portrait was re-launched at the Liverpool Academy in 1835 and secured by William Earle (1760–1839) for whom Gibson later sculpted a memorial relief, also in St James the Less. Earle, who habitually wintered in Rome for his health, was the proprietor of a prosperous family enterprise in Leghorn which is credited with the initiation of the importation into Liverpool of Carrara marble to be used for sculpture. In 1843 Earle's son presented Geddes's Roman masterpiece to the Liverpool Institution

where it hung in close proximity to a portrait of William Roscoe, Gibson's most influential Liverpudlian patron.[131]

In February 1830 Geddes received from Wilkie an extended bulletin on the sudden death on 7 January of Sir Thomas Lawrence which shocked London society and generated intense speculation as to his professional successor. Wilkie himself, whose anticipated nomination for election to the Royal Academy was frustrated, was appointed to Lawrence's other public office as Painter-in-Ordinary to George IV. Of his own last encounter with Sir Thomas, Wilkie recalled the President's regret that Geddes's 'taste and feeling in the Art was not yet appreciated by the public, as he confessed it was by himself', and enjoined Geddes to participate, on his return from Italy, in 'the search for those who have a similar aim with Lawrence' and which 'might bring employers in your way & no doubt with advantage.'[132] Apart from the unedifying scramble for patronage, Wilkie's main concern was the successful retrieval – instigated by Wilkie at his friend's request – of the Old Master drawings

Fig.67 · left · Samuel Bellin after Andrew Geddes
John Gibson, 1839
[Scottish National Portrait Gallery, Edinburgh]

Fig.68 · opposite · Andrew Geddes
John Gibson, 1830
[Walker Art Gallery, National Museums and Galleries on Merseyside]

deposited by Geddes with Lawrence about two years previously and whose ownership, not having been satisfactorily verified, was contested by the executor, Archibald Keightley. Among these was, almost certainly, a Rubens study of St Francis Xavier (Fitzwilliam Museum, Cambridge) which bore the collector's mark of Lawrence.[133] Wilkie's letter of February 1830 was the first of two intimations addressed to Geddes concerning the protracted affair of the Lawrence collection in which he was to become doubly embroiled.

In a lengthy and important epistle of 17 May 1830, John Sheepshanks briefed Geddes on the latest Old Master print sales and market trends and notable recent publications of engravings, especially those of Moon & Boys after Wilkie. In addition, he volunteered an exhaustive account of the scale and immediate implications of the debt crisis then encumbering the Lawrence estate, observing that

> *It must continue yet a matter of doubt whether the effects exclusive for the old drawings, will be found sufficient to pay all the debts, in which event only can they be offered in one lot ... to the King, British Museum, Lord Dudley or Mr Peel [i.e. Robert Peel] for £18,000. Woodburn [i.e. the dealer Samuel Woodburn] tells me that they have cost more than £30,000 & that he is ready to take them at a higher price than the Will puts upon them.*

Sheepshanks's chronicle, which unknowingly anticipated the denouement of the crisis – the refusal of Lawrence's offer to the nation of his entire collection for a fraction of its estimated market value, its consequent dispersal and the invalidation of the artist's bequests – was probably the incidental catalyst for his correspondent's campaign in January 1832 to prevent this self same denouement.[134]

In the meantime, having thanked Geddes for 'the very kind offer of accommodation at Rome with you' Sheepshanks resumed discussion of his earlier plans – frustrated by severe illness – for an extended Continental tour on which, during the initial stages, he would be accompanied by 'Mr. Gibbon the Engraver ... to make Etchings or facsimiles copies of rare prints.' In anticipation of his own eventual arrival in Rome, he enquired whether Geddes might accept a commission for an etched view of 'Claude's house as it now stands' as the frontispiece to a projected catalogue of his own print collection including etchings by the French master [fig.83]. The resulting plate – like that for the related commission of his patron's portrait which may have been executed prior to Geddes's departure for Italy [fig.85] – remained the outright property of Sheepshanks. Geddes's etching was, of course, unbeknown to Sheepshanks or to his protégé, a commemoration of contemporary mythology rather than historical reality![135]

The proposed reunion with Sheepshanks was to be superseded by Geddes's decision to return to Britain later that year, prompted, in part, by the onset of consumption. Over the summer he undertook a restorative visit to Naples, one of the compelling attractions being, as in Rome, the prospect of a second encounter with the spoliated works since repatriated from the Louvre. While in Naples, he probably renewed contact with James Justinian Morier (*c*.1780–1849), the well known Persian diplomat, traveller and author of the picaresque romances *Adventures of Hajji Baba* (1824), whose son had sat the previous year for a half-length portrait now in Aberdeen Art Gallery. The Geddeses' return journey across Italy that autumn became, inevitably, an artistic pilgrimage in the course of which Geddes paused in Florence and in Venice to worship at the all-powerful shrine of Titian, executing a copy of *Flora* and the *St Peter Martyr* installed in the church of SS. Giovanni e Paolo during the post-Napoleonic restitution. From Venice, where, as already noted, he made several purchases of Schiavones, he proceeded through the Tyrol to Munich to immerse himself in the study of Rubens. Finally, after traversing the Brenner Pass in the depths of winter, the Geddeses reached Paris in December and London on 2 January 1831.[136]

CHAPTER TEN

London 1831–1844: Poussin, Hals and the Westminster Competition of 1843

Wilkie's intercessions with Lawrence's executor during Geddes's absence in Italy may well have contributed to the successful retrieval of at least some of the contested Old Master drawings just over one month after Geddes's return to London. In his will which, as Sheepshanks notified Geddes in May 1830, had been published in the British press, Lawrence directed that his collection of drawings 'which in number and value I know to be unequalled in Europe' should be offered for £18,000 to the King on first refusal and then to the British Museum, whom failing, to Sir Robert Peel and the 1st Earl of Dudley. All of these parties having declined the offer, an abortive attempt was made six months after Lawrence's death to secure the collection intact for the nation by means of a public subscription.

On 20 January 1832 Geddes addressed an anonymous petitionary letter to the President and Governors of the British Institution in which he argued, with prescience, both from case precedent and from intimate knowledge of the collection, that, 'the loss of the Lawrence Cabinet of Drawings will be handed down to posterity as ... an eternal stain on the miserable parsimony of (whatever may otherwise be asserted) the richest country in the world.' In 1824 the British Institution, many of whose governors and/or directors were both Members of Parliament and vociferous lobbyists for a national gallery, had played a decisive role in Parliament's ultimate acquiescence in, and funding of, the Gallery's establishment. Prominent among the Institution lobbyists was one of the directors, the connoisseur Richard Payne Knight who bequeathed his own important cabinet of Old Master Italian, Dutch and Flemish drawings to the British Museum in 1824. This was the case precedent elo-

quently, but ineffectively, cited by Geddes in favour of the purchase for the 'National Museum' of the collection of national stature formed privately by Lawrence.[137]

After an equally abortive endeavour by (Sir) Charles Eastlake in 1834 to secure a government-funded purchase for the National Gallery, 'miserable parsimony' prevailed and Lawrence's executor Archibald Keightley was obliged to dispose of the collection to the principal creditor, the dealer Samuel Woodburn, for £15,000 or a quarter of Lawrence's total estimated investment in forming the collection. During the protracted and piecemeal dispersal which followed Woodburn's ten promotional exhibitions in 1835, Geddes was to purchase several of the drawings for his own collection in tribute to one of the most valued and formative friendships of his earlier career.[138]

In 1832 Geddes resumed his regular support of the Royal Academy, being strongly represented that year by a total of seven portraits, including those of John Gibson and Cardinal Weld painted in Rome. In November, together with Clarkson Stanfield, he was at last elected to Associate membership. From the year of his election until his death in 1844 Geddes exhibited annually at the Academy, predominantly portraits, of which a significant number testified to his determination to advertise his retention of an identifiably Scottish clientele and, as occasion permitted, a dual artistic identity.[139]

It was with this resolve that in 1837 he embarked upon one of the most challenging assignments of his career as a portraitist with the collaboration of (and possibly at the instigation of) Dr D. Maclagan, President of the Royal College of Surgeons of Edinburgh, whose own portrait had graced Geddes's retrospective exhibition in 1821. Their objective – formulated in circumstances as yet unexplained – was to secure for Scotland a 'Public Picture' of one of the most formidable and intractable of all potential sitters in public life, the Duke of Wellington. This project, which preceded by a decade the bronze monument to Wellington sculpted for the city of Edinburgh by John Steell, achieved at least partial success. Remarkably, Geddes secured an interview with Wellington at Apsley House and, despite the Duke's abhorrence of the 'Curse of Painters', extracted a grudging provisional agreement of which the only apparent manifestation was a characteristic small whole-length included in the artist's posthumous sale on 11 April 1845.[140]

It was as a subject and landscape painter that Geddes preferred to present himself to the British Institution and, from 1836, at the Royal Scottish Academy. (This implicit transfer of allegiance from the troubled Royal Institution was preceded by his conspicuous absence from the Edinburgh exhibitions during the most intensive phase of the power struggle between the Institution and the secessionist Academy for jurisdiction over the public promotion of modern Scottish painting.) Among the subject pictures there was an increasing preponderance of literary and religious motifs, realised with a variable degree of conviction and an equally variable critical reception. Of these, *Hagar*, exhibited at the Royal Academy in 1842, was acclaimed by the *Art Union* as being 'finely wrought and deeply touching' – in accordance with contemporary sensibility [fig.69]. It clearly demonstrated the affiliation of this type of subject picture with Geddes's other admired specialism of fancy portraiture. The following year, however, his *Spring*, an illustration to James Thomson's poem *The Seasons*, was lambasted in the same journal which, having excoriated Geddes's unfashionable adoption of allegory, pronounced the artist himself to be 'a very unequal painter, sometimes good, at other times exceedingly bad' – a verdict not devoid of justification.[141]

Adverse criticism notwithstanding, Adela Geddes maintained that her husband's *Christ and the Woman of Samaria* (exhibited at the Royal Academy in 1841) was 'undertaken with a view to fame alone' and confirmed his 'ability for the highest walk of art.' In the penultimate year of his life, Geddes seemingly made one final bid for a revitalised career as a history painter subsidised by the State. Thirty years later, in the course of her extended correspondence

with the Edinburgh antiquary David Laing, preparatory to his pioneering catalogue of Geddes's etchings, the artist's widow sought advice as to an appropriate recipient for ' a Cartoon of Mr. Geddes, "Samson Agonistes". I have had it rolled up for many years ever since it was exhibited in Westminster Hall ... The heads all having been from life are expressive. Dimensions 14 ft by 12.' The obvious precedent, in terms of scale and compositional procedure, was the *Discovery of the Regalia* of 1818–21. The context, however, was surely that of the Westminster cartoon competitions occasioned by the decoration of the new Palace of Westminster.[142]

In 1841 a Select Committee was formed to debate the promotion of the fine arts in relation to the reconstruction of the Houses of Parliament after the devastating fire of 1834. This Committee was shortly superseded by a Royal Commission under the Presidency of the Prince Consort which determined to promote history painting (in the sense of epic narrative) in fresco as a genre beyond the capacity of private patronage – in emulation of the employment of the Nazarenes by Ludwig, Crown Prince of Bavaria at his new palace in Munich. The first and best-remembered of the ensuing competitions was announced by the Committee in 1842. In 1843 the exclusively British participants were to present monochrome cartoons in chalk or a similar medium, measuring between ten and fifteen feet in height and length, and with figures not under life-size, for frescoes illustrating episodes from British history or from the works of Spenser, Milton or Shakespeare. Sir Robert Peel, by then Prime Minister, was among the three lay judges of this competition which was accompanied by a public exhibition of all one hundred and forty submissions in Westminster Hall between 1 July and 2 September. Milton accounted for no fewer than forty submissions, the preference being given to *Samson Agonistes*. Geddes was not amongst the prize-winners.[143]

It was arguably as a connoisseur-dealer that Geddes achieved lasting distinction during his final years of declining health in London. In 1834 he showed at the Royal Academy a portrait of his longstanding friend and patron,

Fig.69 · Andrew Geddes
Hagar
[National Gallery of Scotland, Edinburgh]

the Berwickshire landowner Sir John James Steuart of Allanbank (1779–1879), of whom a three-quarter length, one of at least two recorded oils by Geddes, was presented to the Scottish National Portrait Gallery in 1962 by the sitter's collateral descendent Naomi, Lady Mitchison [fig.70]. The following June Steuart married his second wife Katharine Munro, daughter of another patron of Geddes, Alexander Munro 'Tertius', Professor of Anatomy at the University of Edinburgh.[144] Steuart's marriage may have necessitated the otherwise unexplained sale on 23 May 1835 at Christie's of most, or conceivably all, of his Old Master collection. Geddes was invited to collaborate as an anonymous associated vendor, presumably in order to lend the sale greater substance and credibility. Steuart's own collection, whose quality and true extent it is difficult to estimate, may well have been formed during the period of his closest involvement with the Institution for the Encouragement of the Fine Arts in Scotland of which he became a founder-director in 1819. Judging by the evidence of the 1835 sale, Steuart's collection was mainly Northern Euro-

pean in character. Geddes, whose Old Master properties accounted for fifty-two out of the total of ninety-eight lots, contributed (as observed elsewhere), *The Betrothal* by Ochtervelt, the 'Rembrandt' *Old Woman Plucking a Fowl*, the De Witte *Church Interior* and the Van der Helst portrait group of a lady and child, all of which he had attempted to sell to the Earl of Hopetoun in 1820. In addition, he offered his three Andrea Schiavones, including *Christ Disputing with the Doctors*, and the Rubens portrait then identified as Nicolaas Rockox, Burgomaster of Antwerp, which he had reproduced as an etching.[145]

There was one further item (lot 64) indicative of Geddes's interest in Frans Hals, a small panel portrait of Johannes Hoornbeek, supposedly engraved by Jonas Suyderhoef. Purchased at the auction by Geddes's brother-in-law Andrew James, 'Mr Watteau', it was inherited by the artist's niece Sarah Ann James and is now in the Emory Ford collection in Detroit, described as a copy of the original of 1645 in the Musée Royal des Beaux-Arts in Brussels.[146] Of far greater moment, and not included in the 1835 collaborative sale, was the single most impressive testimonial of Geddes's connoisseurship of Northern European Old Master painting since his acquisition of *The Toilet of Bathsheba* at the dispersal of Alexandre Delahante's stock-in-trade in 1814. The exclusion from the 1835 sale of the *Young Man Holding a Skull* by Hals [fig.71] may indicate that its purchase by Geddes for Steuart had yet to be effected or, equally, that Steuart, having recognised its exceptional quality, had decided to retain the ownership.[147]

Geddes's motivation in rationalising his own Old Master collection was presumably that of 'trading up'. In 1844 Adela Geddes recalled of their occupation of Poussin's supposed residence on the Pincio in Rome that her husband, as an ardent admirer of Poussin, afterwards had the gratification of obtaining a 'splendid specimen' of his work as the culmination of a lifetime's aspiration. Painted in 1640, the year of Poussin's departure from Rome for Paris,

Fig.70 · Andrew Geddes
Sir John James Steuart of Allanbank
[Scottish National Portrait Gallery, Edinburgh]

Fig.71 · Frans Hals
Young Man Holding a Skull (Vanitas), c.1626–8
[National Gallery, London]

the *Landscape with St John on Patmos* [fig.62] had been admired in London in 1801 by Andrew Wilson's mentor and co-adjutor, the great Scottish entrepreneur, William Buchanan, following its recent purchase in Paris by the dealer Bryan for Sir Simon Clarke of Oakhill in Hertfordshire. Geddes's opportunity arose in 1840 when the Clarke collection was dispersed at Christie's, the purchase price being a mere £90.6s as distinct from the £1000 originally paid by Sir Simon in or about 1801. Of the Old Master paintings retained by Geddes until his death in 1844, the Poussin was the outstanding picture of those which passed through his posthumous sale in 1845. Having been bought in, it remained in his widow's possession until at least 1867 when the second sale of her husband's property took place that autumn.[148]

In 1839 Geddes undertook the climactic pilgrimage of his artistic career, a voyage to Holland to pay his last homage to Rembrandt in The Hague and in Amsterdam, and in particular to Rembrandt as an original printmaker 'of whose admirable etchings he possessed so many fine specimens.' While in Amsterdam, Geddes's calling card proved sufficient – when accompanied by an explanatory note expressing his fascination with Rembrandt – to secure an introduction to Hendrik Six, Heer van Hillegom and his private collection, Six being the lineal descendant of the celebrated connoisseur and Burgomaster of Amsterdam, Jan Six, whose friendship Rembrandt has commemorated both in oils and through the medium of etching.[149] In The Hague the Geddeses sought an entrée to Johan Gijsbert, Baron Verstolk van Soelen (1776–1845), Minister of State and proprietor of the most extensive print collection to be formed in Holland since the Napoleonic era. The Baron's holdings of Rembrandt totalled no fewer than twenty-five drawings and 815 etchings. Having been denied access to this superlative collection due to the Baron's absence from home in The Hague, Geddes was fortunate enough to secure a personal invitation following a chance encounter in the Trippenhuis in Amsterdam where he had gone to inspect the Rijksmuseum's Rembrandt etchings. Before leaving Holland, Geddes despatched to the Baron, as a mark of his gratitude, some samples of his own etchings.[150]

It is just conceivable that a souvenir of this excursion has survived in the form of a small undated oil landscape by Geddes in the National Gallery of Scotland, whose subject has been variously interpreted as a scene on the Thames and, more plausibly, as an actual or imaginary view in Holland [fig.72] The Rembrandtesque conception of the composition, which, by extension, raises the possibility that the landscape was actually a tributary pastiche rather than a reconstruction from nature, was highlighted by the translation of the oil into a drypoint with significant variations in detail. In the drypoint the area of the sky was substantially reduced to redress the balance between land and sky and to emphasise the Rembrandtesque, elongated format of the landscape motif, while the narrative element of the foreground figures was excised and the tonal range simplified in the interests of luminosity.[151] Whatever the precise status of the oil, the Rembrandtesque allusion was sufficiently convincing to justify the acquisition of the picture by William Seguier (1772–1843), older brother of Geddes's erstwhile fellow student at the Royal Academy Schools, John Seguier, and a friend of Wilkie since the same period. A picture restorer and dealer to trade, the elder Seguier rose to become Superintendent of the British Institution, then Keeper of the National Gallery in London. In his related capacity as picture consultant to some of the foremost connoisseurs of the day, he had advised George IV on the development of the collection of Dutch and Flemish paintings at Buckingham Palace.[152]

Several months before the opening of the exhibition in Westminster Hall and the presumed launch of his cartoon of *Samson Agonistes*, it became apparent that Geddes was experiencing the terminal stages of the consumption which had first afflicted him in Italy. After rallying temporarily, he suffered a second prolonged attack during the spring of 1844 but refused all medical assistance in his determination to complete his submissions to the Royal Academy's annual exhibition. On 5 May, his wedding anniversary, he expired without a struggle in the arms of his wife at his house in Berners Street. Of his passing, his former contemporary at the Academy Schools, Benjamin Robert Haydon, noted in his journal entry on the Academy's exhibition that, 'The Pictures of those Artists who have died since it opened are Melancholy – Geddes, a Man of pure Taste, but no power ...' Haydon's characteristically acerbic wit masked a tribute to Geddes both as a creative artist and as a connoisseur whose sincerity would have been fully endorsed by Sir Thomas Lawrence.[153]

CHAPTER ELEVEN

Adela Geddes's Legacy

Almost immediately after Geddes's death his widow Adela began the process of creating a permanent monument which was to occupy her, both directly and vicariously, for the next thirty years. By December 1844 she had published the *Memoir* which has remained the fundamental primary source on Geddes and of which a presentation copy was despatched to the artist's patron, the Prime Minister Sir Robert Peel, in 1845. Having been appointed sole executrix and heir to her husband's entire moveable estate,[154] it was presumably through financial necessity that Adela Geddes resolved on the disposal by public auction of his entire collection of Old Master prints, drawings and paintings, together with a substantial proportion of his own original works, comprising finished oils, compositional sketches in oil and a range of drawings of comparably diverse status.[155] With a commendable sense of its appropriateness to 'A Man of pure Taste', the Council of the Royal Academy organised a selective tribute to Geddes by purchasing from his posthumous sale his full-scale replica of Titian's *Sacred and Profane Love*

in the Villa Borghese and his copy of the four-volume *Recueil Jullienne* of Watteau's collected works.[156]

In May 1843 Geddes had executed two portrait drawings of the four-year-old Nevile Reid II (1839–1913), nephew of Lady Carmichael of Skirling, to whose family Adela Plimer had served as governess in her youth [fig.73]. Six months after the artist's death the young Reids were left orphaned by the sudden death of their mother the Honble Caroline Napier, sister of Lady Carmichael, their father having predeceased her. The children's guardianship had been entrusted to their aunt by marriage, Lady Napier, wife of the 8th Lord Napier of Merchiston who, being unable to take up residence with her wards, engaged the widowed Adela Geddes to manage the household, probably in the course of 1845. Many years later Nevile Reid was to recall her as a clever but irascible 'small woman with deep set eyes and large prominent eyebrows and a most uncompromising gold-brown wig which she wore of the same shade to the latest day of her life.'

Fig.72 · Andrew Geddes
Landscape in the Manner of Rembrandt
[National Gallery of Scotland, Edinburgh]

Fig.73 · Andrew Geddes
Nevile Reid II, 1843
[Private Collection]

Following the second sale from her husband's collection in 1867,[157] Mrs Geddes retained for her own enjoyment a modest selection of his original works, in particular his definitive Lawrentian self-portrait from the 1820s and the portrait of Agnes Boyd as the alter ego of Rembrandt's mother [figs.23 & 50]. In her will, drawn up in 1878, Mrs Geddes appointed as co-executor and residuary legatee her niece Sarah Ann James, the daughter of Ann Plimer and 'Mr Watteau', to whom she officially bequeathed all of the pictures then in her possession at 19 Brunswick Gardens in Kensington. Among the other recipients of monetary legacies were her goddaughter Isabella, daughter of the Revd John Thomson of Duddingston and widow of the Scottish figure painter Robert Scott Lauder, Nevile Reid II, his wife, and his sister Clara Vernon Reid. Despite the formal provisions of this will in favour of Miss James, Adela Geddes evidently distributed among the Reid family, on account of their personal association during the early years of her widowhood, a number of her husband's original works. Among those allocated to Nevile Reid II was the unmistakably Rembrandtesque *Peckham Rye* with the effect of an approaching thunderstorm, the prototype for one of Geddes's finer essays in the drypoint medium.[158]

Almost a year before finalising this will, Adela Geddes appears to have made provision for an alternative bequest to the National Gallery of Scotland which was clearly intended as Geddes's designated monument in his native Edinburgh. In the event, this bequest of 20 March 1877 was translated into an outright gift within her lifetime. That autumn the Board of Trustees for Manufactures, as the custodians of the Gallery, accepted for integration into the annual rehang of the Gallery in December the Lawrentian self-portrait of the artist, the Rembrandtesque portrait of his mother, and *Hagar*.[159]

Prior to her own death on 12 February 1881, the artist's widow had the satisfaction of participating in the creation of another monument built upon the foundation of her own *Memoir* of Geddes published in 1844. Geddes's sudden death, following his prolonged decline into ill-health, as well as the essentially private and non-commercially ori-

ented nature of his printmaking, may well have prevented the destruction or cancellation of his etching plates as the usual preventative measure against unauthorised exploitation. Ironically, the exploitative intentions of one major London print seller, either Tiffen or Graves, were frustrated by the fragmented dispersal of Geddes's copper plates at his posthumous sale in April 1845. The majority of those plates eventually came into the hands of the Scottish literary antiquary David Laing (1793–1878), son of the Edinburgh bookseller William Laing, at whose shop the younger Laing had first encountered George Chalmers, the author of *Caledonia*. From about 1812 – the year when Chalmers sat to Geddes for the portrait commissioned by Archibald Constable – he had been Laing's antiquarian mentor [fig.74].

Laing's initially unfocused and exploratory proposal for the publication of a new limited edition of Geddes's etchings, pulled from the surviving plates, was to develop into a major research project relating to the history and practice of 'original' etching by Scottish artists, as exemplified by Wilkie and Geddes. For the best part of two years, from 1873 to 1875, Laing was in regular correspondence with Adela Geddes, to whom he received a personal introduction in 1874 from his fellow antiquary and impassioned collector, James Gibson Craig (1799–1886).[160] As Member of Parliament for Edinburgh, Craig had been one of the chief promoters of the National Gallery of Scotland. The outcome of Laing's collaboration with the artist's widow was the publication in 1875 of his pioneering catalogue of Wilkie's and Geddes's etchings which, although issued in a limited edition of a hundred copies, assisted in perpetuating the reputation of Haydon's 'Man of pure Taste' into the twentieth century.[161]

Fig.74 · Sir William Fettes Douglas
David Laing, 1862
[Scottish National Portrait Gallery, Edinburgh]

PETER BLACK

Andrew Geddes: Herald of the Etching Revival

... Geddes alone can take permanent rank among the greatest etchers (and that in spite of his very limited output) by virtue of the great sympathy with, and understanding of humanity which he was able to express in his few plates.

(E.S. Lumsden, *The Art of Etching*, London 1925)

Andrew Geddes was born into an age that talked of history painting but chose to immortalise the living through so many thousands of portraits in marble, on canvas, and printed in ever larger numbers by the mezzotint engravers. The few at the top of the profession, like Raeburn, Reynolds and Lawrence, could charge extraordinary prices which only the very rich could afford. The expectation that artists would paint portraits affected talent at all levels by forcing participation in a production process that ensured a surprising homogeneity of portraiture between 1770 and 1840. Geddes may not have commanded prices as high as those of Raeburn or Lawrence, but his art was the richer for having had the chance to develop his talent as an etcher, an area in which he can be said to have achieved more than any British artist of his generation. In his etchings, and in the influence they were to have later in the nineteenth century, Geddes struck a decisive blow against the commercialism that dogged printmaking throughout Europe in the late eighteenth century. Just as there seemed to be no place for paintings other than portraits, there was an expectation that all prints would be formulaic interpretations made by professional engravers rather than autographic works conceived in, and for, the medium by the painter-etcher.

Geddes established a distinct position for himself as a portrait painter, but what he achieved as an etcher needs to

be weighed against the prevailing indifference to artists' etchings. In 1820, there simply was no market for etchings, or any printed works of art by living artists sold singly. This had long been so, and etchers who wished to put their work before the public tended to produce bound collections of their work. In 1826 Geddes gathered a selection of ten plates for publication in this way. Geddes's friend Wilkie had brought out a similar edition only two years earlier. Neither edition proved popular, the experience of Geddes and Wilkie matching that of other artists of the period. If there were no convenient hook on which to hang them – which usually meant antiquarian interest – etchings were difficult to sell, and some did not see the light of day until long after they had been produced, as happened with John Crome (1768–1821), whose widow published his etchings posthumously in 1834.

Geddes was virtually the only artist who produced portrait etchings in the years from 1812 to 1826, a time when the craze for collecting portrait engravings (mainly mezzotints) was still at its height. Geddes's landscape prints have been associated with those of etchers such as Crome, J.S. Cotman (1782–1842) and E.T. Daniell (1804–1842). With Crome and Daniell, Geddes also shares a determined rejection of neoclassical ideas in favour of a natural image of landscape inspired by seventeenth-century Dutch etchers, notably Rembrandt, Ruisdael and their circles. In some ways the most instructive comparison with Geddes is not with his fellow etchers, but with major figures from contemporary painting who might in other circumstances have produced more etchings than they did, but instead commissioned professional engravers to make prints for them. The reproductive mezzotints of Turner's *Liber Studiorum*

(1807–1819) and Constable's *Various Subjects of Landscape* (1833) were necessary manifestos for their work as painters. Coincidentally, these prints influenced the public taste for landscape which was to become the dominant theme of etching in the period from 1850 to 1940. David Wilkie is another major figure who experimented with etching at the same time as Geddes, but he seems to have preferred interpretation by professional engravers because – like Turner and Constable – he saw publication as the path to fame and wealth.

Geddes made some fifty plates, principally in etching and drypoint, which fall into three main categories. The most important are the twenty or so portraits, mentioned in Lumsden's tribute quoted above. E.S. Lumsden (1883–1948) was an Edinburgh etcher and author of a valuable book on the history and technique of etching, *The Art of Etching*, published at the very height of the etching boom in 1925.[1] Geddes's portraits would – even without his paint-

ings – constitute a valuable contribution to early nineteenth-century portraiture. The other important component is formed by the dozen landscapes, some of scenes in Scotland but most set in countryside around London, which were created in a natural style that grew from an appreciation of Dutch landscape prints. The third (and smallest) category comprises copies after Old Masters. Some of these are early experiments in the medium of etching, while others (some securely datable to 1822–6) are versions of paintings which were part of Geddes's collection, or his stock as an art dealer, by Andrea Meldolla (Schiavone), Van Dyck, Rubens and Jordaens.[2] The motivation behind these reproductive images is more complicated than the few Rembrandt copies, which can safely be regarded as early

Fig.75 · Andrew Geddes (after Schiavone)
Christ Disputing with the Doctors in the Temple, published 1826
[National Gallery of Scotland, Edinburgh]

and as being part of the artist's self-education. Elements of study can also be found in these works. Three are based on paintings by Van Dyck whose graphic work includes some of the greatest of all portrait etchings and who was, with Rembrandt, Geddes's principal source of inspiration. Andrea Meldolla (?1522–1582), by whom Geddes owned various paintings, one of which is the subject of the etching *Christ Disputing with the Doctors in the Temple* [fig.75], was one of the first Italian artists to take up etching. These prints must have played some part in Geddes's dealing in pictures and yet he included examples among the selection published in 1826. They are therefore something personal: images which the artist quotes as a composer might transcribe and experiment with a theme written by another. One of the Van Dycks, the *Infanta Isabella*, of *c.*1826 [fig.39], is also a technical experiment, combining effects of drypoint with a creative use of 'foul biting'. (Foul biting is used to describe what is usually a technical deficiency. Lines drawn too close to one another allow the acid to undermine the etching ground and create tone, an effect which Geddes was seeking.) E.S. Lumsden, the Edinburgh etcher who owned the plate, describes this in some detail.[3] Like his predecessor Geddes, Lumsden was a self-taught artist, and Geddes's prints were among those which he collected and studied as technical models for his own work.

There is insufficient evidence to permit a precise chronological sequence of Geddes's prints. There is some internal documentation in the form of dates, and the portrait etchings tend to follow versions in oil which can be dated by their inclusion in exhibitions. The earliest dated plate is from 1812, the portrait of *George Chalmers* the antiquary, and author of *Caledonia* [fig.76]. The portraits were almost all made between 1812 and 1826. The landscapes seem to have developed later than the portraits, though there is less evidence for dating them than for the portraits. A limiting date is supplied for the ten prints in the publication of 1826, which included two landscapes, *Peckham Rye* [fig.84] and *Trees in Hyde Park. The Field of Bannockburn and the Bore Stone* [fig.82] is dated 1826. The drypoint called *Whim, Peebles-shire* can be dated by association with the portrait Geddes made of Archibald Montgomery exhibited at the Royal Academy, London in 1822, whose Peeblesshire seat was called *The Whim* [fig.54]. Of the Old Master reproductions one is dated 1822 (*Nicholas Rockox, after Rubens*).

This plate and the *Old Woman Looking at a Ring, after Jordaens* were included in the publication of 1826.

It is not recorded how Geddes came to make his first plates. Some deductions can be made, however, from the subject-matter. Further, it is known that Geddes was brought up surrounded by the etchings in his father's collection, and that his circle included printmakers. Although Edinburgh in the 1790s was home to a number of professional engravers, it was a bleak place for an artist minded to produce etchings. Etching was the province of caricaturists and amateurs rather than serious artists. The English artist Paul Sandby (1725–1809) had made etchings in Edinburgh while based in Scotland from 1747 to 1752. John Clerk of Eldin (1728–1812), who had contact with Sandby and was a patron of the etchers Alexander and John Runciman, had produced a series of landscapes in the 1770s. Among the

Fig.76 · Andrew Geddes *George Chalmers*, 1812
[The British Museum, London]

better known figures active in Geddes's time was David Deuchar (1745–1808), a seal engraver who made competent etched copies after Dutch Old Masters, but whose original work is weak. There was also the eccentric figure of John Kay (1742–1826) who carried on a practice like that of Matthew and Mary Darly in London, centred on a shop selling mild caricatures of newsworthy people [fig.2].

Adela Geddes implies in her privately printed *Memoir* that the artist's father encouraged Andrew in the study and collecting of art, but opposed his becoming an artist. Geddes may have attended the Trustees' Academy in Edinburgh, where James Wardrop later remembered him as a student of John Graham, although this statement is not confirmed by any documentation from the Academy during the time of Graham's mastership from 1798 to 1817. Geddes is also said to have attended the private academy of Alexander Nasmyth at 47 York Place.[4] If so, contact with Nasmyth may have provided him with an opportunity to etch. Speculation, however, is not needed to explain Geddes's assured approach to what was at the time an unfashionable medium. The stimuli are to be found in the substantial collection of etchings belonging to his father (with excellent holdings of Rembrandt), and personal links that followed from his father's serious interest in the art of etching. Two friendships are crucial, that with the engraver John Burnet (1784–1868), an exact contemporary, and John Clerk of Eldin (1757–1832), the Edinburgh advocate, and later judge, who was thirty years Geddes's senior [fig.3].

John Burnet, Geddes and Wilkie were part of the same circle in London from 1806, Burnet and Wilkie (and possibly Geddes) having attended the Trustees' Academy together in the years from 1800 to 1805.[5] Geddes and Burnet are likely to have been acquainted as boys since both were sons of excise officers. Burnet served an apprenticeship with the engraver, Robert Scott (probably from 1799 to 1806), before setting up independently in London. Either in Edinburgh or in London, Burnet had the knowledge, tools and enthusiasm to introduce Geddes to etching which would have been part of his training as a line engraver. The firm evidence of Burnet and Geddes's relationship relates to the years from 1808 to 1820 when both were established in London. In 1814 they travelled to Paris together to study and copy plundered paintings gathered in the Musée Napoléon and which were about to be repatriated. The fol-

lowing year Burnet engraved a Rembrandt painting, the *Toilet of Bathsheba*, which Geddes acquired in 1814 at the Delahante sale [figs.26 & 27], and in 1819 Geddes contributed designs for plates to an edition of the works of Robert Burns, the engraving of which was done by, and under the supervision of, Burnet.[6]

The other formative friendship documented was with John Clerk who was a friend of David Geddes, the artist's father. Clerk, Geddes senior and another friend, Colin Macfarquhar (*c.*1745–1793), all had important Rembrandt collections and knew each other through their interest in prints. Clerk's father, John Clerk of Eldin, was not just a Rembrandt collector but the etcher of a series of landscapes made in the 1770s which are – with those of Sandby – virtually the only Scottish antecedents to Geddes's landscape prints. Adela Geddes provides an anecdote about the loan of a drawing to Geddes when he was a small boy which indicates the closeness of the ties with Clerk; both Clerk and Geddes senior were clients of Thomas Philipe, an art dealer and auctioneer with knowledge of printmaking such that from 1808 to 1810 he was employed to rearrange and catalogue albums of prints for the British Museum's new Department of Prints and Drawings.[7]

The earliest prints made by Geddes are, by common agreement, the studies or copies he made after Old Master etchings. *The Boy with Spoon*, and *The Beggar Woman Leaning on a Stick, after Rembrandt* are both signed with initials 'AG' in a way that differs markedly from the elegant monogram that appears on the plate of the portrait of George Chalmers of 1812, which is the earliest dated plate. The signature on the Chalmers portrait is a sophisticated monogram 'AG ft' (Andrew Geddes fecit) consciously modelled on the style used by seventeenth-century artists.[8] These copies could be images chosen from the Old Master prints in the Geddes collection to suit the dimensions of what are small scraps of copper, one of which is known to have been the recycled plate from a benefit ticket. While there is no reason to link the fact or the dates of Geddes's earliest essays in etching with David Deuchar, they do resemble distinctly Deuchar's copies published in variable sets in 1803 in Edinburgh (titled *A Collection of Etchings, after the Dutch and Flemish Schools...*). Whether or not it is connected, Deuchar's publication is interesting evidence of the developing taste for Dutch and Flemish prints.

Geddes grew up in a house that was filled with art of a quite different kind from that which a Scottish artist needed to practise in order to survive. Geddes's gods were Titian, Poussin, Watteau, Rubens, Van Dyck and Rembrandt, but included lesser artists who were important as etchers. The surviving biographical information that concerns Geddes's early art education (his widow Adela's more or less reliable *Memoir*) stressed that Geddes worked on his own initiative, copying drawings in his father's collection, and in those of his father's fellow collectors to which he had access. The group of early copies/studies are a reflection of this method of study which is manifested equally in Geddes's drawings. That Geddes admired Rembrandt to the point of dressing up in his image emerges from a rare self-portrait etching [fig.77] (described as *Oval Portrait of Rembrandt*, a plate abandoned and re-etched), which is paralleled by the self-portrait in oil in the style of Rembrandt [fig.25]. This etching was long assumed to be a version of a Rembrandt self-portrait, but the features of the young man do not resemble those of Rembrandt, although as the general presentation, the clothing, and especially the iron gorget and velvet cap make clear, Geddes intended the viewer to make the identification.

Portraiture formed the basis of Geddes's practice as a painter, and portraits form the most important group within his work as a printmaker. The portraits vary in type, and divide – like the paintings – into standard formats. The portraits of *Sir William Allan, Agnes Geddes, The Artist's Mother, Francis Jeffrey, Alexander Nasmyth* and *Molesworth Phillips* are versions of, or translations of, existing paintings, but they were not conceived as reproductions.[9]

Fig.77 · Andrew Geddes
Self-portrait as Rembrandt
[National Gallery of Scotland, Edinburgh]

Fig.78 · Andrew Geddes
Agnes Geddes, The Artist's Mother, 1822
[National Gallery of Scotland, Edinburgh]

The portraits of *The Artist's Mother* [fig.78] and *Alexander Nasmyth* [fig.79] are masterpieces of this more finished type of portrait. Both are dark, richly worked images, in each case thought out in terms of the printmaking medium and almost entirely in drypoint. *The Artist's Mother* is one of the most Rembrandtian of Geddes's prints, executed in a confident combination of drypoint, mezzotint and etching, the drypoint scraped to retain luminosity between the marks.[10] The *Alexander Nasmyth* goes a step beyond *The Artist's Mother* with even richer drypoint work in the background to provide a contrast with the sitter's pale flesh.

The more finished portraits stray to some extent from the intrinsic qualities of etching or drypoint as a medium although they show the extent to which Geddes was consulting the prints of Rembrandt as models for his own work. They also reveal that they are the work of an artist familiar with commissioning mezzotint engravings of his portraits. Rembrandt's portrait prints vary from slight sketches to genre subjects integrating the figure into a professional or personal context. Geddes's prints reflect this range, and the most finished of all of his prints is the densely worked *Dull Reading* [fig.80] which is a double portrait of Elizabeth Nasmyth (daughter of Geddes's mentor), and her husband the actor, Daniel Terry. This is a

genre piece that quotes heavily from Rembrandt, and has obvious links with Wilkie. It may have been inspired by Rembrandt's *St Jerome in a Dark Chamber*, a print recorded among the Rembrandts in Geddes's collection.[11]

Besides *The Artist's Mother*, the most celebrated of the portrait prints is that of *Sir William Allan* [fig.81], an image often singled out as an illustration of Scottish art of the Romantic period. It is not a portrait in quite the same sense as Geddes's small full-length painting of Wilkie, though it, too, is a valuable and powerful image of a fellow artist. The story is that Allan had returned from Russia and the Caucasus in 1814, bringing with him the Circassian armour he is wearing, and which turns up as a studio prop in a number of Allan's paintings. The image is surprisingly rich

Fig.79 · below left · Andrew Geddes
*Alexander Nasmyth, c.*1825
[National Gallery of Scotland, Edinburgh]

Fig.80 · below right · Andrew Geddes
Dull Reading, before 1826
[National Gallery of Scotland, Edinburgh]

Fig.81 · right · Andrew Geddes
Sir William Allan, 1815
[National Gallery of Scotland, Edinburgh]

in associations, beginning with Rembrandt whose etchings are immediately called to mind by the technique, especially the atmospheric hatching used behind the figure to suggest the smoke of battle. At the same time Allan's bow, and his alert pose, are reminiscent of Raeburn's full-length portrait of *Nathaniel Spens* (1793), a member of the Royal Company of Archers of Edinburgh; Allan's eastern exoticism pitted against the native. The plate bears the date 18 June 1815, which one would naturally assume to record the date Geddes signed the finished work. This may be so, but the date is memorable as that of the Battle of Waterloo, and Allan, who certainly had first-hand experience of war in Europe, is portrayed as if he were present at Waterloo. The image of Allan as monumental soldier contains echoes of Géricault's great Salon painting of the *Charging Chasseur* of 1812, including the brightly lit background scene of figures fleeing a burning cannon.

The most striking and characteristic group of Geddes's portraits are those in which the sitter's head is isolated as a

fragment, creating an apparently spontaneous, sketch-like statement of character. Early states of the more Rembrandt-like portraits, such as *Alexander Nasmyth*, and the *Portrait of Agnes Geddes, the Artist's Mother*, show that this was how he began work on the plate, mirroring the painter's procedure on canvas, beginning with the character-defining features. While the *Alexander Nasmyth* and the *Artist's Mother* proceed beyond the fragmentary stage to become complete half-length portraits, there is a group that are frozen in this vivid, sketch-like state despite the fact that the related paintings present the figure in relation to a background: *Barrington Pope Blachford, David Bridges, Junior, Henry Broadwood* [fig.46], *George Chalmers* [fig.76], and *William Martin*. Within this group are the brightest and most lively of Geddes's portrait prints, especially the *Henry Broadwood* and the *George Chalmers*, which echo the early states of some of Van Dyck's portraits for the 'Iconography' series in which the head was etched by the master before he handed the plate on to the engraver for completion. Broadwood's ruff is deliberately suggestive of a seventeenth-century portrait, but the resemblance is closest of all with the *George Chalmers* in which Geddes has consciously emulated Van Dyck's touch, depicting the sitter's hair with a few judiciously spaced lines, some curling upward to break the outline of the head, and patches of white suggestive of light falling on the sitter. The drypoint used to suggest Chalmers's fur collar again mirrors Van Dyck's technique, particularly in the portrait of *Jan van den Wouwer*.

Fig.82 · below left · Andrew Geddes
The Field of Bannockburn and the Bore Stone, 1826
[British Museum, London]

Fig.83 · right · Andrew Geddes
Claude Lorrain's House in Rome, c.1830
[Victoria and Albert Museum, London]

Fig.84 · below right · Andrew Geddes
Peckham Rye, c.1826
[National Gallery of Scotland, Edinburgh]

The landscapes seem, in general, to be later than the portraits, and although it is unfair to judge on the limited selection represented, Geddes seems to have regarded the portraits as more important: only two landscapes feature among the ten works in the publication of 1826. Possibly the artist regarded the making of a landscape – a private activity – as a relaxation from portraiture, which was his source of income. Four of the landscape prints are etchings, each of which has an element of calculation in the image: *The Field of Bannockburn and the Bore Stone* [fig.82] of 1826, is important as the first printed image of the Bore Stone in which Bruce is said to have raised the royal standard against the English in 1314. Geddes would have been aware of Burns's celebration of the battle in 'Scots wha hae wi' Wallace bled' (1794), thanks to which the place was soon to be developed as a sacred site in national history (and the stone itself destroyed by souvenir hunters). The choice of etching rather than drypoint as technique may imply that the plate had been commissioned (since more impressions can be taken from an etched plate). In 1830, when he was in Rome, Geddes was commissioned by the collector John Sheepshanks to make an etching of *Claude Lorrain's House* [fig.83] which (according to an old, but mistaken tradition) stood at the intersection of Via Sistina and Via Gregoriana, close to Geddes's lodgings. Sheepshanks wanted the image for a catalogue of Claude's etchings he was compiling. Two other etchings show Geddes reacting to the landscape with an eye trained in Dutch naturalism, _Halliford on Thames; Stump of a Tree in Centre_, and _Trees in Hyde Park with a Cow Feeding_ which, as Laing identified, shows Geddes emulating the work of Naiwincx.

With the exception of the etchings mentioned and _Peckham Rye_ (a drypoint to which aquatint was added as an after thought), Geddes's landscape prints were executed in drypoint: _Whim, Peebles-shire_; _View in Richmond Park (?), A Small Bridge to the Right_; _View in Richmond Park (?), A Fountain on the Left_; _Landscape: A View on a Hill, with Trees and Figures_; _Halliford on Thames: A Group of Trees within White Palings_; _Halliford on Thames: Long Row of Trees_; and _Landscape in the style of Rembrandt_. It is striking how free they are from conventions of either technique or iconography, the norms of both of which are represented among Geddes's contemporaries by Turner. Geddes made foreign journeys to study works of art, but no trace of the picturesque or classical aesthetic can be found in his landscape prints. In this respect Geddes's prints reveal a kinship with Constable, the leading artist of the day whose leaning was towards Dutch landscape modes rather than the classical, and who – like Geddes – was happy to celebrate ordinary and familiar scenes.

Although drypoint is the simplest of the intaglio techniques, and although since the time of Whistler and Haden the making of drypoints has become routine, the fact remains that Geddes is the first British artist to use the technique for landscape. Geddes would have been familiar with the effects available with the technique from Rembrandt, who used drypoint both in combination with etching and on its own, especially in his landscapes. Geddes owned one of Rembrandt's two monumental New Testament subjects carried out entirely in drypoint, the _Christ Presented to the People: Oblong plate_. Also among his Rembrandts was the landscape (in etching and drypoint) _Cottage with a White Paling_ which was model for his own beautiful drypoint, _Peckham Rye_ [fig.84], which transports Rembrandt's scene from the Diemerdijk on the south-eastern edge of Amster-

dam to the village on the south-eastern edge of London.[12]

The publication which Geddes prepared in 1826 summarises his achievement as an etcher to that date and it tells quite a lot about the situation for an aspiring etcher of the time. Geddes printed a prospectus for his publication in which he expressed the hope that it would stimulate interest and allow him to sell his work in etching which he was coming to regard as a rather expensive hobby.[13] Although the artist clearly intended the publication to make his work as an etcher better known, only one copy is known to be preserved in a public collection, in Perth Museum and Art Gallery. The etchings were loosely contained within the board portfolio rather than being bound in, which allowed Geddes to vary the prints included, and to insert additional rare proofs for some of the specialist collectors among his acquaintance. A couple of works are datable after 1826: for example, the view of _Claude Lorrain's House_ which was commissioned by John Sheepshanks in a letter of 1830 to Geddes in Rome, and the small portrait of _Pieter van Laer, after Peter van Laer_, which Geddes saw in Florence on his return from Italy in 1830. We have the word of Adela, the

Fig.85 · Andrew Geddes
John Sheepshanks, c.1826–8
[Victoria and Albert Museum, London]

artist's widow, that the bulk of Geddes's etchings were made before their marriage in 1827, and so it does seem as if the commercial failure of the publication brought Geddes's printmaking effectively to an end. Besides Geddes's visit to Holland in 1839 to visit the Rijksmuseum – another pilgrimage to view works of art – there is little suggestion in Geddes's later work of his continuing to etch. On the visit to Holland he chanced to meet one of the great Dutch Rembrandt collectors, Baron Verstolk van Soelen, who received him in his house in The Hague. Geddes made him a present of some of his etchings.

Much of Geddes's work looks surprisingly modern when contrasted with that of his contemporaries. Geddes's instincts led him to use the medium of copper for what it does best, in two distinct ways. On the one hand the autographic trace of the creating hand is a vital part of the process of making a portrait by means of etching, since it provides the response of artist to sitter, in a way that the more sculptural effect of engraving cannot. On the other hand, Geddes understood the appropriateness of informality and spontaneity in landscape, using vigorous drypoint lines to suggest light and movement, and hence life.

With only a small output, printed in very limited numbers by the artist rather than a professional printer, at a time when no market existed for such things, Geddes nonetheless found admirers among print collectors of his time. In addition to being a painter and etcher, Geddes was an art dealer and connoisseur of real learning, and he had a network of contacts among sitters, collectors and fellow artists that ensured the survival of his work as an etcher. Geddes's prints in institutional collections can often be traced back to those early collectors who bought, or received gifts of etchings, from Geddes. The National Gallery of Scotland in Edinburgh has an extensive collection of his paintings and drawings. Although its holdings of prints are small compared to the two main London collections, it can claim to hold the earliest acquisitions made by any institution, since some of its prints were acquired in 1827 for the (Royal) Institution for the Encouragement of the Fine Arts in Scotland, by Geddes's friend James Skene, on the recommendation of Hugh William Williams. Impressions of Geddes's

prints entered the Department of Prints and Drawings of the British Museum (which is the major holding) in the years immediately following Geddes's death, thanks – initially – to one of Geddes's contacts, William Hookham Carpenter, who was Keeper of Prints and Drawings from 1845 to 1866. Carpenter had known Geddes since the 1820s, and learnt the technique of etching from him. Carpenter bought a group of prints in 1847 from the sale of one of Geddes's closest art dealing colleagues, the expatriate miniature painter Anthony Stewart [fig.5]. In 1852 the department acquired a major group that belonged to the collector Dr E.V. Utterson, and which Utterson had acquired from Geddes in about 1826. Many of Geddes's prints in the Victoria and Albert Museum came from a similar important holding, that of John Sheepshanks, who presented his collection of British art in 1857, and gave prints to the newly founded Department of Prints and Drawings in 1862. Sheepshanks was one of the most important English print collectors of the nineteenth century, with an absolutely sure eye for the best in printmaking, whether of the seventeenth century, or of his own day [fig.85].

In the years that intervened between Geddes's publication and the 1860s, when the exhibition and sale of single etchings became more common, much work was produced in etching that seemed to prolong the reign of engraving. Samuel Palmer, for example, who was from 1853 a member of the Etching Club (founded in 1838) etched in a style quite characteristic of earlier line engravers, and his subjects are bookish, in keeping with the activities of the Etching Club, which focused on the production of volumes of etchings, destined for library shelves rather than the portfolio, or the drawing-room walls. The stirring of interest in 'painter's etchings' was reflected in an article of that title in the *Art Union* in 1840, the year in which Queen Victoria and Prince Albert took up etching, but it would be another twenty-eight years before the publication of P.G. Hamerton's influential work, *Etching & Etchers*, which put Geddes's prints into their proper context as forerunners of the revival which was most visibly promoted by Whistler, and which converted the artist's etching from object for the connoisseur to being a desirable item of interior decoration.

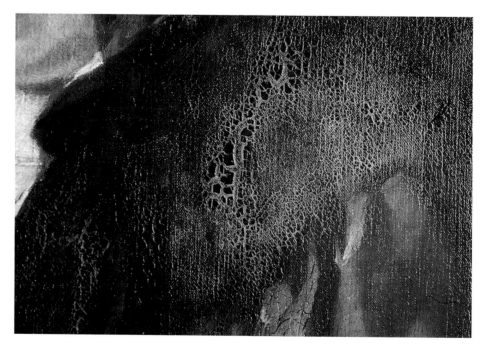

Fig.86 · Detail during cleaning of
The Artist's Mother [fig.23] revealing the widespread drying
craquelure in the paint describing the collar.

LESLEY A. STEVENSON

Andrew Geddes: Aspects of Technique Discussed in the Context of Nineteenth-century British Painting Practice

... Mr Geddes, a very unequal painter, sometimes remarkably good, at other times exceedingly bad.[1]

Andrew Geddes was a largely self-taught painter who moved in intellectual circles and was motivated by an insatiable passion for Old Master paintings. He can also be seen as representing those Scottish artists whose ambitions extended beyond the limits of the Edinburgh art market.

Surveying the works gathered for this exhibition, it is possible to imagine that there are several different hands at work. At first glance, the oeuvre of Andrew Geddes appears peculiarly diverse in subject-matter and approach. Equally, the paintings reveal some inconsistency of quality and condition. A selection of portraits from the National Galleries of Scotland's collections was examined with a view to assessing how far the artist followed the prevalent trend for technical experimentation among painters of his time.[2] The results will not provide a comprehensive survey of technique, but rather offer some general observations concerning the physical nature of Geddes's portraits. The extent to which problematic surfaces are the result of deliberate manipulation of the paint medium rather than external factors – natural ageing, commercial adulteration, subsequent restoration – will also be considered.[3]

CONTEXT

Over the last decade research into the techniques of British artists working during the nineteenth century has generated a considerable body of knowledge.[4] The study of documentary sources allied with close examination and scientific analysis of the works of art has led to a greater understanding of the unique appearance of so many of the paintings created at this time. Curiosity plays a significant role in the search to explain why so many nineteenth-century paintings have deteriorated on ageing. However, frustration with the frequent difficulty – in some cases impossibility – of removing discoloured varnishes safely from paint surfaces has also provided an incentive for the investigations of conservators. Many images of this period are nearly illegible, disrupted by networks of wide-mouthed, round-edged cracks – unsightly, alligator skin-type paint surfaces ravaged by disfiguring pools of poorly dried paint which offer incongruous and unintended glimpses of underlying colours [fig.86].[5] Too readily dismissed as the result of an unstable, bituminous addition to the artist's paint, it is important to examine the context in which the artists were working. An exploration of what exactly artists were using and how the physical properties of these materials seduced them, provides an invaluable insight into contemporary painting technique. It might also be asked whether painters were themselves aware of the disastrous implications these choices had for the future longevity of their art.

Although the early nineteenth century witnessed an unparalleled expansion in the development of artist's materials, there was simultaneously a deep-felt preoccupation with the painting techniques of the Old Masters.[6] This reverence for the productions of the past manifested itself in practical terms. Portrait painters sought to enhance their use of colour, to deepen and enrich areas of shadow, and to improve the tactile quality of their brushwork through copying what they regarded as the methods employed by their highly esteemed predecessors. However, they were unperturbed by the universal ignorance surrounding such matters. Convinced that true genius might only be achieved through the discovery of some long-forgotten and mysterious concoction, many aspiring artists embarked on imaginative and all too often ill-judged, manipulation of their paints and more specifically, the paint medium.[7]

Great masterpieces imported from the Continent by connoisseurs and artists were increasingly sought after, but technical information about them was vague and ambiguous.[8] Alarmingly, elaborate 'investigations' were carried out at the time in a clumsy and destructive fashion by over zealous and inquisitive practitioners. Contemporary accounts of Sir Joshua Reynolds's practical efforts to glean some insight into the supposed 'secrets' have achieved legendary status.[9]

For those artists without access to formal training there was another option available: the rapidly increasing number of artists' instruction manuals appearing on the commercial market. Intended as much for the professional as the amateur artist, these publications presented a wealth of information, describing in detail the 'nuts and bolts' of the profession, listing materials and providing a step-by-step guide to all forms of portrait painting.[10] Thomas Bardwell's *The Practice of Painting and Perspective Made Easy*, published in 1756, was particularly influential and it is against the methods advocated in this volume that the technique of many portraits from this period can be compared.[11] The impact of such publications cannot be underestimated and there are aspects of Geddes's portraiture which indicate his having had access to some technical information, for example, his choice of pigments and application of oil or varnish interlayers during the painting process.

With artists' training becoming more formally established as the century progressed, serious scientific enquiry into the theories and chemistry of art was pursued for the first time by dedicated individuals outwith the immediate fine arts profession. By the middle of the nineteenth century, partly as a reaction to the lamentable physical condition of many publicly displayed works, greater emphasis was spent on the teaching of technical matters – from the initial preparation of a canvas to systems of paint application and varnish.[12]

RESULTS OF EXAMINATION AND ANALYSES

Of the eight portraits studied in detail, four were cleaned in preparation for the exhibition.

All date from the second decade of the nineteenth century. Standard investigative techniques were employed in the conservation studio and more sophisticated forms of analysis were performed by colleagues in the field of scientific research.[13]

While such methods, namely the preparation of cross section samples, provide invaluable information as to the applied sequence of paint layers and the pigments employed in a specific area, it is the identification of the vehicle in which the pigments were ground which is of particular interest to the study of painting technique of this period.

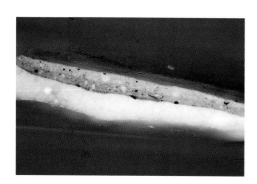

Fig.87 · left
Cross section taken from a small damage on the arm of *Anne Geddes, the Artist's Sister* [fig.50] which shows the thin, warm brown layer the artist applied over the white commercial priming. Above this there are two distinct paint layers which consitute the modelling of the flesh in this area.

Fig.88 · right
Detail of lower right area of the portrait of George Sanders [fig.31] which illustrates the paraphenalia lying around the miniaturist's studio.

Several samples were analysed in order to ascertain whether or not Geddes had succumbed to the temptation of using megilp, that is, a gelled paint medium or bituminous additions to his paint.[14]

SUPPORT AND GROUND PREPARATION

The evidence suggests that Andrew Geddes purchased his painting supports pre-prepared, with a ground or priming layer already applied, from a commercial supplier.[15] He used linen canvases of both tabby and twill weave or wood panels (probably mahogany or oak). While he appears to have painted directly on to the relatively thin, lead white and chalk-based ground layer of the panels, some modification appears to have been undertaken with several of the canvas supports. This took the form of a thin, sparsely pigmented, mid-brown layer applied by the artist over the commercial ground layer [fig.87]. It brings to light a subtle difference of approach observed between the execution of portraits on fabric and solid supports.[16] The two demanded different scales of working, the panels were generally made in a smaller and more restricted range of sizes than canvases. In addition, the intrinsic physical characteristics of the two types of support meant that they absorbed the oil paint differently. Both aspects exerted a marked influence on how the artist would approach his craft. The smooth ground of the panels inspired greater attention to detail, in particular the articulation of both surface texture – whether it be sumptuous patterned carpets and draperies or glimmering pewter – and the resulting play of light on these objects. In this respect the thin paint layer applied over the white preparatory under layer allowed a degree of luminosity that increases the jewel-like quality of the finely observed details [fig.88]. Conversely, the portraits on fabric exploit the tactile nature of the support in a different manner. The portrait of *George Chalmers* [fig.13], for example, reveals an expressive, spontaneous approach which contrasts with the measured application of the two panel portraits of fellow artists, *George Sanders* and *David Wilkie* [figs.31 & 32].

PIGMENTS

Analysis has revealed a conventional range of pigments employed by the artist: lead white, bone black, Naples yellow, Prussian blue, vermilion, earth pigments (ochre, red iron), as well as organic red lakes, including madder. When compared with published studies of the palettes of several near contemporaries – Raeburn, Reynolds and Romney, for example – Geddes's choice proved to be entirely consistent with the prevalent fashion.[17]

PAINT MEDIA

Identification of the paint medium was carried out on a single sample taken from each of six different portraits. The fatty acid ratios found were consistent with the artist's use of a standard heat-bodied linseed oil. Two additional materials were detected in samples from two of the portraits examined. Diterpene resins were found in the sample from *Archibald Constable*, indicating the presence of a hard resin, likely to be Copal.[18] Unfortunately, as no attempt was made to remove the discoloured varnish layers, it is impossible to ascertain whether or not this resin forms part of either the paint or the overlying varnish layer. Copal was used during this period for both purposes.[19]

Wax was found in the sample taken from *George Sanders*.[20] This clearly indicates some manipulation of the paint vehicle. Geddes may have been encouraged in this choice by his good friend, David Wilkie.[21] Like megilp, wax would have been added to the paint in order to improve its handling and texturing properties. It would also have imparted a semi-translucency to the paint, reducing its ability to dry to a hardened film as well as increasing its sensitivity to elevated temperatures and relatively 'mild' organic solvents.

BITUMEN AND MEGILP

In essence there are two materials commonly blamed for the poor state of preservation apparent in works from this period: the dark-brown pigment bitumen or asphaltum and the gelled paint medium, megilp.

The two terms bitumen and asphaltum are often used interchangeably and are listed as both pigment and painting medium in artists' supply catalogues, depending on their preparation. This brown pigment, a varied and complex material chemically, comprises 'the waxy residues from crude petroleum which will, in part, distil between 300 and 540°c'.[22] It has a long history of use and is mentioned by several early authors on painting technique. Available from numerous different countries as a semi-liquid as well as a solid material, it was available pre-prepared from Winsor and Newton from 1835 both in tubes and pots.[23] In common with many artists' materials during the nineteenth century it was frequently adulterated with turpentine, pitch and other balsamic substances.[24]

By the 1830s, authors differentiated between two forms of bitumen – native and artificial – although warnings concerning their use did not distinguish between them. Two basic recipes describe the method of preparation, both involving heating, then grinding and dissolving in either a drying oil or an oil and resin combination. Despite the frequent addition of materials to enhance the drying properties – lead acetate or umber for example – it is clear that the severe deteriorative effect; poor drying and cracking of the paint film caused by the use of bitumen, were recognised at the time:

> *Its fine brown colour, and perfect transparency are lures to its free use with many artists, notwithstanding the certain destruction which awaits the work on which it is much employed*.[25]
>
> *Notwithstanding that painters are frequently aware of the bad results of the use of Asphaltum in pictures, they are tempted, by the beauty of its hue, to try further experiments with it in their own way, and they persuade themselves, that their own special methods of application, will overcome its objectionable tendencies.*[26]

It was also acknowledged that such disastrous effects would not necessarily make themselves visible immediately. According to the Redgraves, cracking:

> *... does not always display itself at once: indeed, under favourable circumstances, they will remain very many years without disruption; but a change in hanging, or in temperature of the room or gallery, and exposure to the sun's rays, and above all varnishing, will though heretofore free from harm, crack them in a few weeks.*[27]

Wilkie is thought to have employed the artificial form of bitumen, a coal tar derivative, in his recipe. The evidence in many of his works of severe deterioration underlines the possibility that this form is the most problematic with regard to paint film-forming defects.

Megilp represents the other regularly employed mixture to which a number of solubility, cracking and yellowing problems can be attributed: 'This was a mixture of drying oil made with a lead drier and mastic varnish. The oil and varnish were prepared separately and then mixed, most commonly in equal parts, by shaking them together briefly. On standing they formed a clear gel, which imparted a rich transparency and a special buttery quality to oil paints. As a result, the paints were said to "keep their place in working, with a flimsy firmness that is perfectly delightful".[28]

Megilp was available in tubes and later in pots from the earliest colourman catalogues, such as those of Winsor and Newton, Reeves, Rowney and Roberson. Reynolds is reputed to have made early use of such a concoction in the latter half of the eighteenth century, while Turner later made extensive use of similar mixtures.[29]

Astonishingly, it seems that artists were well aware of the serious problems caused by the use of both bitumen and megilp. However, so attractive were the properties they imparted and so appealing was their ease of handling, that painters continued to work with them despite regular and public warnings against their use.[30]

Artists' use of such materials has grave implications for the future conservation treatments of their works. In addition to the increased sensitivity of paint layers to the high temperatures frequently used in the past for structural treatments of canvases, the presence of these substances results in little differentiation chemically between the materials used in the paint and in the varnish.[31] The conservator is faced with a paint surface that is soluble in the same organic solvents used for varnish removal. Hence the trepidation with which paintings conservators now regard many works of this period.

PAINT APPLICATION

The Geddes portraits reveal a full range of paint application techniques. Direct, 'wet-in-wet' handling is apparent in the background foliage detail of *Anne Geddes*, whereas with the small full-length panels each thin paint layer has been allowed to dry completely before progressing with the next. The painterly approach of *Anthony Stewart* [fig.5] contrasts vividly with that of the tighter, more conservatively executed *John Clerk, Lord Eldin* [fig.3]. Geddes appears indiscriminate but quite self-conscious in his breadth of pictorial sources. A debt to Raeburn and Lawrence apparent in the portrait of his sister Anne [figs. 50 & 89], co-exists with borrowings from the Italian Baroque in the portrait of *Miss Amelia Penrose Cumming of Altyre* [fig.34], and Rembrandt in the portrait of *The Artist's Mother* [fig.23].

The panel portraits of *George Sanders* and *David Wilkie* exhibit an elaborate and exquisitely considered level of detail and delicacy of handling, characteristics absent from the more derivative portrait of the artist's sister, *Anne Geddes*, or the kit-kat portraits on fabric supports of *Anthony Stewart* and *George Chalmers*. The emphasis on design and carefully harmonised colour suggested in the portraits of his fellow artists, represents a hybrid portraiture-genre form, where the viewer is invited into an intimate celebration of a person's life.

The overall warmth in tonality can be attributed to the use of red pigments in most layers.[32] However, unlike Raeburn, who favoured the generous use of vermilion, the samples taken from the Geddes portraits reveal a more varied number of red pigments with ochres, as well as vermilion and possibly several different transparent organic lakes [figs.89 & 90].[33] A palette leaning towards the warm end of the spectrum was felt to reflect a debt to the Old Masters.

The following remarks from a nineteenth-century commentator concern Wilkie's colouring:

> *Rembrandt's pictures were the foundation of Wilkie's style of colour. Reynolds and other writers had confirmed him in his choice, from their pointing out the advantage a warm coloured picture had over a cold. 'The Pitlessie Fair' and 'The Village Politicians' (especially in the warmth of the shadows) possess more of this character than his picture of 'The Blind Fiddler'...*[34]

Another aspect of Geddes's generally high-colour key was the so-called Old Master 'golden glow'. Derived from Dutch and Italian seventeenth-century art, it proved deeply attractive to artists at this time. To this end coloured glazes, usually resin-rich layers, scarcely pigmented and heavily diluted to achieve the consistency of a thin varnish, were frequently applied to large areas in an effort to push back what were considered disharmonious, jarring areas. Ironically, in many cases it could well be the effects of the

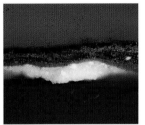

Fig.89 · left
Detail of *Anne Geddes, The Artist's Sister* [fig.50]

Fig.90 · above left
Cross section taken from the red chair in the portrait of *George Chalmers* [fig.13] revealing a build up of paint layers containing combinations of vermilion, bone black, red ochres and transparent lake pigments.

Fig.91 · above right
The cross section shown in fig.89 viewed under an ultraviolet light source. The orange fluorescence of the large particle in the upper centre of the sample is typical of the pigment madder. The white fluorescence along the top of the cross section indicates the presence of varnish layers.

degraded natural resin varnishes on the paint surface that were responsible for the heavily yellowed palette the nineteenth-century artists were so desperate to emulate rather than the Old Masters' original choice of painting materials.

The portrait of *Anne Geddes* exemplifies this. A discrete, warm glaze can be discerned over the landscape background and carried across to the sitter's pale, bare arms resting on her lap [fig.92]. Clearly the existence of such a glaze makes any attempt to remove yellowed varnish layers from the surface extremely complex as they are chemically and visually similiar. *The Artist's Mother* reveals a subtle, yellow-tinged layer over the flesh tones, applied deliberately to imbue the image with a Rembrandtesque effect. Sadly, due to both composition and appearance this layer has often been sacrificed in the hands of past restorers. The result is an imbalance of light and dark passages, an effect exacerbated by the frequent darkening of bituminous layers

or indeed lightening of areas intended to be dark caused by the scattering of light across a cracked and disrupted surface.

THE EXISTENCE OF VARNISH/OIL INTERLAYERS

Integral to traditional painting practice of the period is the presence of 'oiling out layers' between paint applications. These were intended to help unify the layers and prevent 'sinking in' of the medium.[35] Such layers are extremely difficult to identify as instructions insist that only the thinnest suggestion, if any, should remain following removal of excess oil with a cloth. Widely practiced by his contemporaries and regularly referred to in artists' instruction books, many of the cross sections taken from Geddes's portraits

Fig.92 · Detail of *Anne Geddes, The Artist's Sister* [fig.50] showing the subtle, yellow-coloured glaze applied over the background and arm of the sitter (during conservation).

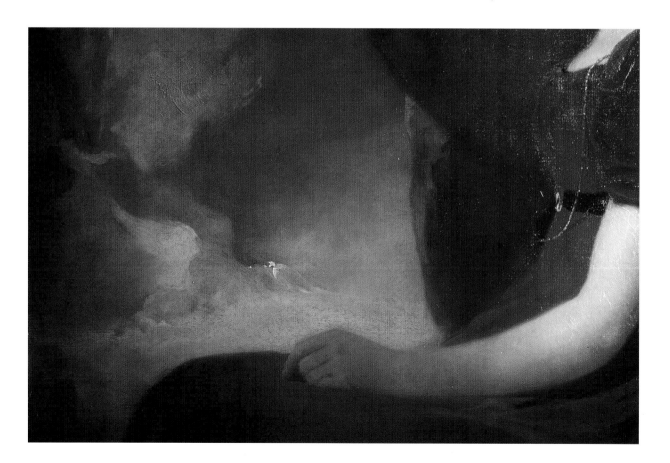

reveal evidence of this technique.[36] This confirms a level of formal technical knowledge probably acquired, like Raeburn, through casual discussion with his contemporaries or from the manuals.

PRESENT CONDITION: CRAQUELURE

The craquelure patterns visible across a painted surface relate directly to the materials and methods employed by the artist. In addition, they can suggest levels of technical proficiency and highlight the possibility of the artist having manipulated an oil paint film. Important external factors also play a part in the development of cracks, such as the climate in which the painting has been kept. Nevertheless, it has been suggested that '… environmental fluctuations do not determine the pattern, they merely develop it to a greater or lesser extent'.[37] With this in mind, the broad range of different crack networks exhibited by the portraits examined allows a simple means of speculation as to how the artist used his materials.[38]

Although analysis did not identify any unstable addition to the oil paint film in these examples, it is immediately apparent from an initial glance that *The Artist's Mother* represents an image dramatically altered from the one Geddes originally intended. Fortunately an etching exists for this work which proved to be of invaluable assistance during the recent conservation treatment.[39] Various factors may be responsible for the round-edged, ductile cracks that are such a prominent feature of the portrait. But it is likely that all in this case relate to the actions of the painter rather than any subsequent considerations. While the presence of a bituminous pigment cannot be discounted entirely, due to the difficulty associated with analysis and the limitations of localised spot testing, the poor drying properties of the paint which have caused the film to contract into these islands may also simply signal weak technique. It is possible that relatively thick paint was applied over layers that had not yet sufficiently hardened or that generous use of a diluent or driers had resulted in shrinkage of the paint film as the solvent evaporated.

It is typical that this phenomenon should occur most acutely – but not exclusively – in the darker passages. Each pigment requires a different amount of medium to produce a workable paint. In general, black and earth brown colours demand a greater amount of oil than lead white. As the pigment itself usually represents the most stable component of a paint formulation, the more medium a paint contains, the less stable it becomes and the more susceptible it is to cracking, solvent abrasion during cleaning and other defects. The portraits examined, irrespective of support, illustrate this. There are discrete, small-scale drying cracks visible in the glaze-like browns of the furniture depicted in *George Sanders* which bear little resemblance to the broad, sharp-edged, branched cracks visible in the heavily lead-white containing paint of Anne Geddes's face. The former is an effect associated with the materials and methods used by the artist, whereas the latter reflects the natural ageing processes paintings inevitably suffer as the different layers expand and contract in response to environmental fluctuations.[40]

CONCLUSION

Although there are limitations to both the scope of this survey and what can be gleaned conclusively from the analytical techniques employed, it is hoped that the information presented contributes to a broader understanding of the present physical appearance of many of Andrew Geddes's portraits.

It is easy with hindsight to criticise nineteenth-century artists for their manipulation of the paint medium. The quest for some long-forgotten painting mixture informed a significant part of artistic activity at the time. Such was the strength of desire to emulate the techniques of the past and so appealing were the handling properties of the materials chosen to achieve this end, that the numerous contemporary warnings about the long term stability of these combinations went unheeded.

However, it has been shown that many factors are responsible for a painting's poor state of preservation and it is imprudent to blame all faults on the choice of one or two 'fashionable' materials. Andrew Geddes painted a number of particularly fine portraits and it is through the examination of those better preserved examples that we should assess his technique. Rather than mourn what has been lost through either the injudicious use of materials, their natural ageing or past restoration interventions, it is the strengths of these surviving works that should be celebrated.

Notes and References

Chapter One · Edinburgh 1783–1803: Rembrandt and the Excise

[1] The unpublished manuscript, *A Catalogue of the Books, Paintings and Prints belonging to David Geddes D. Auditor of Excise*, covering the period from 10 October 1777 to 10 October 1793 (the author's financial year ran from October to October) is in the private possession of the descendants of Margaret Geddes Scott, the youngest sister of Andrew Geddes and youngest child of David Geddes. I am grateful to Antony Griffiths and Sheila O'Connell for help in identifying Philipe's gift. See W. McAllister Johnson, 'From Favereau's Tableaux des Vertus et des Vices to Marolles' Tableaux du Temple des Muses,' in *Gazette des Beaux-Arts*, 1968, vol.72, pp.171–90 in which the volume is described as 'one of the uncontested masterpieces … of seventeenth-century French book production.'

[2] John Fowler Mitchell, *Members of the Scottish Excise Department 1707–1830* (manuscript compiled in 1963, National Archives of Scotland, RH 4/6/1) mentions the 1763 appointment. There are inaccuracies of detail in the other information entered by Fowler on Geddes. See the *Edinburgh Almanack*, 1773, p.122. For McGouan as collector, see infra p.11.

[3] Ed. Hew Scott, *Fasti Ecclesiae Scoticanae*, Edinburgh 1923 (new edition), vol.IV, p.288. For the marriage on 16 February 1766, see the Old Parochial Registers, OPR Edinburgh 685–1/49; for the births of the three children, see OPR 685–1 32/33; for the deaths of the two sons in April and June 1770, see the records of Greyfriars Burials,

OPR 685–1/96. I am indebted to Richard Smith and to his Edinburgh researcher Alison Mowat for this information. The *Book of Disbursements* was presented to Edinburgh Central Public Library (access via the Fine Art Library, Edinburgh City Libraries and Information Services) in 1934 by Andrew Geddes Scott, the direct descendant of David Geddes's youngest daughter by his second marriage. It complements the above-mentioned *Catalogue* (note 1) as a meticulous record of household and culturally-related expenditure from October 1777 to July 1794. The 'Mrs Provand' is less likely to have been Geddes's widowed mother-in-law who died in 1781.

[4] Geddes is listed as Deputy Auditor in the *Edinburgh Almanacks* from 1778 to 1803. See OPR 685–1/51, p.119. The entry was published by the Scottish Record Society in ed. Francis J. Grant, *Register of Marriages in the City of Edinburgh 1751–1800*, Edinburgh 1922, p.274. Agnes Boyd's date of birth is not known.

[5] Most of the birth and baptismal entries from the Old Parochial Registers were transcribed by David Laing for his catalogue, *Etchings by Sir David Wilkie, RA, Limner to HM for Scotland and by Andrew Geddes, ARA with Biographical Sketches*, Edinburgh 1875, pp.6 and 28. The original entries for Andrew (29 May 1783) and Charlotte (parish of St Cuthbert's, Edinburgh) are OPR 685–2/10, p.356; for the others, with the exception of Margaret (untraced), see OPR 685–2/10, p.85 (Anne) and OPR 685–2/11, pp.96 and 224 (Katherine and Grizzel). As Laing observed, the children were baptised by the Revd James Dobie of Mid Calder, Geddes's brother-in-law

by his first marriage. Margaret Geddes married Alexander Scott on 1 July 1828 in Dublin Street at her late mother's lodgings. Scott subsequently emigrated to, and left a will in, America, having apparently deserted his wife in circumstances unknown.

[6] *Book of Disbursements* (see note 3), entries of removal expenses September 1782 and 24 July 1788; Trust, Disposition and Settlement of David Geddes 19 December 1783, registered 16 April 1803 (National Archives of Scotland, RD 3/297, p.699); Register of Sasines (Edinburgh) 1 September 1788 (National Archives of Scotland, RS 27/325, p.149, 2914). For Andrew Geddes's inheritance of the Buccleuch Place property, see p.19 and note 19.

[7] *Book of Disbursements* 1 October 1789. The ledger also includes the earliest reference to the artist – apart from his baptism. On 3 November 1783 David Geddes paid one Dr Gardner for his son's inoculation against smallpox! An extended feature article, 'An Edinburgh Citizen's Account Book', appeared in *The Scotsman* 27 September 1913.

[8] In the late 1820s the Royal High School was transferred to the Greek Doric premises in Regent Road, designed by Thomas Hamilton. Adela Geddes, *Memoir of the late Andrew Geddes, Esq., A.R.A.*, London 1844, pp.6–7. This is still the prime source on the artist's life and career. For the circumstances of its compilation, see *Adela Geddes's Legacy*, pp.83–4 and note 153.

[9] An anecdotal account of Martin appeared in *A Series of Original Portraits and Caricature Etchings by the late John Kay, Miniature Painter, Edinburgh*, Edinburgh

1837, vol.I, pp.140–4, accompanied by a Kay etching depicting Martin in action at a sale [fig.2]. See also Adela Geddes, ibid., p.14. The National Gallery of Scotland holds annotated published catalogues for some of Martin's print auctions from 1783 to 1793 and including the posthumous sale of the collection of Alexander Steuart of Dunearn on 13 February 1787 from which David Geddes made purchases. Martin received his Burgess ticket in 1786. Further information on Martin is held in the National Library of Scotland's unpublished *Directory of Edinburgh Booksellers*.

[10] See the essay by Peter Black in this publication and Campbell Dodgson, *The Etchings of Sir David Wilkie & Andrew Geddes. A Catalogue*, London 1936 (for The Print Collectors' Club), p.33, Cat.9. The rapid sketch of Martin was listed by the artist in his private memorandum of pictures completed in 1813 among the David Laing MSS in Edinburgh University Library, La.IV.26, Fo.89. For David Laing, see *Adela Geddes's Legacy*.

[11] Letter from Philipe, Pall Mall Court, London, 11 March 1791, to David Geddes at the Excise Office, Edinburgh in the Laing MSS, La.IV.26, fos.39–40. David Laing, ibid., p.7, makes an otherwise unsubstantiated and probably confused statement that Philipe operated in a similar capacity in Edinburgh 'for many years' before moving to London. David Geddes's paintings collection was of far lesser import. One of his Edinburgh agents for the purchase of paintings was the jobbing portrait painter, copyist and picture restorer John Medina the Younger (1721–1796). See note 21.

[12] The Department of Prints and Drawings, the British Museum, and the National Library of Scotland both hold annotated copies of the *Catalogue of the Valuable Collection of Prints, Antient and Modern Masters of all Schools, Formed with superior Taste and Judgment, during a Period exceeding Forty Years, by David Geddes, Esq. of Edinburgh ...* (auctioneer, T. Philipe, London 30 April – 5 May 1804). See p.19 and note 21. Lot 360 of the 3rd day of Geddes's posthumous sale at Christie's on 10 April 1845 (note 155) was 'a volume containing 107 pen sketches, by Adam Elsheimer, drawn with great freedom and effect.' See Keith Andrews, *Adam*

Elsheimer. Paintings, Drawings, Prints, Oxford 1977, in which this album is provisionally identified as the one acquired by the Städelsches Kunstinstitut in Frankfurt in 1868 (ibid., pp.41,45–6) and note 39. For his subject picture celebrating the Old Master 'Holy Trinity', see p.49 and note 77.

[13] The 'madness' for Rembrandt's autograph original etchings, as distinct from reproductive mezzotints by British artists, was described by Charles Rogers in *A Collection of Prints in Imitation of Drawings*, London 1778, vol.II, p.215. See Ellen G. D'Oench, '"A Madness to Have His Prints": Rembrandt and Georgian Taste 1720–1800' in Christopher White et al, *Rembrandt in Eighteenth-Century England*, New Haven 1983, pp.63–81. David Geddes's private library included at least two catalogues of Rembrandt's works, notably Daniel Daulby's *A Descriptive Catalogue of the Works of Rembrandt and of his Scholars, Bol, Livens, and Van Vliet*, Liverpool 1796.

[14] McGouan described his diverse collecting activities in a letter to Lady Strange 4 March 1797 in the Strange MSS (National Library of Scotland, MS 14254, fos.90–1). Wilkie's observation on McGouan is quoted in John Burnet, *The Progress of a Painter in the Nineteenth Century*, London 1854, p.19. Burnet refers additionally to the Rembrandt prints owned by John Clerk, later Lord Eldin, and by the drawing master George Walker. Another of Geddes's immediate colleagues in the Excise, John Caw, left his mixed collections to the Society of Antiquaries of Scotland in 1782 and was one of a trio of middle-class cognoscenti portrayed by David Allan in 1783 in *The Connoisseurs* (National Gallery of Scotland, NG 2260).

[15] A brief account of Erskine appeared in John Kay, ibid., vol.II, pp.57–9. Some information on his print collection and private library is contained in his testament and inventory of 24 January 1794 (National Archives of Scotland, CC8/8/129(2)). The 'Luxembourg Gallery', a luxury folio volume with extremely high quality engravings, has been identified by Antony Griffiths as *La Gallerie du Palais Luxembourg peinte par Rubens, dessiné par les Sieurs Nattier, et gravée par les plus meilleurs graveurs du temps. Dédiée au Roy. Se vend à Paris chez le*

Sr Duchange graveur du Roy en son Académie Royale de Peinture et Sculpture rue St Jacques au dessus de la rue des Mathurins. Avec privilège de sa Majesté, 1710. Macfarquhar's testament providing for the disposal of his print collection was drawn up on 16 August 1791 and registered on 8 April 1793 (National Archives of Scotland, RD4/253, pp.668–83). His ten day London sale from 11 May 1796 was advertised in the *Edinburgh Evening Courant* 31 March 1796, Philipe and Martin being named as agents for Mr King the auctioneer. An annotated copy of the sale catalogue is in the National Gallery of Scotland. The Elsheimer/Goudt volume was lot 1004.

[16] Andrew Geddes's brief attendance at Edinburgh University is recorded in the *Ledger of Class Attendance: Class Lists 1796/7 Latin and Greek* and the *Ledger of Matriculation 1786–1803*, vol.II (entries for 1796 and 1797 only) (Edinburgh University Library, Department of Special Collections). I am grateful to Arnot Wilson, University Archivist, for his assistance in checking the records. For Wardrop, who matriculated as a student of Classics in 1795, see p.19 and note 23. On Geddes's involuntary recruitment to the Excise, see Adela Geddes, ibid., pp.8–9. The younger Geddes is not listed on the staff of the Scottish Board of Excise in the published *Almanacks* until 1804 (see note 22). John Fowler Mitchell, ibid., (note 2), claimed that he was signatory for the Auditor of the Aberdeen Salary Book on 5 July 1796 and the Argyle South Salary Book in December. This would fit with Adela Geddes's assertion that her husband was employed in the Excise 'for nearly five years', vetting the accounts, but refrained from drawing his salary.

[17] Evidence of Philipe's agency in marketing Clerk of Eldin's etchings is provided in a letter to Clerk from Robert Murray, Edinburgh, 10 December 1777 (National Archives of Scotland, GD 18/4685). In 1786, at the suggestion of the 11th Earl of Buchan, founder of the Society of Antiquaries of Scotland, a set was presented to George III.

[18] Adela Geddes, ibid., pp.7–8 and Julia Lloyd Williams et al, *Dutch Art and Scotland. A Reflection of Taste*, Edinburgh 1992, p.161. Lot 137 of the 5th day's sale of Eldin's collection comprised twenty-nine Geddes etchings

on India paper. See the *Catalogue of the Extensive, Genuine, and Highly Valuable Collection of Pictures, late the Property of the Hon. John Clerk of Eldin, one of the Senators of the College of Justice* (auctioneers, Thomas Winstanley & Sons of Liverpool at Clerk's residence 16 Picardy Place, Edinburgh, 14–27 March 1833). Eldin's collection was said to include every Rembrandt print catalogued by Daniel Daulby (see note 13). On the importance to young Scottish artists of the availability of Eldin's collection of Rembrandt prints, see John Burnet, ibid., pp.18–19. Another collector singled out by Burnet, but who is not known to have had any immediate connection with either of the Geddeses, was the drawing master George Walker of the Hunter's Square Academy. His print collection, auctioned by Thomas Philipe in London on 22 February 1814, included only a small quota of Rembrandt etchings despite the claims advanced by Burnet.

Chapter Two · The Order of Release, 1803: the Trustees' Academy, Alexander Nasmyth's Academy and the Royal Academy Schools

[19] David Geddes's death was reported in the *Scots Magazine*, April 1803, p.292. His burial took place at Greyfriars Kirk, Edinburgh, on 17 March (Register of Greyfriars Burials OPR 685–1/98 in which he is misleadingly described as Auditor of Excise). I am grateful to Richard Smith and Alison Mowat for this information. For Andrew Geddes's inheritance and a description of the Buccleuch Place third storey lodging, see the Register of Sasines for Edinburgh 8 October 1804 (National Archives of Scotland, RS 27/528, p.219, 10857).

[20] Letter from Philipe, Golden Square, London 20 June 1803, to Geddes at the Excise Office, Edinburgh, in the Laing MSS (note 11), La.IV.26, Fos.41–2. Geddes's excise appointment in 1803 is recorded by Laing in his prefatory essay to his 1875 catalogue, ibid. (note 5), p.6. Laing may have verified the statement by direct investigation of Excise records. Andrew Geddes's next appointment was noted in the tabulated listing of the Board of Excise in the *New Scots Almanack* in 1804.

[21] See note 12. The National Library of Scotland's copy of David Geddes's print sale catalogue is annotated with prices and purchasers, principally dealers, including Woodburn, Colnaghi, Graves, Molteno and Philipe himself. The Library also holds a priced and annotated copy of *A Catalogue of the Valuable and Choice Collection of Pictures the Property of the Late Mr David Geddes of the Excise* (auctioneer, William Martin at 94, South Bridge Street, Edinburgh, 24 February 1804. See note 11.

[22] Laing MSS, La.IV.26, fos.43–4. Geddes is still listed under the Board of Excise in the *Edinburgh Almanack* for 1805. His name was omitted from the *British Almanack* from 1806 onwards. The tradition of his self-education as an artist derives, essentially, from his widow's *Memoir* of 1844. Despite the inaccuracies of detail in this memoir, the tradition does deserve some credence. See notes 23 and 26 for the conflicting evidence of James Wardrop and Wilkie's biographer Allan Cunningham.

[23] See note 24. Autobiographical notes of Dr James Wardrop, transcribed by his daughter Mrs Shirley, among the Wardrop MSS (National Library of Scotland, Acc.5653, vol.I, p.4). Wardrop, who settled permanently in London in 1809, was appointed Surgeon Extraordinary to the Prince Regent in 1819 and, following the latter's coronation as George IV in 1821, attended him during the Royal visit to Edinburgh in 1822. Geddes's fine half-length portrait (from the Shirley collection and now in the Royal College of Surgeons of Edinburgh) probably dates from this period. It is reproduced in Alastair H.B. Masson, *Portraits, Paintings & Busts in the Royal College of Surgeons of Edinburgh*, Edinburgh 1995. A smaller half-length Geddes portrait of Wardrop senior, indicative of the artist's close study of the portraiture of Sir Henry Raeburn, is in Aberdeen Art Gallery. In 1850 the younger Wardrop presented two paintings to the newly founded National Gallery of Scotland: *The Beheading of St John The Baptist*, then attributed to Domenico Fetti and now reattributed to Hendrik Terbrugghen (NG 28) and a 'Spanish School' *Battlefield* now described as Italian school of the seventeenth century (NG 85). The remainder of Wardrop's picture collection was auctioned posthumously by Messrs Foster of Pall Mall on 31 March 1869.

[24] Nasmyth opened a private academy in his studio in St James's Square (transferred to 2 Princes Street by 1799) following his failed application for the Mastership of the Trustees' Academy in 1786. See J.C.B. Cooksey, *Alexander Nasmyth HRA 1758–1840. A Man of the Scottish Renaissance*, Haddington 1991, especially ch.6 and Appendix H. Walker first advertised private classes in Edinburgh in the *Caledonian Mercury* on 2 November 1782. For his Hunter's Square academy (for young ladies) and his private collection of Old Master paintings, see his correspondence with the 11th Earl of Buchan 1804–13 (Edinburgh University Library, Department of Special Collections, Gen. 1429/22/3).

[25] For the early history of the Trustees' Academy, see J. Mason, 'The Edinburgh School of Design', in *Book of the Old Edinburgh Club*, 1949, vol.27, pp.67–96; David and Francina Irwin, *Scottish Painters at Home and Abroad*, London 1975, pp.90–8; and Patricia Brookes, *The Trustees' Academy, Edinburgh 1760–1801: The Public Patronage of Art and Design in the Scottish Enlightenment*, Ann Arbor 1989 (UMI reprint of doctoral thesis, Syracuse University 1989). The extant records of the Academy, later the School of Design, are preserved among the Board of Manufactures papers (National Archives of Scotland, NG 2; and numerous references including inconsistently detailed returns of student admissions, throughout the Board Minutes, NG 1). Graham's reformed Academy was promoted in the *Edinburgh Evening Courant* on 1 July and 21 November 1799.

[26] Wardrop's testimony was reiterated, independently, by Allan Cunningham in *The Life of Sir David Wilkie*, London 1843, vol.II, p.65, as follows: 'In his countryman, Andrew Geddes, a student from the Edinburgh Academy, he [Wilkie] was not slow to perceive a resolution to excel united to that calm perseverance in study and love of nature which he felt in himself: this was sufficient to win the regard of Wilkie.'

[27] See Allan Cunningham, ibid., vol.I, pp.33–7 and vol.II, p.391 and John Burnet, ibid. (note 14), p.205. Burnet's acquaintance with Geddes may well have originated in a shared parental connection with the Excise. As Burnet recounted in his *Autobiography*

(published in the *Art Journal*, 1850, pp.275–7), the circumstances of his own birth in Edinburgh were determined by his father's transfer to the city following his appointment as General Surveyor of Excise, an appointment which coincided with David Geddes's prolonged tenure of office as Deputy-Auditor. An informative obituary of Burnet appeared in *The Athenaeum*, 6 June 1868, 2119, p.797. Allan Cunningham, ibid., vol.I, p.102 (letter from Wilkie to his father, undated, spring 1806, on completion of *The Village Politicians*) and p.89 (undated letter from Wilkie to his father, 1805, concerning Wilkie's renewal of acquaintance with former contemporaries from the Trustees' Academy).

[28] Applicants for admission to Graham's two-year course of free tuition were accepted on personal recommendation for a probationary period of six weeks. The Trustees abandoned the less practicable – in a Scottish context – procedure requiring the ability to draw from the cast. The terms of admission to the Royal Academy Schools, applicable to Wilkie, were summarised in the RA Council Minutes of 15 January 1805 (RA Archives, London). Wilkie's highly finished chalk study after a cast of the antique group of the *Dancing Faun* (National Gallery of Scotland, D.4915) has been related, plausibly but not conclusively, to his enrolment on 28 November 1805.

[29] See Sidney C. Hutchison, 'The Royal Academy Schools 1768–1830', in the *Walpole Society*, vol.XXXVIII, p.163. Hutchison transcribed the ledger entry as follows: 1807 – January 15/906 Geddes, Andrew. The omission of Geddes, as distinct from his co-entrants, from the contemporary record in the RA Council Minutes (vol.IV, 1807–12, p.3) and the absence of any reference in the General Assembly Minutes may be indicative of an unorthodox admission procedure (information from Mark Pomeroy, RA Archivist). The beginning of Wilkie's acquaintance with Geddes at the Schools is mentioned in Adela Geddes, ibid., pp.9–10.

[30] Adela Geddes, ibid., p.9. Stewart exhibited at the Royal Academy from 1807 but had evidently reached London by June 1794. The Geddes conversation piece, which is probably nearly contemporary with a half-length portrait of Stewart dated 1812 and in the

Scottish National Portrait Gallery [PG 430, fig.5], was presented by Mrs Geddes in her widowhood to the Reid family and has been inherited by descent. Stewart's daughter and pupil Margaret married John Seguier, Geddes's fellow-student at the Royal Academy and later Superintendent of the British Institution in succession to his artist brother William, also an influential dealer and collector. See p.82 and note 152.

[31] See note 24. Cooksey, ibid., ch.6, pp.52–3, and ed. Samuel Smiles, *James Nasmyth Engineer. An Autobiography*, London 1883, pp.50–1.

[32] Geddes's *Draught Players* was last recorded with the Glasgow dealer MacNicol in 1959 (archive photograph in the National Gallery of Scotland). In 1908 it was lent to the Scottish National Exhibition in Edinburgh by Alfred N.G. Aitken. For Wilkie's *Card Players*, see the catalogue (by Professor Hamish Miles) of the exhibition *Sir David Wilkie 1785-1841*, Richard L. Feigen & Co., London, 1994, Cat.6. Other examples of this type of compositional study in Geddes's preferred medium of black chalk are held by the British Museum (*Cottage Interior*, inv.1918-10-2-1) and the National Gallery of Scotland, D.5440 (d) and D.5440 (c) whose composition may also allude to the Rembrandt 'spirited sketches – interior of sick chamber' which were dispersed in Geddes's posthumous sale at Christie's (3rd day's sale, 10 April 1845, lot 329).

Chapter Three · The Return to Edinburgh 1810–14 and the Incorporated Society of Artists

[33] Geddes's acquisition of the York Place apartment is recorded in the Register of Sasines for Edinburgh on 27 February 1810 (National Archives of Scotland, RS 27/651, p.173, no.14633). From 1811 to 1814 he was listed at this address in the *Post Office Annual Directory* for Edinburgh. By 1816 his widowed mother was living at 20 Dublin Street off York Place (and by 1824 at 39 Dublin Street). It was at this address that Geddes appears to have lodged, whether by preference or by necessity, on periodic return visits to the city from 1819. He had presumably relinquished his interest in the York Place

property in the meantime. In 1813 he gave his York Place studio as his contact address when exhibiting at the Royal Academy, but by 1815 this had changed to 5 Conduit Street in London.

[34] See Duncan Thomson et al, *Raeburn: The Art of Sir Henry Raeburn 1756-1823*, Edinburgh 1997, pp.24–7. For Wilkie's involvement with Raeburn's London reconnoitre, see Allan Cunningham, ibid., vol.I, p.280 and p.299.

[35] The unpublished manuscript minute book and the printed exhibition catalogues of the Associated Artists are in the library of the Royal Scottish Academy. I am grateful to Joanna Soden, Librarian and Curator of the RSA, for alerting me to the existence of this material. A brief account of the Society is given in D. and F. Irwin, ibid., ch.11, pp.186–7. For a contextual discussion, see Duncan Forbes, 'Art and Anxiety in Enlightenment Scotland: The Society of Incorporated Artists 1808–1813' in *Scotia: Interdisciplinary Journal of Scottish Studies*, Virginia 1997, vol.XXI, pp.1–17.

[36] Plimer ceased to exhibit with the Associated Artists from 1808. The account of his career in George C. Williamson, *Andrew & Nathaniel Plimer, Miniature Painters. Their Lives and their Works*, London 1903, is conspicuously incomplete. Geddes's memoranda were published in entirety by David Laing, ibid., pp.9–10. The 1812 list is, unaccountably, no longer among the Laing MSS in Edinburgh University Library. For the 1813 and 1814 lists, see La.IV.26, fo.89. The tradition ascribing the first encounter of Adela Plimer and Andrew Geddes to 1803 was rehearsed in the obituary of Geddes in the *Art Union*, London 1844, p.292. The unexplained circumstances which delayed their marriage were presumably both financial and professional. Adela's date of birth, previously unknown, is recorded as 22 August 1791 in the Baptism Registers of St George's, Hanover Square, London (Westminster City Archives). For the Plimer/Geddes marriage, see pp.66–7.

[37] The drypoint of Plimer was excluded from Laing's 1875 catalogue, presumably on account of Adela Geddes's strictures in her letter to him of 4 November 1874 (Laing MSS,

La.IV.17., fos.3507–11). The copper plate had already been destroyed. See also Campbell Dodgson, ibid., p.35, cat.no.12 (note 10). Campbell Dodgson questions the identification of this print, being unfamiliar with the above correspondence as the rationale for its exclusion by Laing. For Geddes as painter-etcher, see the essay in this publication by Peter Black.

[38] See note 35. The Artists' exhibitions were open to non-members and amateurs. The Nasmyths were admitted to membership on 27 May 1809; Geddes was proposed – outcome not recorded – on 1 June 1811. The Life academy project was first mooted on 25 November 1809. Rather ill-advisedly, the Artists' Committee approached the Board of Trustees for Manufactures for discretionary use of the Trustees' Academy premises in Picardy Place outwith class hours. In 1810 the Trustees, unimpressed by pleas of poverty and protective of their own jurisdiction over art education in the Scottish capital with or without provision for study from the life, rejected the Artists' petition which had been modified to exclude an enlightened but contentious proposal for the engagement of female as well as male models. The Artists eventually rented premises from one of their own Committee members, the animal painter James Howe (see the minute book, 16 December 1809, 2 and 5 June 1810 and 6 February 1811).

[39] James Nasmyth, ibid., pp.56–7. The most comprehensive public collections of Geddes's drawings are in the National Gallery of Scotland and the British Museum. The holdings of landscape drawings represent a small fraction of his total output, as may be gauged from the catalogue of his posthumous sale at Christie's, 8–13 April 1845. Several of the titles reflect his abiding interest in the transitory effects of nature. The Christie's Archives copy of this catalogue, annotated with prices and purchasers, is interleaved with a manuscript inventory of additional lots including landscape drawings. Lot 361 of the 3rd day's sale comprised 'Van Goyen's Sketch Book: A volume containing a collection of 181 spirited sketches of landscapes, by Van Goyen, in black lead', another probable influence on Geddes's drawing style. For the so-called 'London Sketchbook' (British Museum, 1946.7.13.1076 (1–182)), see Hans-

Ulrich Beck, *Jan van Goyen, 1596–1656* (Amsterdam 1972), vol.I, pp.257–64. For Geddes's ownership of an album of Elsheimer sketches, see note 12. Geddes's 1810 landscape, as exhibited by the Associated Artists, is discussed in D. and F. Irwin, ibid. See also fig.10. David Geddes owned a small number of unspecified prints after Rubens landscapes. Geddes's own collection of Bolswert's reproductive engravings was dispersed in the 1845 sale as lot 48.

[40] Patrick Gibson (a friend of Geddes) in *Edinburgh Annual Register*, Edinburgh 1816, p.457; Sara Stevenson and Helen Bennett, *Van Dyck in Check Trousers. Fancy Dress in Art and Life 1700–1900*, Edinburgh 1978, especially pp.19–30. Buchan's commissioned 'closet pictures' averaged 15 × 12½ inches. For the Caledonian Temple of Fame, see Helen Smailes, *A Portrait Gallery for Scotland. The Foundation, Architecture and Mural Decoration of the Scottish National Portrait Gallery 1882–1906*, Edinburgh 1985, pp.10–14 and bibliography. Geddes later reproduced as an etching the Van Dyck self-portrait from the collection of the Duke of Grafton. See Campbell Dodgson, ibid., p.50, cat.no.48.

[41] See John Clive, *Scotch Reviewers. The Edinburgh Review 1802–1815*, London 1957. Constable's portrait comprised the first entry in Geddes's private memorandum of pictures painted in 1813. The earlier conversation piece featured as no.12 in the 1812 memorandum (see note 36) and was photographed by the Scottish National Portrait Gallery prior to Dowell's Edinburgh sale of 2 November 1962 (lot 103). Craigcrook was purchased from Constable in 1814 by the future Lord Advocate, and later editor of the *Edinburgh Review*, Francis Jeffrey, a patron of Geddes in 1820. See p.55.

[42] Constable correspondence, National Library of Scotland, MS 670, fo.13. Geddes's print after his own oil portrait of Chalmers, executed in etching with an admixture of drypoint in later states, is dated 1812 and, given the circumstances of the original commission, may have been produced either in London or in Edinburgh. Campbell Dodgson (ibid., p.30, cat.no.5) mistakenly associates contemporary references to the distinguished Scottish theologian Dr Thomas Chalmers (see pp.45–6) with the author of *Caledonia*.

[43] Both drawings are in the Scottish National Portrait Gallery (PG 196 and PG 2674) and are listed as nos.16 and 22 in Geddes's memoranda of pictures, 1812 and 1813 (see note 36). Alexander Murray had been engaged by Constable to prepare a new edition of James Bruce's *Travels* in 1802. He referred affably to the artist, evidently then in London, in a letter to Constable of 6 June 1812 (National Library of Scotland, MS 681, fo.243). An impression of Burnet's etching is in the Scottish National Portrait Gallery (SPV 181-1).

[44] On the prevalence of portraiture, see Duncan Forbes, ibid., p.8, citing commentaries in the *Scots Magazine*, April 1813, p.246 and the *Edinburgh Star*, 24 May 1811, p.4. For Geddes's 1812 exhibits, see the *Scots Magazine*, 1812, pp.351–2, in which only the portrait of Skirving is identified by name. Exhibit 127 may have been either the portrait of the artist's mother or that of Mrs David Bridges senior (see p.32 and fig.20) both of which would fit the generalised description.

[45] On Wilson's acquaintance with Wilkie, who may have introduced him to Geddes, see Allan Cunningham, ibid., vol.I, pp.130–1. Wilson, who had recently returned to London after three years in Genoa, was employed as Professor of Drawing at Sandhurst. The sale of his Genoese Old Masters was recorded in the revelatory *Memoirs* of Buchanan. As Old Master picture consultant to the Scottish nobility, Wilson was to attain a stature and influence far exceeding that of his landscape painting. On this subject, see the introductory essay by Hugh Brigstocke in *William Buchanan and the Nineteenth Century Art Trade: 100 Letters to His Agent in London and Italy*, 1982 (published privately by the Paul Mellon Centre for Studies in British Art). For Wilson's subsequent association with Geddes, see pp.47–50 and p.69.

[46] The oil portrait of Skirving is no.1 on Geddes's list for 1812 and that of his brother, no.9 on the list for 1813 (note 36): Campbell Dodgson, ibid., pp.36–7, cat.nos.14–15, and Stephen Lloyd, *Raeburn's Rival: Archibald Skirving 1749–1819*, Edinburgh 1999, especially p.76. The impression in the Scottish National Portrait Gallery of the 6th state of the print is inscribed on the reverse in Geddes's hand: 'And: Geddes fecit / Aquaforti [*sic*] by Mr Skirven [*sic*] Portrait Painter in Pastel'.

[47] Nasmyth's and Geddes's association with the Dilettanti Club and Allan's painting are described by James Nasmyth. See ed. Samuel Smiles, ibid., pp.35–6 and, for Bridges, ed. William Ruddick, *John Gibson Lockhart, Peter's Letters to His Kinsfolk*, Edinburgh 1977, Letter XLVII, pp.114–17 (first published 1819). The Bridges portraits, of which the originals were inherited by the 'Director General's' brother James Bridges and remain in the possession of his direct descendent, were all included in Geddes's 1812 inventory, as published by David Laing, ibid., p.9 (note 36). For the related etching, see Campbell Dodgson, ibid., p.29, cat.no.5.

[48] For the circumstances of the Society's schismatic disintegration, see Duncan Forbes, ibid. Patrick Nasmyth wrote to his father 11 October 1814 from London, approving of the latter's resignation and announcing his own (National Library of Scotland, MS 2521, fo.143).

[49] Geddes's cabinet portrait of Robison passed through Christie's, London, on 20 April 1990 (lot 39) with an attribution to Julius Caesar Ibbetson (1759–1817) based upon a misreading of the signature (in initials only) and a presumed lineage from the early skating pictures of Ibbetson which are among his best known and most popular works. See James Mitchell, *Julius Caesar Ibbetson (1759–1817), 'The Berchem of England'*, London 1999 (for John Mitchell & Son). The landscape setting was wrongly identified in the sale catalogue as Craiglockhart rather than Duddingston. Robison's portrait, no.17 in the artist's 1813 memorandum, was selected for inclusion in his 1821 retrospective exhibition in Edinburgh. See infra., p.34. For Raeburn's portrait of the elder Robison, see Duncan Thomson et al, ibid., pp.120–1, cat.no.33.

[50] Raeburn's portrait of Walker is discussed at length in Duncan Thomson et al., ibid., pp.88–90, including a possible precedent in the life size full-length of another member of the Club, the lawyer William Grant of Congalton, by Gilbert Stuart, painted and exhibited in London in 1782. By the early 1790s, the provisional date now assigned to the Raeburn, Grant had repatriated this portrait, entrusting it temporarily to the custody of his friend, the banker and Maecenas, Gilbert Innes of Stow at whose residence in the centre of Edinburgh it could well have been seen by Raeburn (research in progress by the present author). On the Edinburgh Skating Club, see Margaret Elliot, 'The Edinburgh Skating Club 1778–1966', in *The Book of the Old Edinburgh Club*, vol.XXXIII, part 2, Edinburgh 1971, pp.96–136 (and on Robison, p.100 and p.121) and Merlin Waterson, 'Hissing along the polished ice', in *Country Life*, 2 April 1981, pp.872–4.

[51] The small full-length of Agnes Boyd and Geddes's Rembrandtesque self-portrait are in the private possession of the descendants of the artist's younger sister, Margaret Geddes Scott. Agnes Boyd's portrait was no.3 in his 1812 memorandum. For the wider influence of *The Artist's Mother* by Rembrandt (now ascribed by some to Jan Lievens), see Christopher White 'Rembrandt's Influence on English Painting', pp.21–2 and Ellen G. D'Oench, p.77 in Christopher White et al, ibid. (note 13). See also Christopher White, *The Dutch Pictures in the Collection of Her Majesty the Queen*, Cambridge 1982, pp.101–3, cat.no.158 and Julia Lloyd Williams et al, ibid., p.116, cat.46 (note 18). For Geddes's 1822 drypoint of Agnes Boyd Geddes, see the essay by Peter Black. The Rembrandtesque oil was presented to the National Gallery of Scotland in 1877 by the artist's widow. The self-portrait, which does not correspond to any specific Rembrandt prototype, may have been painted in 1816 – the last digit of the date in the original inscription is uncertain – and thus after Geddes's acquisition of *The Toilet of Bathsheba*. See ch.4.

Chapter Four · The Parisian Interlude 1814, the Artist as Dealer and the Alternative Lure of London

[52] See *Annals of the Fine Arts*, London 1819, vol.III, 1818, p.277. The same journal had carried an editorial the previous year, 'Fidelia on the Frauds of Picture Dealers', including a commentary on the phenomenon of the gentleman amateur dealer with particular reference to Sir William Hamilton and a postscript on the proliferation and implied degradation of picture dealing across the social classes and professions including 'tradesmen' (ibid., London 1818, vol.II, 1817, pp.201ff and p.209). The British Institution had been founded in 1805. It promoted itself as a complementary organisation to the Royal Academy, particularly through the facilities for the study of Old Master painting which were accessible to both amateur and professional artists through the Institution's school, opened in 1806, the year of Geddes's arrival in London. The Institution, the prototype for its counterpart formed in Edinburgh in 1819 (see p.47), played a decisive role in the establishment of the National Gallery in 1824. See the article on the Institution by Jordana Pomeroy, 'Creating a national collection', *Apollo*, August 1998, pp.41–9.

[53] The 'Carracci' is now considered to have been a copy after *Christ Appearing to St Anthony Abbot During his Temptation* in the National Gallery, London. Geddes is recorded as the purchaser of both pictures (lots 25 and 33) in the National Art Library's annotated copy of *A Catalogue of the Distinguished Collection of Valuable Original Pictures First Class of the Italian, Dutch and Flemish Schools ... the Property of A. Delahante Esq. Returning to Paris* (auctioneer H. Phillips, London, 3 and 4 June 1814. For the circumstances of the onward sale to Lawrence, see p.68. Curiously, Geddes's interim ownership was not noted by the dealer John Smith in his *A Catalogue Raisonné of the Works of the Most Eminent Dutch, Flemish and French Painters*, London 1836, pt.VII, p.13. The picture was first recorded in the Willem Six sale in Amsterdam 12 May 1734, no.56.

[54] An impression of Burnet's engraving is in the British Museum (1861-11-9-293; fig.27). Geddes informed Clerk that he had despatched a batch of the prints to Scotland, including one presentation impression, in a letter of 26 July 1815 from London (National Library of Scotland, MS 9994, fo.32). For Oswald, see Adela Geddes, ibid., p.11.

[55] On Wilkie's and Haydon's Parisian excursion, see Allan Cunningham, ibid., vol.I, ch.XI, p.389ff. For the Musée Napoléon, see ed. Jean Tulard, *Dictionnaire Napoléon*, Paris 1987, pp.1209–11 and Cecil Gould, *Trophy of Conquest. The Musée Napoléon and the Creation of the Louvre*, London 1965. Gould reproduces Benjamin Zix's drawing of the marriage procession of Napoleon I and Marie-Louise through the Grande Galerie in 1810. The looted paintings displayed in the

background included most of the major works by Rubens from Belgium and Raphaels from the Vatican, notably *The Transfiguration*. Margaret Geddes Scott, the artist's youngest sister, recalled that her brother developed a particular proficiency in French, fostered, no doubt, by the availability in David Geddes's private library of a significant number of 'classics' of French literature from Rabelais to Rousseau, some in translation and some in the original (memorandum of W.D. Scott, nephew of the artist, to David Laing, 25 March 1875, Laing MSS, La.IV.17, fos.3577–80). For Geddes in Italy, see Adela Geddes, ibid., p.17, and ch.9.

[56] Geddes's passion for Rubens extended, predictably, to collecting. In 1822 he executed an etching after a Rubens portrait, then in his possession (and now unlocated) and reputedly representing Nicolaas Rockox, Burgomaster of Antwerp (Hildegaard van de Velde of the Stichting Nicolaas Rockox in Antwerp has confirmed that the etched image does not correspond to any of the known portrait types of Rockox.) For Geddes's creative dialogue with Rubens's 'Chapeau de Paille', as purchased by Sir Robert Peel, see p.64 and for his ownership of Rubens drawings, see note 133. On 23 May 1835 Geddes, as the anonymous 'Friend' of Sir John James Steuart of Allanbank, entered in the mixed sale of their respective Old Master collections a 'finished sketch' by Rubens for the Whitehall ceiling, *The Archangel Michael Driving Down Discord from Heaven* (lot 81). The allocation of specific lots to the two associated vendors is identified by annotations in Christie's Archives copy of the sale catalogue.

[57] See note 54. The parish records for St James's Garlickhythe are in the Department of Manuscripts of the Guildhall Library in the City of London. Summary references to the commissioning of Geddes's altarpiece are in the Vestry Minutes (MS 4813(8)) 30 January and 6 February 1815 and 14 January 1816. See also MS 4841 (Faculty 1 December 1815 for repairs to the church).

[58] A less convincing model for the Geddes altarpiece, as proposed by D. and F. Irwin, ibid., pp.199–200, was Titian's *Assumption of the Virgin*, removed from Verona Cathedral and then also on display in the Louvre. Geddes is not known to have executed any

further religious paintings to commission although the survival of two drawings, both dated 1817, indicates that a second, possibly unrelated, project may have been contemplated. These are a watercolour study for a triptych of the Apostles Peter, Paul and John in the National Gallery of Scotland (D.2285) and a drawing in coloured chalks of six unidentified Apostles, probably a study for a reredos, in the British Museum (1927-2-12-32).

[59] Letter from Wilson to Bridges from Sandhurst (where Wilson was currently Professor of Drawing) 12 May 1815. In a second letter of 19 October 1816 Wilson made a similarly optimistic prediction concerning Geddes's prospects in Scotland. Geddes's cordial relationship with Bridges may be gauged from the fact that he provided an introduction for Wilkie in a letter of 17 July during the latter's excursion into Scotland in 1817. All these letters are preserved in a volume of Bridges's correspondence in the private possession of descendants of his brother James. Adela Geddes recalled Lawrence's and Turner's approval of her husband's altarpiece in a letter to David Laing, 28 November 1874 (Laing MSS, La.IV.27, fos.3516–17). See also p.57.

[60] Ed. William Ruddick, ibid. (note 47), Edinburgh 1977, Letter L, p.126 (first published in 1819). Lockhart's other nominees for the Scottish succession to Raeburn were John Watson (1788–1864), who assumed the additional surname of Gordon from 1826 to avoid conflation with his uncle George Watson, and William Nicholson (1781–1844) who experimented with etching after his own original portrait drawings, more or less contemporaneously with Geddes.

[61] For Geddes's London exhibition reviews, see *The Examiner*, 16 June 1816, p.381 and 29 June 1817, p.415. Ward's mezzotint was published on 14 October 1818 in both London and Edinburgh, one of the Scottish agents for the receipt of subscriptions being David Bridges junior. A related prospectus is in the Innes of Stowe Muniments among the business and personal correspondence of Gilbert Innes of Stowe (National Archives of Scotland, GD 113/4/163, bundle 1, no.39). The 1823 cabinet portrait of the Duke of York in the National Portrait Gallery, London,

exemplifies, with its high finish, Wilkie's exploitation of the small full-length format and invites comparison with the contemporary portraiture of Geddes. This format was also occasionally adopted by Alexander Nasmyth.

[62] The three artists' portraits were all relaunched in Geddes's one-man retrospective exhibition in Edinburgh in 1821 (see p.00). Wilkie's pronouncement was occasioned by Geddes's portrait of another fellow artist, John Butler Danvers ARA, exhibited at the Royal Academy in 1832. See Adela Geddes, ibid., p.19.

[63] Ed. William Ruddick, ibid., Letter XLVII, pp.116–7. On Allan's Orientalism, see D. and F. Irwin, ibid., pp.207–13 and Julie Lawson et al, *Visions of the Ottoman Empire*, Edinburgh 1994, pp.24–5. In 1818 Allan sat to William Nicholson for a half-length oil portrait in Circassian costume (Scottish National Portrait Gallery, PG 1022). In 1864 the Royal Scottish Academy declined, on the recommendation of Sir William Fettes Douglas, the proffered sale from R. Evans of Southampton of Geddes's Circassian portrait of their second President, 'in the manner of Rembrandt … a Picture which Mr. Evans stated had made a favourable impression at the Royal Academy when exhibited there, and was supposed to have contributed to the election of Mr Geddes as an Associate of that Body' (Minutes of the RSA Council meeting 13 July 1864, p.205, RSA Library). The vendor evidently confused the circumstances of Geddes's final successful election in 1832 with the two abortive bids in 1817 and in 1818, in which Geddes polled precisely two votes and one vote respectively. See ed. Kathryn Cave, *The Diary of Joseph Farington*, New Haven and London 1994, vol.XIV, p.5096 and vol.XV, p.5284. At the British Institution Geddes showed in 1818 *The Circassian* (framed dimensions 9'2" × 6'3") and in 1824 *A Circassian in the costume of his country* (framed dimensions 3'1" × 2'6") of which the second corresponded closely to the description of Allan's portrait as included in Geddes's 1821 retrospective exhibition. See p.54.

[64] The Gordon Cumming family of this generation, notably Cumming-Bruce's brother the second baronet, were enthusiastic patrons of the sculptor Lorenzo Bartolini for his bust

portraiture and of George Sanders – who had sat to Geddes in 1816 – for full-scale portraiture in oils as distinct from miniatures. Cumming-Bruce's sister-in-law Eliza Maria Campbell, daughter of Lady Charlotte Campbell or Bury and niece of the Duke of Argyll, was herself a gifted amateur artist and, in later life, a patron of Landseer, Sanders, James Giles and Sir William Ross, as well as being an internationally renowned pioneer collector of fossil fish. Geddes's portrait is mentioned, together with concurrent commissions to Bartolini and the Scottish sculptor Laurence McDonald, in the letter from Cumming-Bruce to the second baronet from Florence 15 January 1824 (Gordon Cumming of Altyre papers, National Library of Scotland, Dep. 175, Box 160 (3)) and an 1855 inventory of the furnishings of Altyre House (Dep. 175, section II, Box 93 Inventories of Plenishing).

[65] On Geddes's relationship with Lawrence, both as portrait painter and collector, see ch.7. The Raeburn portrait of Lady Gordon Cumming is reproduced in Duncan Thomson et al, ibid., p.27 with a comparative illustration of *Mrs Jens Wolff*. See Richard E. Spear, *Domenichino*, New Haven and London 1982, p.238, cat.85 and col.pl.6; and Michael Helston et al, *Guercino in Britain, Paintings from British Collections*, London 1991 (for the National Gallery and the Burlington Magazine Publications), cat.27 (reproduced).

[66] From 1819, and possibly earlier, after re-adjusting the balance of priorities between Edinburgh and London, Geddes lodged with his mother and unmarried sister at 20 Dublin Street during business reconnoitres in Scotland. For Wilson's and Bridges's shared estimation of his simultaneous progress in the two capitals see note 59. Scott's alternative sobriquet for Mackenzie, 'The Addison of the north', also relocated him within the context of the Scottish Enlightenment and was based on his achievements as an essayist and editor of *The Mirror*, a weekly periodical modelled on the *Spectator*. Mackenzie's enduring nationwide reputation may be gauged from the extended obituary in the London Journal *The Annual Biography and Obituary* in 1832 (vol.XVI, pp.10–23). R. Rhodes's large-scale line engraving after Geddes was issued by Colnaghi in February 1822.

[67] For the circumstances of Wilkie's early acquaintance with Chalmers and initiation of the Smith portrait commission in 1817, see the essay by J. Patricia Campbell, 'The Chalmers Portraits' in ed. A.C. Cheyne, *The Practical and the Pious. Essays on Thomas Chalmers (1780–1847)*, Edinburgh 1985, ch.XII, pp.196–204, which draws upon the four-volume biography of Chalmers by his son-in-law William Hanna, *Memoirs of the Life and Writings of Thomas Chalmers*, London 1849–52, and unpublished correspondence among the Chalmers papers in New College Library, University of Edinburgh (see note 68).

[68] As early as March 1818, when sending his own sketch of Chalmers to Smith in Glasgow, Wilkie recommended the selection of Geddes on the basis of his recently completed portrait of Principal Baird, and for considerations of convenience and availability since 'Mr Geddes usually comes to London in May & goes back to Edinb. in the Winter. On one of his Northern excursions he might accomplish such a work as this.' (Letters from Wilkie, Collessie near Cupar, 29 September 1817 and from Kensington, 16 March 1818, to Smith, in the National Library of Scotland, MS 10995, fos.3–5 and 11–12. See also letters from Wilkie to Chalmers 21 December 1818, 29 January 1819 and 17 August 1821 and from Geddes to Chalmers 29 April 1819 in the Chalmers Papers, New College Library, University of Edinburgh, CHA 4.9.49, CHA.4.14.39, CHA.4.18.64 and CHA.4.11.45. Wilkie reviewed the successful realisation of his initiative in a letter to Geddes of 30 December 1821 (Laing MSS, La.IV.26.,fos.45–6.)

[69] Unsourced and undated photographs of the companion portraits of Thomas and Grace Chalmers are held by New College Library. The original oils are both in an English private collection (information from Professor Duncan Macmillan 2000). Geddes's portrait of Dr Chalmers was reproduced as a steel engraving by G.B. Shaw for the frontispiece of vol.I of Hanna's biography in 1849. Geddes promoted the subscription for Ward's mezzotint in conjunction with his own one-man exhibition in *The Scotsman*, 29 December 1821. The choice of Ward, one of the foremost British practitioners of mezzotint, for the prints of Henry Mackenzie and Chalmers, was clearly a strategic one. For

Campbell Dodgson's conflation of Thomas with George Chalmers, see note 42. Geddes's undated letter to Utterson is interleaved in the copy of David Laing's catalogue (1875) in the Department of Prints and Drawings at the British Museum.

Chapter Five · Edinburgh 1819: the Founding of the Royal Institution, Geddes and the Hopetoun and Ellesmere Van Dycks

[70] On Wilson's early career, see pp.29–30 and note 45. Of Aberdonian landed extraction, James Skene of Rubislaw (1775–1864) was a gentleman amateur artist and etcher, in which capacity he was associated with Walter Scott in an unrealised project for a descriptive volume on Edinburgh with illustrations by Skene. In 1829 Skene published independently, with the commendation of Scott, *A Series of Sketches of existing localities alluded to in the Waverley Novels*. Having been appointed Secretary to the Board of Trustees for Manufactures in 1830, he was entrusted with the organisation of the fund for a Scott memorial, launched in October 1832. Wilson's letter from Florence of 6 September 1831 is among the important Wilson/Skene correspondence in the National Library of Scotland (Acc.10608). Geddes participated as a collector-cum-dealer in the inaugural Old Master exhibition of the Institution (see p.48) and as a contemporary practitioner, in the Institution's *Exhibition of Living Artists* in 1828 (from London) and in 1829 (from Italy). Having been elected an Honorary (Artist) Member in 1824, he did not support the rival Scottish Academy as an exhibitor until 1836. See p.62. In 1829, with the exception of Nasmyth, most of the artists who had refused to join the dissident Academy in 1826 capitulated.

[71] Concerning the British Institution, see note 52 and p.37. In 1821 Steuart published with Colnaghi of London two sets of etchings each, inspired by the works of Scott and Byron, followed in 1828 by *The Visions of an Amateur*. Steuart is represented in the National Gallery of Scotland by a substantial corpus of sketches and a few etchings (D.4635, D.4716–38, D.4771 and D.4821). For his transactions with Geddes as a dealer, most especially in the purchase of Hals's *Young Man Holding a Skull* (National Gallery, London), see pp.79–80.

[72] For a contemporary commentary on the Edinburgh Institution, see *The Edinburgh Magazine and Literary Miscellany*, Edinburgh 1819, pp.290–6. On its cultural-political context and the divergence between founding aspirations and measurable achievement, see Duncan Forbes, ibid. (note 35).

[73] See Colin Thompson et al, *Pictures for Scotland*, Edinburgh 1972, pp.27–8, for Wilson's letter of December 1829 to the Directorate of the Institution. Wilson resigned from the Trustees' Academy in 1826 and returned to Italy where he was chiefly occupied in dealing rather than in landscape painting. An adroitly self-interested visionary, he had originally destined his outstanding Genoese Van Dyck for the collection of the Earl of Hopetoun. Wilson's policy vis-à-vis the Institution was vindicated in 1859 when its collection, including the *Lomellini Family*, was subsumed in the new National Gallery of Scotland. Concurrently with the *Lomellini Family* negotiation, he acquired the *St Sebastian Bound for Martyrdom* from the Balbi family in Genoa (National Gallery of Scotland) and two Van Dycks from the Spinola collection for Sir Robert Peel. See the Wilson/Skene correspondence (note 70) and Brigstocke, ibid. (note 45).

[74] Geddes's purchase must have been made after 1814 when a Thomas Philipe was still conducting auction sales. Memorandum from Andrew Wilson, incorporating Geddes's testimony, to Lord Hopetoun 11 January 1821 in the Hopetoun Muniments, Bundle 620 (National Register of Archives of Scotland, Survey 888, Marquess of Linlithgow). I am grateful to Mrs Pat Crichton, archivist at Hopetoun House, for access to the original manuscripts. See also [Edward Morris], *Foreign Catalogue. Walker Art Gallery*, Liverpool 1977, pp.59–60.

[75] Prior to *Infanta Isabella*, Lord Hopetoun bought via Wilson a Cuyp *Landscape with Cattle* from the London dealer Bernard Pinney after its authenticity and condition had been vetted by Geddes (letter from Wilson to the Earl 2 October 1820 and letter from Geddes to the Earl 12 February 1821 in the Hopetoun Muniments, ibid.). See also Basil Skinner, 'Andrew Wilson and the Hopetoun Collection', in *Country Life*, 15 August 1968, vol.44, pp.370–2. The Van Dyck

Ecce Homo was bought via Wilson from a Mr Berry of Glasgow and not, as stated by Skinner, from Geddes.

[76] For the detailed provenance of the 'Rembrandt', see Arthur K. Wheelock, Jr., *Dutch Paintings of the Seventeenth Century*, New York and Oxford 1995, for the National Gallery of Art, Washington. It was offered again in Geddes's posthumous sale on 12 April 1845 at Christie's (lot 646) and again at Christie's on 30 November 1867 (lot 53) during the second dispersal of his stock-in-trade, instructed by his widow, when it was acquired by the dealer Alimonde. The Wilson/Pinney 'Rembrandt' was a copy or version of the picture in the National Gallery, London. For the 1828 transaction, see p.68 and letter from Geddes to Lawrence 8 August 1828 in the Lawrence correspondence (Royal Academy Archives, LAW 5/261.). Of the remaining pictures declined by Lord Hopetoun, the Van der Helst was submitted as a bargain to the (Edinburgh) Institution in 1828 (letter from Geddes to Francis Cameron, 29 January 1828, in Royal Institution papers, National Archives of Scotland, NG 3/4/10(8)). The De Witte *Church Interior* and one of his two Jacob Ochtervelts passed through his 1835 joint sale with Steuart of Allanbank at Christie's on 23 May 1835 (lots 80 and 42) together with the 'Rembrandt' (lot 94). For Ochtervelt's *The Betrothal*, see Susan Donahue Kuretsky, *The Paintings of Jacob Ochtervelt (1634–1682)*, Mont Clair 1979, pp.83–4, cat.72.

[77] Concerning Geddes's etching of *Infanta Isabella*, see the essay by Peter Black, Campbell Dodgson, ibid., p.49, cat.46 and E.S. Lumsden, *The Art of Etching*, New York 1962, pp.262–3 (reprinted from the 1925 first edition). Geddes's Old Master conversation piece (now lost) was included in his posthumous sale at Christie's on 11 April 1845 (lot 574).

[78] For Geddes's etching of *Philip IV of Spain* by Van Dyck, see Campbell Dodgson, ibid., p.50. cat.no.47. The private publication of Geddes's variable portfolios of etchings in 1826 is discussed by Peter Black. See also p.64. One impression of *Philip IV* was included in the only known surviving example of this portfolio (Perth Museum & Art Gallery). The set seen by Campbell Dodgson in

the possession of E.R. Boase of Edinburgh included another. None of the impressions was dated by the artist. The chronologically tenable, although now invalidated, identification of the subject as Philip IV seems to date from Laing's catalogue of 1875. Laing probably 'corrected' by updating the alternative identification proposed by Adela Geddes, an occasionally unreliable witness, whose conviction may or may not have corresponded to that of her husband in this instance. See the Laing MSS, La.IV.17, fos.3586–7 and Adela Geddes, ibid., p.20. Geddes's copy after Titian was sold at Christie's on 12 April 1845 (lot 665).

[79] Unaccountably, in view of Adela Geddes's statement to Laing, Geddes's Van Dyck has not been traced in Bridgewater catalogues prior to its listing by Bourke and Cust in *Bridgewater Gallery*, London 1903, cat.41. The security of the traditional attribution has been questioned. For the 'Stafford Gallery', see Mrs Steuart Erskine, 'The Bridgewater and Ellesmere Collections in Bridgewater House', in *Connoisseur*, May 1903, pp.2–10 and Colin Thompson et al, ibid., pp.122–7 for the subsequent history of the collection in relation to the Sutherland Loan to the National Gallery of Scotland.

Chapter Six · Retrospective and Royal: the Discovery of the Regalia and the Edinburgh Exhibitions of 1821 and 1822

[80] Scott's own lively accounts of the proceedings in letters to the MPs J.B.S. Morritt and J.W. Croker are quoted in John Gibson Lockhart, *The Life of Sir Walter Scott, Bart*, London 1893 (new popular edition), ch.XL.

[81] Of the seven commissioned illustrations of the Regalia, only four, by Allan, Geddes and Lizars, are now extant for certain. The three representations of the Crown, including the oil study by Geddes, were included in a special exhibition on *The Honours of Scotland* mounted by the former Scottish Record Office at Register House 13 May – 10 September 1955, but could not be located in 2000. The surviving illustrations (SP 12/2/16(4–7)) are associated with the original Minutes of the Commissioners' meetings and copies of their official report which was received in

Whitehall by John Cam Hobhouse for the Prince Regent on 27 February 1818 (Regalia Papers, SP 12/2, National Archives of Scotland). The Minutes of 7 and 10 February 1818 record the admission of the artists and the inspection of their illustrations, the Revd Thomson being named first in order of precedence, perhaps in deference to his brother the Commissioner.

[82] See Katrina Thomson, *Turner and Sir Walter Scott. The Provincial Antiquities and Picturesque Scenery of Scotland*, Edinburgh 1999, ch.1 and fig.4. J.M.W. Turner, who produced twelve designs of scenes in Edinburgh and the locality may have encountered Geddes during his related visit to Scotland in 1818. For the contractual arrangements, see Katrina Thomson, ibid., ch.II, pp.23–4. Scott, Turner, Lizars and the Revd John Thomson were all co-proprietors. Geddes's small oil at Abbotsford, executed on panel, is a conspicuous example of the technical problems which beset so many of his paintings of this period and which are partially attributable to his Rembrandtesque aesthetic. See the essay by Lesley Stevenson in this publication.

[83] Letter from Geddes to Abraham Cooper RA 6 January 1843 in the Egerton MSS (British Library, London), MS 2075 fo.93. Geddes's portrait of Scott was then in the possession of their mutual friend Sir John James Steuart of Allanbank. Presumably after his death in 1849, it was acquired by Geddes's brother-in-law Andrew James (see p.67) and inherited by the latter's unmarried daughter Sarah Ann James. Adela Geddes vouched for its authenticity as a unique original in a letter to David Laing 5 June 1875 (Laing MSS, La.IV.17, fos 34–5). In 1823 Geddes himself supplied an attenuated reproductive drawing (Scottish National Portrait Gallery) for an engraving by F.C. Lewis executed in 1824 under Geddes's supervision.

[84] Geddes's copy in 'oils' after Wilkie's study of the Duke of Buccleuch passed through Geddes's sale on 12 April 1845 (lot 602). See Allan Cunningham, ibid., vol.II, p.16. For the Oxford drawing, see David Blayney Brown, *Sir David Wilkie. Drawings and Sketches in the Ashmolean Museum*, London 1985, cat.24 (reproduced). Wilkie subsequently executed a more polished

drawing of the Duke (Private Collection) which was engraved by F.C. Lewis by 1821 as a private plate. See also Geddes's posthumous sale on 9 April 1845 (lot 205). I am grateful to Professor Hamish Miles for information concerning the Wilkie portrait drawings of the Duke of Buccleuch.

[85] Geddes provided an extensive commentary on the Regalia picture in *Catalogue of Mr. Geddes's Pictures Now Exhibiting in Bruce's Great Room, Waterloo Place, Edinburgh 1821*, see p.50. Allan Cunningham, ibid., vol.II, p.16. In 1822, on the occasion of Wilkie's and Geddes's joint excursion to Edinburgh in the company of William Collins, Wilkie executed a commemorative watercolour of the moment of the rediscovery of the Regalia, clearly from vicarious recollection (Scottish National Portrait Gallery, PG 2069). Unusually, he also chose to celebrate the occasion through a Rembrandtesque subject picture of the burial of the Regalia in Kineff Church in 1652 during the Cromwellian invasion of Scotland and following the Scottish coronation of Charles II, the last coronation at which the royal insignia had been deployed. A highly wrought compositional study for this picture was recently purchased from Agnew's by the Fitzwilliam Museum in Cambridge.

[86] The *Courant*'s review, possibly by Geddes's friend the landscape painter Patrick Gibson, an accomplished art critic, was quoted in entirety by David Laing, ibid., pp.13–14. Geddes's start on the picture in 1818 'with figures as large as life' was reported in London by the *Annals of the Fine Arts* (vol.III, London 1819, p.526). Three autograph oil sketches related to the Regalia picture passed through the artist's posthumous sale at Christie's on 11 April 1845 (lots 463 and 468). Letter from Wilson 2 October 1820, Edinburgh, to Lord Hopetoun in the Hopetoun Muniments, Bundle 620. For critiques of the Regalia picture, see *The Examiner*, London 1821, p.332, *European Magazine* LXXIX, London 1821, p.433, *The Literary Gazette and Journal of the Belles Lettres*, London 12 May 1821, p.296 and *Magazine of the Fine Arts*, 1821, vol.I, p.209. Professor Hamish Miles kindly allowed me access to his collection of Royal Academy exhibition reivews. On 22 November 1821, the *Edinburgh Evening Courant* claimed,

possibly without foundation, that the picture had 'excited ... much notice in London – with many of his other performances.'

[87] Williams held two substantial one-man exhibitions at the Calton Convening Rooms in 1822 and 1826. For the Haydon and Geddes one-man exhibitions, see the *Edinburgh Evening Courant* 22 November, 1 and 15 December 1821 (as already quoted). For the etching of Jeffrey, see Campbell Dodgson, ibid., pp.32–3, cat.no.8. See also *The Scotsman* 29 December 1821, 'Mr. Geddes's Exhibition'. The same issue carried an advertisement for the publication by subscription of Ward's mezzotint after Geddes's portrait of Dr Chalmers. See p.46 and note 69.

[88] See David Wainwright, *Broadwood by Appointment. A History*, London 1982, pp.94 ff. I am indebted to John Raymond for information on the Broadwood dynasty. For Henry Broadwood's interest in Watteau, see Selby Whittingham, 'Watteau and "Watteaus" in Britain *c*.1780–1851' in ed. François Moreau and Margaret Morgan Grasselli, *Antoine Watteau (1684–1721), Le Peintre, Son Temps et Sa Légende*, Paris and Geneva 1987, p.273. On the Geddes etching, see Campbell Dodgson, ibid., p.30, cat.4. Concerning Andrew James, Geddes's brother-in-law from 1827, and his sobriquet 'Mr Watteau', see pp.67 ff.

[89] Francis Haskell, *Rediscoveries in Art: Some Aspects of Taste, Fashion and Collecting in England and France*, Ithica 1976, p.57; Selby Whittingham, ibid., p.273 and bibliography and 'What You Will; or some notes regarding the influence of Watteau on Turner and other British Artists', part 2 in *Turner Studies*, Winter 1985, vol.5, no.2, pp.29–48. Whittingham quotes on Watteau's 'Rubénisme', Matthew Pilkington's account of Watteau in the 1829 edition of *A General Dictionary of Painters*. Pilkington was actually rehearsing a long-established tradition concerning Watteau as the epitome of the 'Rubénisme' movement in France which originated in the so-called Quarrel of Colour and Design in the French Academy in 1671–2. One such Geddes 'pasticcio', a *Fête Champêtre*, was sold at Christie's on 14 February 1947 (lot 33) from the collection of Miss C.M. Reid and may have had a provenance from Adela Geddes (archive photograph in the National Gallery of Scotland).

[90] Details of the 1821 election were confirmed by Mark Pomeroy, Royal Academy Archivist. Wilkie deplored the failed candidature of both his friends in a letter to Geddes of 30 December 1821 during the Edinburgh exhibition of the Regalia picture (Laing MSS, La.IV.26, fos.45–6, and Allan Cunningham, ibid., vol.II, pp.65–7). Adela Geddes, in response to an enquiry from Laing, stated in a letter of 5 June 1875 that she sold for four guineas apiece portrait heads of Lord President Hope, the Duke of Buccleuch and the Lord Justice Clerk David Boyle of Shewalton. The latter fragment was at Kilkerran, having been inherited by the sitter's daughter, Lady Dalrymple Fergusson. See the Laing MSS, La.IV.17, fos.3534–5.

[91] Allan Cunningham, ibid., vol.II, pp.82–3 and W. Wilkie Collins, *Memoirs of the Life of William Collins, Esq. RA*, London 1978 (EP Publishing reprint), pp.198–200. Turner and Geddes were certainly well acquainted by 1825 (see p.57). They probably met in 1818, possibly through Thomson of Duddingston, when Turner was in Scotland making drawings for Scott's *Provincial Antiquities*. See Katrina Thomson, ibid. For the bonanza of artistic production generated by George IV's visit, see the catalogue by Basil Skinner, *Visit of George IV to Edinburgh 1822* for the Scottish National Portrait Gallery exhibition of 1961. On Scott's stage management of the proceedings, see Basil Skinner, 'Scott as Pageant-Master – The Royal Visit of 1822' in ed. Allan S. Bell, *Scott Bicentenary Essays. Selected Papers Read at the Sir Walter Scott Bicentenary Conference*, Edinburgh 1973, pp.228–37.

[92] The Royal Command was issued to William Adam, Lord Chief Commissioner of the Jury Court and one of the Regalia Commissioners, who wrote of the projected exhibition to James Skene on 19 August 1822 (letter among the Skene of Rubislaw MSS, National Register of Archives of Scotland, Survey 0464).

Chapter Seven · The Later 1820s: the Ascendancy of Lawrence, and Geddes's 'Chapeau de Paille'

[93] Undated letter from Lawrence, Russell Square, London to Geddes, annotated on the reverse, probably by Adela Geddes, 'Sir Thomas/Lawrence opinion of the Ascension [sic]

picture' (Laing MSS, La.IV.26, fos.81–2). See also pp.39, 57 and note 59. The cause and nature of the dispute were not disclosed.

[94] Letters from Lawrence to Geddes 20 November 1826 and 26 August 1828 (National Library of Scotland, MS 9994, fos.34 and 36). The drawings for which Lawrence thanked Geddes in 1828 were almost certainly Old Masters rather than original works by the Scottish artist. For Geddes's crusade to secure the Lawrence cabinet, see Adela Geddes, ibid., pp.26–32, and infra. p.56. Concerning Lawrence as collector of Old Master drawings and the ultimate dispersal of his estate, see Douglas Goldring, *Regency Portrait Painter. The Life of Sir Thomas Lawrence PRA*, London 1951, pp.296 ff and Denys Sutton, 'Oxford and the Lawrence Collection of Drawings' in *Italian Drawings from the Ashmolean Museum, Oxford*, London 1970 (for Wildenstein's), pp.vii–xxxiii.

[95] The Rembrandt is discussed, without reference to the ownership of James or the possible ownership of Geddes, in ed. Eva Benesch, Otto Benesch, *The Drawings of Rembrandt*, New York 1973, vol.V, p.248, cat.no.885 (illustrated fig.1160); and ed. L. Demonts, Frits Lugt, *Musée du Louvre Inventaire Général des Dessins des Ecoles du Nord. Ecole Hollandaise. Rembrandt, ses Elèves, ses Imitateurs, ses Copistes*, Paris 1933, vol.III. This appears to be the only known drawing of this particular subject with a joint Lawrence and Esdaile provenance. James and Geddes married the Plimer sisters Ann and Adela in 1827. See ch.8. Most of Andrew James's collection, other than the portion retained by his daughter Sarah Ann, was auctioned by Christie, Manson & Woods on 28 April 1873. Rembrandt's *Christ Among the Doctors*, with an Ottley, Lawrence and Esdaile provenance specified, was lot 69. For Geddes's purchases from the Esdaile collection in 1840, see pp.67–8 and note 116. The immediate purchaser of the Geddes Rembrandt drawing in 1845 was W.B. White according to the annotated copy in Christie's Archives of the *Catalogue of the Valuable Collection of Pictures & Drawings by Old Masters, Etchings; Books; and Articles of Taste and Vertu, Formed by that Elegant and Accomplished Artist, Andrew Geddes, Esq. ARA, Deceased, also his own Original Works*, Christie and Manson 8–13 April 1845.

[96] The Gallery's picture, which was presented in 1951 by Mrs H.F. Rose, a direct descendent of the artist's youngest sister Margaret Geddes Scott, probably corresponds to the 'half-length' (in the sense of 50 × 40 inches) portrait of Miss Geddes, no.3 in Geddes's Memorandum of pictures painted in 1812. See David Laing, ibid., p.9. A full-length portrait of Margaret Geddes (1799–1884) as a young girl seated in a landscape – in private possession inherited by descent – displays a similar affinity with Lawrence in composition and handling. See the letter from Adela Geddes to Laing 23 September 1874 concerning her late husband's self-portrait: 'As I consider the portrait I have of Mr. Geddes the only likeness of him in my opinion would you like me to send it down to you as a loan of course the dress is unfinished it was painted about the time of our marriage 1827.' (Laing MSS, La.IV.17, fo.3491).

[97] Geddes's drawing of Charlotte Nasmyth (British Museum, 1949-8-12-10) is now badly discoloured through past over-exposure to light. His conversation piece of the Terrys in the manner of Dutch seventeenth-century genre, was published by Geddes as an etching touched with drypoint in 1826. See Campbell Dodgson, ibid., p.37, cat.16 and the essay by Peter Black. The original oil, included in the Robert Vernon gift to the National Gallery in 1847 and later transferred to the Tate Gallery (now Tate Britain) has since deteriorated beyond retrieval. For the technical deficiencies partially occasioned by Geddes's aesthetic priorities, and those of many of his contemporaries, see the Tate exhibition catalogue by Robin Hamlyn et al, *Robert Vernon's Gift: British Art for the Nation 1847*, London 1993, and the essay in this publication by Lesley Stevenson.

[98] The three Geddes portrait drawings of 1823 were lots 112–14 in Graham Robertson's posthumous sale at Christie, Manson & Woods on 22 July 1949. One of the drawings of Miss Walford, in private possession in 1962, is known from a photograph in the archives of Tate Britain. The undated half-length portrait of Greatorex, together with a half-length of his wife, possibly painted in the 1830s and now unlocated, were in the same sale (double lot 140), together with a similarly unlocated Geddes oil of Mrs Walford. The Lawrentian three-quarter-length of her

daughter, which was presented to the Tate Gallery in 1940 by Graham Robertson, has been arbitrarily identified as the portrait of Mrs Greatorex which Geddes showed at the Royal Academy in 1840. The whole conception of the picture and the costume of the sitter are indicative of a production of the 1820s.

[99] The Montgomery commission was presumably associated with the production of a Geddes landscape etching most convincingly identified as a view on the Whim estate (as distinct from Oatlands). This identification is corroborated by an autograph inscription on the impression of the first state in the Victoria and Albert Museum (inv.13432). Geddes's interest in the group portraiture of Lawrence is also illustrated by his execution of a drypoint, published privately in 1826, after the Lawrence of Lady Henrietta Drummond, daughter of the 9th Earl of Kinnoull, and her child. See Campbell Dodgson, ibid., p.31, cat.6 and p.40, cat.22.

[100] The Duke of York sat to Lawrence on at least three occasions for portraits exhibited at the Royal Academy in 1814, 1816 and 1822. See Kenneth Garlick, *Sir Thomas Lawrence. A Complete Catalogue of the Oil Paintings*, Oxford 1989, pp.289–90, cat.nos.858 (a) – (c) (reproduced). Geddes's portrait, signed and dated 1825, has been disfigured by severe craquelure and discolouration. A full-length of the Duke, of unstated dimensions, was included in the Geddes sale at Christie's on 11 April 1845 (lot 585). In his letter to Geddes on 2 April 1826, Wilkie deplored the loss of 'Your friend the Duchess of Rutland' (Laing MSS, La.IV.26, fos.55–6). I am grateful to J.R. Webster, Archivist, and Andrew Norman, Comptroller of the Belvoir Estate, for facilitating access to the picture at Belvoir Castle.

[101] Letter from Turner to Holworthy, endorsed 7 January 1826, in ed. John Gage, *Collected Correspondence of J.M.W. Turner*, Oxford 1980, pp.96–8. Gage confuses the subsequent death of the 5th Duke of Rutland with that of the Duchess. Dr Selby Whittingham, author of the revised entry on Geddes for the *New Dictionary of National Biography*, has suggested that Geddes may have belonged to the Turner-Holworthy circle at Belvoir. Turner may well have acted as intermediary (for Geddes and Turner, see

p.52). The Rutlands were also patrons, for full-scale portraiture, of Geddes's acquaintance or friend George Sanders. The Rutland conversation piece by Geddes is no longer traceable (information from J.R. Webster). Adela Plimer, in noting the royal approbation of the York portrait, refers to two large conversation pieces of the Rutland family completed shortly before her marriage to Geddes in 1827 (ibid., p.15). Letter from Williams to Geddes 23 July 1826 in the Laing MSS La.IV.26, fos.61–2.

[102] See p.35 and note 59. Letter from Wilson to Geddes July 1823 in the Laing MSS, La.IV.26, fos.51–2; *Annual Biography and Obituary*, London 1824, vol.VII, XIX, *Sir Henry Raeburn, RA*, pp.378–91. On Raeburn's studio at 32 York Place, see p.23 and Duncan Thomson et al, ibid., p.24 (with illustrations).

[103] Letter from H.W. Williams (1773–1829) to Geddes 23 July 1826 (mentioning Colvin Smith) and 26 June 1826 in the Laing MSS, La.IV.26, fos.61–2 and 57–8. In 1822 Williams's one-man exhibition of his own watercolours of Greece had been the artistic sensation of the year in Edinburgh. The two-volume edition of *Select Views of Greece*, illustrated with engravings, appeared in 1829. Geddes was facilitating the sale to Sheepshanks of a rare set incorporating proofs before letters and 'Unique Etchings of some of the subjects.' For Geddes's important relationship with the connoisseur print collector, see pp.69 ff and the essay by Peter Black. On Colvin Smith, see *The Scotsman* obituary 22 July 1875 and R.C.M. Colvin Smith, *The Life and Works of Colvin Smith, RSA, 1796–1875*, Aberdeen 1939. For Watson Gordon, see D. and F. Irwin, ibid., pp.308–10.

[104] See note 70. Letter from Geddes to Francis Cameron, Institution Secretary, 10 April 1824 among the Royal Institution papers (National Archives of Scotland, NG 3/4/6 (15)). The printed catalogue of the *Fifth Exhibition of Modern Pictures* in 1826 listed James Skene as Secretary and, as the Artist Honorary Members, Wilkie, Geddes, Burnet, Patrick or 'Peter' Nasmyth, and the Revd John Thomson. Wilson, also Manager of the Institution, featured among the twelve Artist Associates, as did Alexander Nasmyth, Allan, George Watson and his nephew

Watson Gordon and 'Grecian' Wiliams. Although finally elected an Associate of the Royal Academy in 1832, Geddes never secured – and possibly did not seek – membership of the Royal Scottish Academy.

[105] The full text of the 1826 prospectus was published by David Laing, ibid. One set of these unbound etchings, in a pasteboard portfolio stamped with an unidentified collector's mark 'E' is in Perth Museum and Art Gallery. Another set was presented to General James R. Hope, younger son of the Earl of Hopetoun (purchaser of *Infanta Isabella*), about 1835 (letter from Hope to Geddes, watermarked 1835, in the Laing MSS, La.IV.26, fos.79–80). See the essay by Peter Black. For the Bannockburn etching, see Campbell Dodgson, ibid., p.41, cat.no.23. Two related oil studies were entered in Geddes's posthumous sale on 11 April 1845 (lots 469 and 470).

[106] Letter from H.W. Williams, Edinburgh, to Skene 15 March 1827 in the Royal Institution papers (National Archives of Scotland, NG 3/4/9 (23)). In 1858, effectively coinciding with its own demise, the Institution gifted some unspecified Geddes etchings to the National Gallery of Scotland which opened to the public the following year. A number of the Gallery's impressions of Geddes etchings bear the inked stamp of the Royal Institution but were not necessarily acquired through the gift of 1858.

[107] The trade consortium comprised L.J. Nieuwenhuys of Brussels and J. Foster and John Smith of London. Peel paid the princely sum of £2725. See Gregory Martin's critical catalogue for the National Gallery, *The Flemish School circa 1600–circa 1900*, London 1970, pp.174–81. The unsourced press eulogy of the Rubens, dated 7 March 1823, is among the *Presscuttings from English Newspapers on Matters of Artistic Interest*, vol.v. p.1275 in the National Art Library. Lawrence's portrait of Lady Peel (The Frick Collection, New York, c.1826) was evidently conceived as a tribute to her husband's purchase.

[108] A second autograph version of *Summer*, also on canvas support, is in the possession of a direct descendant of the artist's youngest sister Margaret Geddes Scott. Yet another variant (?) passed through Sotheby's Gleneagles sale 23/24 August 1976 (lot 401),

reputedly (and implausibly) dated 1820. The former may correspond to 'Summer – *an idea from the Chapeau de Paille*' in the artist's posthumous sale 1845 (lot 535), described as an autograph original in oils. The Rubens drawing of *Hélène Fourment* was lot 347 on 10 April 1845. It is just conceivable – given the disputed ownership of some of the Old Master drawings in Lawrence's estate and related claims upon the estate by Geddes (see pp.70 and 73) – that the Geddes Rubens corresponded to the superb full-length drawing in black, white and red chalks, with an incomplete provenance including Lawrence, now in the Museum Boymans van Beuningen in Rotterdam. See Hans Vlieghe, *Rubens Portraits of Identified Sitters Painted in Antwerp*, London and New York 1987, p.90, cat.no.96a and fig.86.

[109] Letter from Geddes, London, to Francis Cameron of the Royal Institution 18 May 1828 in the Royal Institution papers (National Archives of Scotland, NG 3/4/10 (40)). The seemingly unsubstantiated identification of the sitter as Charlotte Nasmyth, who sat to Geddes for a portrait drawing in 1823 (British Museum, 1949-8-12-10, see pp.59–60), was first ventured by William Darling McKay in *The Scottish School of Paintings*, London 1906. The artist's own title for the fancy picture, *Summer*, was published without further gloss in the catalogues of the British Institution and the Edinburgh Royal Institution in 1826 and 1828 respectively. For the artistic lineage of Rubens's full-length portrait of Hélène or Susanna Fourment (Calouste Gulbenkian Foundation, Lisbon) as a prelude to *Summer*, see Sara Stevenson and Helen Bennett, ibid., pp.24–30. Geddes's other exhibit in 1828, *Head of a Polish Jew*, belonged to an Orientalist sub-division of fancy portraiture of Rembrandtesque inspiration and variable ethnicity. Other near-contemporary examples of this genre were painted by Raeburn (the problematic *Portrait of a Jew* in the National Gallery of Scotland, NG 2108), Margaret Carpenter (1823, Scottish Private Collection) and Martin Archer Shee. Wilson's letter to the Institution's directorate from Genoa 25 December 1829 is among the Wilson/Skene correspondence in the National Library of Scotland (Acc.10608). See also Colin Thompson et al, ibid., pp.27–8.

Chapter Eight · London 1827: Marriage and 'Mr Watteau'

[110] After his naturalisation as a British citizen in 1726, Handel composed some of his greatest works, including *Messiah* in Lower Brook Street. Geddes's former residence at number 58 (now number 23) will form part of the Handel House Museum scheduled to open in 2001. For the history of Brook Street, excluding the Lower Brook Street section within the Conduit Mead Estate, see ed. F.H.W. Sheppard, *The Survey of London: The Grosvenor Estate in Mayfair*, London 1980, part II, vol.XL, ch.I. I am grateful to John Greenacombe, General Editor of the *Survey of London*, for his assistance concerning the status of, and tenancies at, 58 Lower Brook Street. Geddes last appeared in the rate books for Brook Street in 1830, but in conjunction with his successor in the tenancy, Henry Webber (see ch.9 for Geddes's excursion to Italy).

[111] Geddes's marriage to Adela Plimer in 1827 (see infra) remained childless. William Collins (1788–1847), a close friend of Wilkie, married Harriet Geddes, sister of Margaret Geddes Carpenter. See W. Wilkie Collins, ibid. (note 91), pp.208–14. In 1874 or 1875 Adela Geddes was obliged to inform David Laing that Margaret Geddes Carpenter was not a blood relative of her late husband. See the miscellaneous notes supplied to Laing in connection with his critical catalogue of 1875 in the Laing MSS, La.17, fo.3588. Most recently, the description of Andrew Geddes as Collins's father-in-law was repeated by John Gage in his edition of *Collected Correspondence of J.M.W. Turner*, Oxford 1980, p.246. I am indebted to Richard J. Smith, author of a forthcoming critical biography of Margaret Carpenter to be published by Antique Collectors Club in 2001, for detailed genealogical information.

[112] Richard Smith's interim account of Mrs Carpenter appeared in ed. Delia Gaze, *Dictionary of Women Painters*, London and Chicago 1997, vol.I, pp.348–50. Mrs Carpenter's portrait of Geddes was included in his posthumous sale in 1845 (lot 554) and is now unlocated. It was then sold at Christie, Manson & Woods on 20 June 1891 (lot 8) from the collection of Sarah Ann James (1827/9–90), daughter of Ann Plimer and

Andrew James, from whom the picture may have been inherited. For James as 'Mr Watteau', see p.67. Dr Selby Whittingham, seconded by Charles Sebag-Montefiore, has provided invaluable assistance concerning the James family genealogy and Andrew James as a collector. Campbell Dodgson (ibid., pp.18–19) discusses briefly Carpenter's role in developing the British Museum's holdings of Geddes etchings. See also the essay by Peter Black.

[113] Nathaniel Plimer's supposed date of death (1822) cannot be verified from the surviving records of St George's, Hanover Square, or St Marylebone in Westminster City Archives. The Geddes/Plimer marriage was no.345 in the 'Register of Marriages', vol.19, for St George's, Hanover Square. The brief narrative of Adela Plimer's connection with the Gibson Carmichaels is in the unpublished reminiscences of Nevile Reid in the possession of his direct descendants. Documentation on the Gibson Carmichael cabinet portrait is held in the Gallery's archival file on NG 2438. For Geddes's earlier acquaintance with the Plimers in Edinburgh, see p.24 and note 36.

[114] For James, see Selby Whittingham, ibid. (note 88), pp.269–77, especially pp.273–4. The Department of Prints and Drawings at the British Museum holds several sheets of studies by Geddes after Watteau, all with the provenance from the collection of the Scottish portrait painter James Hall of Dunglass (1800–1855), who had purchased them at Geddes's posthumous sale in 1845 (1927-2-12-18, 1927-2-12-19, 1927-2-12-20, 1927-2-12-21, 1927-2-12-26, 1927-2-12-27, 1927-2-12-28, 1927-2-12-29, 1927-2-12-30, and 1927-2-12-33).

[115] Miss James was named as a co-executor and beneficiary of the will of her aunt Adela Geddes (25 July 1878, proven 12 March 1881) who bequeathed to her all of her pictures and works of art. The two James sales took place at Christie's on 20 June 1891 (lots 1–35A in a Mixed Sale of Ancient and Modern Pictures) and 22 June 1891 (Modern Water-colour Drawings and Drawings by the Old Masters). The British Museum purchased quite a substantial number of Watteau drawings at the second sale (information from Antony Griffiths). Charles

Sebag-Montefiore has drawn to my attention the Arundel Society's 1878 folio volume, *Twenty-Six drawings by Antoine Watteau, Reproduced from the Original Works, the Property of Miss James, Recently Exhibited in the Bethnal Green Branch of the South Kensington Museum.*

[116] G. Waagen, *Galleries and Cabinets of Art in Great Britain*, London 1857, vol.IV (Supplement), pp.213–7. See p.57 and note 95 and *Catalogue of the Collection of Etchings by Rembrandt of Colonel Turner, Deceased ... Also The Collection of Drawings & Etchings by Rembrandt and Some Fine Proofs and Impressions after the Works of Sir Joshua Reynolds of the late Andrew James, Esq.*, Christie, Manson & Woods, London 28 April 1873 (annotated copy in Christie's Archives). For Geddes's purchases from the Esdaile sale at Christie's on 17 June 1840, see Frits Lugt, *Les Marques de Collections de Dessins & d'Estampes*, Amsterdam 1921, p.492. His purchases may not be listed in entirety. Lugt does not mention *Christ Among the Doctors*.

[117] See Selby Whittingham, ibid., pp.274–5 (note 88) for a more detailed history of Geddes/James Watteaus. Lot 655 of the 5th day of the Geddes sale on 12 April 1845 was *The triumphs of Ceres* by Watteau, date of acquisition unknown.

[118] Letter from Wilkie, Rome, to Geddes, Lower Brook Street, London 2 April 1826 in Laing MSS, La.IV.26, fos.55–6, transcribed by Allan Cunningham, ibid., vol.II, pp.276–82. Letter from Thomson, Duddingston, to Geddes, London, 1 September 1828 in the Laing MSS, La.IV.26, fos.63–4. Thomson enquired as to the possibility of travelling with Geddes as far as Paris in order to visit the Louvre in his company. For *The Toilet of Bathsheba*, see p.37 and note 53 and fig.26. Letter from Geddes to Lawrence 8 August 1828 in the Lawrence correspondence, Royal Academy Archives, LAW 5/261.

[119] See Adela Geddes, ibid., p.18. She observes, with particular reference to Titian as well as Schiavone, that 'Venetian art was what he [ie Geddes] fully appreciated and delighted in; and although he had seen the "Pietro Martire" in the Louvre [by Titian and in 1814], it was with redoubled pleasure he studied it in the church of San Giovanni e Paolo' in 1830. For the 1826 etching, see

Campbell Dodgson, ibid., p.46, cat no.36. Geddes's first Schiavone oil painting is not catalogued in Francis L. Richardson, *Andrea Schiavone*, Oxford 1980, and is apparently unrecorded. All three Schiavones, together with the Jacopo Pontormo *Venus and Cupid* declined by Lawrence, were included in the Steuart/Geddes mixed sale at Christie's on 23 May 1835 (lots 95–8), then again in Geddes's posthumous sale at Christie's on 12 April 1845 (lots 647, 650 (Pontormo), 652 and 653) with two Venetian overdoors by Schiavone, pendants representing *Apollo and Daphne* and *The Rape of Europa* (lots 644 and 645). The final Geddes sale at Christie's on 30 November 1867 included *The Holy Family* (lot 57) and *Christ Disputing with the Doctors* (lot 55), wrongly described as a purchase made by Geddes in Venice.

Chapter Nine · The Italian Sojourn 1828–1830

[120] Adela Geddes, ibid., pp.15–18, gives quite an informative chronicle of the Italian sojourn which was to compensate for the frustration in 1821 of the artist's plans for a Continental tour with his friend and patron Alexander Oswald. For Wilson's later achievements as a dealer in Rome and Genoa, see ed. Colin Thompson, ibid., *Wilson's Correspondence with James Skene of Rubislaw* (National Library of Scotland, Acc.10608) and note 45. Allan Cunningham, ibid., vol.II, pp.384–5, quoting from Wilkie's journal reminiscences of a festival dinner at the Palazzo Astili in January 1817, hosted by the expatriate Scottish artists and cognoscenti and attended by Thorwaldsen and Camuccini. The second celebrity was the Edinburgh-born Neo-classical portrait and figure sculptor Thomas Campbell (1791–1858).

[121] Turner reported to Wilkie his admiration of Geddes's recent copy of Veronese's *St John Preaching* in the Borghese collection. See Allan Cunningham, ibid., vol.III, p.13. Letter from Geddes to Sheepshanks from 49 Via della Croce, Rome, 11 April 1829 in the Laing MSS, La.IV.26, fos.65–6. Laing (1875), ibid., p.17, reproduces Geddes's letter of 10 January 1826, accompanying his gift of his own etchings. See also p.62 and note 103 and the essay by Peter Black.

[122] In 1836 the bulk of Sheepshanks's print collection, excluding the etchings by Rembrandt and Van Dyck – coincidentally of particular interest to Geddes – was acquired by the British Museum via the dealer William Smith. See Martin Royalton-Kisch, 'John Sheepshanks (1787–1863) and his Dutch and Flemish Etchings' in ed. Antony Griffiths, *Landmarks in Print Collecting*, London 1996, pp.65–79. For the Sheepshanks holdings in the Victoria and Albert Museum, see ed. Richard Redgrave, *Inventory of the Pictures, Drawings, Etchings &c in the British Fine Arts Collections in the New Gallery, South Kensington, Being for the Most Part the Gift of John Sheepshanks Esq. and Mrs Ellison*, London 1863, especially pp.18–19 concerning the Geddes etchings: and Ronald Parkinson, *Victoria & Albert Museum: Catalogue of British Oil Paintings 1820–1860*, London 1990, pp.109–10. Geddes's genre painting may have represented a commission. His copy after Giorgione was purchased by Sheepshanks after Geddes's posthumous sale in 1845 (lot 660). The 'Giorgione' original, since assigned to a follower of Titian, is now in the collection of the Duke of Northumberland at Alnwick. See Selby Whittingham on Geddes in 'Byron and the Two Giorgiones' in *Byron Society Journal*, 1986, vol.14, pp.52–5.

[123] See note 121. None of these landscapes has been traced with the exception of *Carrara* which probably corresponded to *The Quarries of Carrara* (Scottish Private Collection), sold on 8 April 1845 (lot 517) from the artist's collection.

[124] Adela Geddes, ibid., pp.16–17 and her letter to David Laing 2 October 1874 in the Laing MSS, La.IV.17, fos.3492–3. See also the essay by Peter Black. A fascinating account of the Poussin and Claude myth, 'La Maison de Nicolas Poussin, Via del Babuino à Rome' by Donatella Livia Sparti appeared in *Nicolas Poussin (1594–1665). Actes du Colloque Organisé au Musée du Louvre par le Service Culturel du 19 au 21 octobre 1994*, Paris 1996, vol.1, pp.147 ff. For the 1840 purchase, see pp.77–8. Letter from Wilson to James Skene of Rubislaw from Genoa 6 April 1830 commending Geddes's connoisseurship of Poussin (Wilson/Skene correspondence, National Library of Scotland, Acc.10608).

[125] *Diario di Roma* 2 December 1829, 3, 11 and 14 April (report pp.21–4 listing all the office bearers and 'Consiglieri') and 6 November 1830. I am grateful to the staff of the Archivio Storico Capitolino, Biblioteca Romana, in Rome for making this journal available at very short notice. The Biblioteca also holds an account of the history of the Società published in 1919 and a pamphlet commemorating its centenary in 1929, neither of which I was able to inspect (information from Dr Paola Pavan, Director of the Archivio Capitolino). Eric Forster, author of a forthcoming biography of John Gibson, has confirmed the identification of the British painter 'Williams' as Penry Williams rather than Hugh 'Grecian' Williams of Geddes's acquaintance.

[126] Letter from Wilkie, London, to Geddes, 49 Via della Croce, Rome, 14 December 1829 in the Laing MSS, La.IV.26, fos.67–8. Adela Geddes, ibid., makes no mention of the Società or its 1830 exhibition. See D. and F. Irwin, ibid., p.202, plate 69 and p.434 and note 47 concerning the *Diario di Roma*. An inscription on the reverse of the fancy portrait reads: 'Anno 1830 / Exhibited [*sic*] in the Capitol in the First Exhibition of Artists of All Nations in Rome / AG'.

[127] Geddes's promising association with the Società presumably ended with his departure from Rome in 1830. Mary Talbot, granted the rank of Princess by Ludwig I of Bavaria, and her husband were the last of the Dorias to live continuously in the Palazzo Doria Pamphilj and were avid art collectors, specialising in the Italian Cinquecento. I am grateful to the late Principessa Orietta Doria Pamphilj Landi for background information and especially for showing me Geddes's fancy portrait of the Ladies Talbot. In 1827 the philanthropic Princess Teresa Doria became the subject of Wilkie's *A Roman Princess with her Attendant Washing the Female Pilgrims' Feet* (Royal Collection), exhibited at the Royal Academy in 1829 and composed with the aid of a portrait drawing executed at his request by Frances Mackenzie, one-time inamorata of Thorvaldsen (information from Professor Hamish Miles).

[128] The Shrewsbury commission is apparently undocumented. A third preparatory study ahead of Lady Gwendoline Talbot, is also in the National Gallery of Scotland (D.4098). Four drawings relating to the picture, including the present three, passed through Geddes's sale on 9 April 1845 (lot 303). In the British Museum there is a small drawing, probably from recollection, by Geddes after Claude Lorrain's *Imaginary View of Delphi with a Procession* in the Doria Pamphilj collection (British Museum, 1927-2-12-54).

[129] Gustav Waagen, *Treasures of Great Britain*, London 1854, vol.I, pp.396–415 on the Peel collection and J. Mordaunt Crook, 'Sir Robert Peel: Patron of the Arts' in *History Today*, 1966, XVI, pp.3–11. Peel purchased Wilkie's *John Knox Preaching Before the Lords of the Congregation* (Tate Britain) from the Royal Academy exhibition in 1832. Adela Geddes, ibid., p.16, mentions the 'recent' purchase by Peel of her late husband's portraits of Camuccini (shown at the Royal Academy in 1838) and Gibson. The following year she sent Peel a presentation copy of her *Memoir* (letters from Adela Geddes in the Peel papers, British Library, Add. MSS 40557, fos.386 and 387). Both portraits passed through the sale of the residual collections from Drayton Manor by Robinson, Fisher & Harding of London on 29 and 30 November 1917 (lots 26 and 91).

[130] Impressions of Bellin's rare mezzotint are held by the British Museum and the Scottish National Portrait Gallery. Since the letterpress makes no mention of Peel's ownership of the original oil, he may not have concluded the purchase until after 1839. I am grateful to Eric Forster for copies of Gibson's letter of 16 October 1847 to Mrs George Lawrence, wife of the Mayor of Liverpool, concerning his visit to Drayton Manor with Peel (typescript A14 among the Gibson/Lawrence correspondence in the Walker Art Gallery, Liverpool). For Gibson's description of the Peel portrait as a replica, see T. Matthews, *The Biography of John Gibson RA, Sculptor*, Rome 1911, p.12.

[131] Information on Earle's trading activities was volunteered by Eric Forster. The portrait of Gibson owned by Earle was the likelier of the two possible submissions to the Royal Academy exhibition of 1832. In 1828 Geddes again showed a portrait of Gibson at the Academy, probably the Peel variant as engraved by Bellin in 1839. For the critical reception of the Earle portrait in 1835, see the *Liverpool Courier* 18 September 1835, p.318, and, for its display at the Institution from 1843, see ed. Lady Elizabeth Eastlake, *Life of John Gibson, RA, Sculptor*, London 1870, p.31. A third and far less ambitious Geddes oil portrait of Gibson was sold by T.R.G. Lawrence & Son of Crewkerne, Somerset, on 17 March 1977, lot 166 (photograph in the Witt Library, Courtauld Institute of Art, London). This was assigned a provisional date of 1816–17, a supposition based on an estimation of the sitter's age and not substantiated by any known connection with Geddes during the period of Gibson's early studies in London.

[132] Letter from Wilkie, Kensington, to Geddes, 11 Trinità dei Monti, Rome, 22 February 1830 in the Laing MSS, La.IV.26, fos.69–70, quoted in part by Adela Geddes, ibid., pp.19–20. Wilkie discussed these issues in greater depth in a letter of 7 February to Andrew Wilson, transcribed in Allan Cunningham, ibid., vol.III, pp.31–4.

[133] See L. Burchard and R-A. D'Hulst, *Rubens Drawings*, Brussels 1963, pp.181–3 and cat.no.115, and Michael Jaffé, 'The Interest of Rubens in Annibale and Agostino Carracci: Further Notes' in *The Burlington Magazine*, November 1957, vol.XCIX, pp.375–9. In a letter of 17 February 1830 'W. Geddes', whom Jaffé mentions as an unidentifiable collector of Old Master drawings, reclaimed from the Lawrence estate '4–5 drawings by Rubens probably together in a portfolio – a port. of A. Caracci – a battle as if copied from an antique Bas relief and one or two others (slight drawings)'. These drawings were delivered to the claimant on 12 February 1831 (*Claim upon Works of Art, Books etc., under the Estate of the Late Sir Thos. Lawrence*, Victoria and Albert Museum, MS 86, H.19, Claim no.244). The claimant was surely Andrew or 'A' rather than 'W' Geddes. See also note 132. On the reverse of Wilkie's letter to Geddes of 22 February 1830, there is a transcript of a letter to Wilkie from Keightley dated 23 February and referring to Geddes's claims upon the Lawrence estate.

[134] David Laing, ibid., pp.24–5. Extracts from Sheepshanks's original letter in the Laing MSS, La.IV.26, fos.71–2 and verso.

[135] Sheepshanks's commissioned prints, see the essay by Peter Black, and Campbell Dodgson ibid., pp.35–6, cat.no.13 and pp.44–5, cat.no.33. Campbell Dodgson perpetuates the nineteenth-century myth concerning the location of Claude's house.

[136] David Laing, ibid., p.25, reproduces the elder Morier's letter to Geddes from Naples 27 May 1830, mentioning the artist's impending visit and the commissioned portrait of 1829 (Laing MSS, La.IV.26, fos.73–4). For the final phase of the Italian sojourn, see Adela Geddes, ibid., pp.17–18 and, for the Schiavone purchases, p.68 of this publication.

Chapter Ten · London 1831–1844: Poussin, Hals and the Westminster Competition of 1843

[137] On Geddes's presumed recovery of the contested Old Master drawings, see note 133. His impassioned plea for the preservation of the Lawrence cabinet was published in full in Adela Geddes, ibid., pp.26–32. On the case precedent cited in his letter, see ed. Michael Clarke and Nicholas Penny, *The Arrogant Connoisseur: Richard Payne Knight 1751–1824*, Manchester 1982, especially ch.7.

[138] The majority of Lawrence's drawings were widely scattered. The most significant group in public ownership are the finest of the Raphael and Michelangelo sheets, presented to the University of Oxford in 1845 by public subscription and now in the Ashmolean Museum. On the Lawrence affair, see William T. Whitley, *Art in England*, New York 1973 (reprint), vol.2, especially pp.178–80 and pp.276–80. Geddes's purchases from the Lawrence cabinet passed through his own posthumous sale, possibly in entirety, on 10 April 1845. For Geddes's putative ownership of *Christ Among the Doctors* from the Lawrence collection, see p.57 and note 95, and for his purchases of Rembrandt drawings owned by Lawrence and Esdaile successively, see note 116.

[139] Adela Geddes, ibid., p.20. The 'very dear friend' who persuaded Geddes to stand for election was probably Wilkie. Geddes's election was recorded in the *General Assembly Minutes* on 4 November 1832 (Royal Academy Archives, GA IV 1826–41). Amongst the later exhibited portraits which are still

located, *Mrs Harris Prendergast* (1838) is in the National Gallery of Scotland and the double portrait of Alexina and Catherine Lindsay is in the National Portrait Gallery, London, both having been exhibited in 1838. The ambitious Van Dyckian fancy portrait of the daughters of George Arbuthnot 'in the costume of Charles I' (dated and exhibited 1839) was sold from family possession at Christie's on 22 November 1985 (lot 113).

[140] The small whole length of Wellington was lot 528 on 11 April 1845, the 4th day of the artist's sale at Christie's. See the extended letter from Geddes to Dr Maclagan from 15 Berners Street, London, 5 October 1837 in the National Library of Scotland, MS 10695, fo.5. Geddes gave a detailed account of his interview with the Duke, but the precise circumstances of his mission were obviously not explained to Maclagan as his collaborator.

[141] As an Honorary Member of the Edinburgh Royal Institution, Geddes made his final contribution to its modern exhibition from Rome in 1829. The priority which he had attached to his Italian landscapes is discussed on p.66. For the exhibition critiques, see the *Art Union*, 1842, vol.IV, p.122 and 1843, vol.III, p.167. Geddes was diagnosed with consumption during his stay in Italy. An example of Geddes's late genre pictures, painted during the penultimate year of his life, is the so-called *Boy with a Hurdy-Gurdy* – clearly not the original title – in the Walker Art Gallery in Liverpool. In 1844 he showed *An Italian Minstrel* at the Royal Academy.

[142] Adela Geddes, ibid., p.20. Letter from Adela Geddes to Laing from London 4 November 1874 in the Laing MSS, La.IV.17, fos.3507–11. In a follow-up letter of 21 November 1874 (La.IV.17, fos.3514–5) she reported that she had cut up the Milton cartoon, retaining only the heads, since the composition as a whole was badly rubbed through having been stored rolled up. Prior to the 1843 competition, Geddes had experimented with decorative painting in the form of large easel painting. Reminiscent of Rubens's 'Peace and War' presented to the National Gallery in London by the Duke of Sutherland in 1828, *The Education of Pan* (Kirkcaldy Art Gallery) was commissioned by

the proprietor (probably Robert Brown) of Newhall in Midlothian as a mural.

[143] See T.S.R. Boase, 'The Decoration of the New Palace of Westminster 1841–1863' in *Journal of the Warburg and Courtauld Institutes*, London 1954, vol.17, pp.319ff, especially pp.324–30 and David Robertson, *Sir Charles Eastlake and the Victorian Art World*, Princeton and Guildford 1978. Eastlake was Secretary of the Commission. Geddes is not mentioned by Boase or Robertson among the unsuccessful competitors in 1843. See also ed. Frederick Knight Hunt, *The Book of Art, Cartoons, Frescoes, Sculpture and Decorative Art as applied to the New Houses of Parliament and to Buildings in General, with an Historical Notice of the Exhibitions in Westminster Hall and Directions for Painting in Fresco*, London 1846, and Henry G. Clarke, *A Handbook Guide to the Cartoons now Exhibiting in Westminster Hall*, London 1843. Dr Selby Whittingham, who kindly checked at very short notice *The Book of Art*, has suggested that cat.no.36, a *Samson Agonistes* measuring 11 × 14 feet, may be identifiable as Geddes's cartoon. None of the participants in 1843 was named by Hunt.

[144] The artist's posthumous sale on 11 April 1845 included half-length and three-quarter-length oil portraits of Steuart (lots 551 and 556). Geddes's portrait of Monro 'Tertius' has remained in family possession.

[145] On Steuart of Allanbank, see p.47 and note 71. Geddes's friend William Hookham Carpenter, husband of the portrait painter Margaret Carpenter and Geddes's predecessor in the tenancy of the house at 58 Lower Brook Street in London (see p.61), published two of Steuart's compilations of his own etchings, *The Visions of an Amateur* in 1828 and *Gleanings from the Portfolio of an Amateur*. See also W.G. Constable, 'A Sketchbook by James Stuart in the Avery Library' in *Print Collectors' Quarterly*, 1942, vol.29, pp.237–49. The Christie's sale catalogue of 23 May 1835, of which Christie's Archives copy is annotated by lot with the identities of the two vendors, is the only published record of Steuart's collection.

[146] Miss James sale at Christie's, 20 June 1891, lot 31. See Seymour Slive, *Frans Hals* (National Gallery of Art: Kress Foundation

Studies in History of European Art), New York 1974, vol.iii, pp.84–5, cat.165 (the Geddes and Andrew James provenance is not listed).

[147] Seymour Slive, ibid., pp.37–8, cat.no.61 and Neil Maclaren (revised by Christopher Brown), *The Dutch School 1600–1900: National Gallery Catalogues*, London 1991, vol.i, pp.160–1 and plate 142. The evidence for Geddes's involvement in the transaction – the third party and/or previous provenance of the Hals remain unknown – is provided by J.V. Hodgson, *A Catalogue of the Pictures at Elton Hall*, London 1924, p.29, no.24. Subsequent literature has repeated Hodgson's statement that, on Steuart's death in 1849, the picture was inherited by his 'daughter' Mrs Woodcock. Both of Steuart's marriages were childless, a fact confirmed by his collateral descendant, Lady Mitchison, and the baronetcy consequently became extinct in 1849. 'Mrs Woodcock' was possibly a niece by marriage, Steuart's first wife having been Elizabeth Woodcock (died 1828), only daughter of Elborough Woodcock. See ed. G.E.C. *Complete Baronetage*, Exeter 1904, vol.iv, p.353. One of the beneficiaries of Steuart's will was indeed a Mrs Woodcock, Steuart's sister Sophia, described as the wife of the Revd Elborough Woodcock (National Archives of Scotland, sc 70/4/6, p.480).

[148] See Anthony Blunt, *The Paintings of Nicolas Poussin. A Critical Catalogue*, London 1966, p.59, cat.86, referring to the Clarke sale at Christie's on 8 May 1840 (lot 39). The Poussin was lot 651 on the 5th day of Geddes's posthumous sale on 12 April 1845. Two figures are noted on the marked copy of the sale catalogue in Christie's Archives – 400 and 350 guineas. In 1861 Adela Geddes lent the picture to the winter exhibition at the Royal Academy, London (cat.22). By the second Geddes sale at Christie's on 30 November 1867, market prices had plummeted: the Poussin (lot 56) was bought in for exactly £32 11s! It was also in 1840 that Geddes purchased from the Esdaile sale at Christie's Rembrandt drawings formerly in Lawrence's possession. See notes 116 and 138 and p.73.

[149] Adela Geddes, ibid., pp.21–2. Rembrandt's famous three-quarter-length oil portrait of Jan Six is in the Six Collection in Amsterdam. In 1647 Rembrandt executed an etching of Six within an interior reading and in the following year, an elaborately etched illustration to his patron's play *Medea*. Geddes's own patron John Sheepshanks reputedly travelled widely in Germany, Holland and France to enrich his private collection (testimony of Geddes's friend the engraver John Burnet, cited by Martin Royalton-Kisch in ed. Antony Griffiths, ibid., p.66) and was contemplating one such expedition in 1830 when in correspondence with Geddes in Rome. The calibre and Northern European emphasis of Sheepshanks's print collection were evidently known to cognoscenti in Holland since, in 1836, when he disposed of his collection, an offer of purchase was made by Brondgeest, one of the leading Amsterdam printsellers (see ed. Antony Griffiths, ibid., p.65). A letter, or letters, of introduction from Sheepshanks could well have contributed to the cordiality of Geddes's reception in Holland as recalled by his widow.

[150] For information concerning Baron Verstolk van Soelen and collections housed at his mansion at Lange Voorhout 74 in The Hague (now the premises of the Museum Het Paleis), I am indebted to Robert-Jan te Rijdt, Curator of Drawings at the Rijksprentenkabinett of the Rijksmuseum. See also the essay by Peter Black. Apart from Geddes, the Baron was among the principal purchasers, via his agents, from the Esdaile sale on 17 June 1840. See note 166.

[151] Campbell Dodgson, ibid., p.45, cat.34 and plate xxxvii, reproducing both the oil and the first state (British Museum) of the related drypoint. The handling of the drypoint is slightly reminiscent of *The Goldweigher's Field*, one of the most sought-after of all Rembrandt landscape prints and of which Geddes himself owned an impression.

[152] John Seguier (see p.21) married the daughter of Geddes's early London mentor and friend, the miniaturist Anthony Stewart. On William Seguier as a specialist dealer in the 'black masters', see John Burnet, ibid. (note 14), pp.70–3; Judy Egerton, *The British School: National Gallery Catalogues*, London 1998, pp.388–98; Alastair Laing, 'William Seguier and Advice to Picture Collectors' in ed. Christine Sitwell and Sarah Staniforth,

Studies in History of Painting Restoration, London 1996, pp.97–120. Seguier's ownership of the National Gallery of Scotland's landscape is recorded on a label on the reverse attached by the last owner, Kenneth Sanderson ws (died 1943), a self-taught connoisseur collector of Geddes's etchings. Sanderson's adoption of the shorthand 'Seguier' points to William as the likeliest candidate of the entire Seguier dynasty.

[153] Adela Geddes, ibid., pp.23–4. Selby Whittingham kindly volunteered Haydon's epitaph on Geddes from ed. W.B. Pope, *The Diary of Benjamin Robert Haydon*, Cambridge, Massachusetts 1960–3, vol.v, p.372 (entry for 27 June 1844). The *Art Union* obituary of September 1844 (pp.291–2) was based on Adela Geddes's work in progress.

Chapter Eleven · Adela Geddes's Legacy

[154] See note 129 concerning Peel. In his testament (a disappointingly brief document without an inventory) Geddes termed himself 'portrait and historical painter' (Public Record Office, London, Prerogative Court of Canterbury, pro b11/2001 quire 545, fo.355).

[155] *Catalogue of the Valuable Collection of Pictures and Drawings by Old Masters, Etchings; Books; and Articles of Taste and Vertu; formed by that elegant and accomplished Artist, Andrew Geddes, Esq., ara, Deceased; also, his own Original Works ...*, Christie & Manson, London, 8–13 April 1845. Frequent reference has been made to this catalogue as an invaluable source of documentation on Geddes's private collection as well as his original work. Annotated copies are held by the National Library of Scotland and by Christie's Archives, the latter being of particular importance for its inclusion of manuscript lists as additional lots ex catalogue, and including 'finished sketches in oil' encompassing landscape, portraiture and subject pictures.

[156] C.R. Leslie and Clarkson Stanfield proposed the purchase of the Titian copy. The Watteau *Recueil* was purchased by the Academy's librarian Thomas Uwins and is still in the Library. See the 'Royal Academy Council Minutes', cx (1844–52), 2 and 9 April 1845 (Royal Academy Archives). Among Geddes's

artist contemporaries, the most assiduous bidder at his sale appears to have been the semi-professional gentleman portrait painter James Hall of Dunglass (1800–55). Hall's own posthumous sale at Christie's on 18–19 April 1855 included on the first day's sale (lots 167–74) a large number of Geddes drawings, mainly bound in sketchbooks, of which some were acquired by the British Museum.

[157] See p.67 and note 113. The typescript reminiscences of Nevile Reid have remained in the private possession of his descendants. Christie's Archives hold an annotated copy of the mixed sale of *Ancient and Modern Pictures*, by Christie, Manson & Woods on 13 November 1867 of which lots 53–81 were reputedly all from Geddes's estate but which included at least one picture (by William McTaggart) executed after Geddes's death.

[158] Adela Geddes died on 12 February 1881. The final version of her will, dated 25 July 1878 and proven on 12 March 1881, is in the Public Record Office, London. In 1939 *Peckham Rye* was lent by Nevile Reid III to the *Exhibition of Scottish Art* at the Royal Academy in London. Among the lobbyists for Geddes's representation in this supposedly definitive exhibition was the Scottish etcher E.S. Lumsden (1883–1943), owner of several of Geddes's copper etching plates and among his most committed latter-day champions. See the essay by Peter Black.

[159] Letter from the Board Secretary to Adela Geddes 2 November 1877 in the Board Letterbook (National Archives of Scotland, NG 1/3/36, p.337). The intended bequest of 20 March is mentioned on a label attached to the reverse of the self-portrait (Scottish National Portrait Gallery). The so-called *Boy with a Spaniel* in Glasgow Art Gallery and Museum bears a not dissimilar label. Although this picture may originally have been associated with the bequest to the Edinburgh gallery, the picture passed into the Reid family, presumably as another individual bequest or gift. The operational will of 1878 superseded, by implication, all previous wills or codicils, but did not specify any gifts of pictures other than the all-encompassing gift to Miss James.

[160] On Gibson Craig, see Colin Thompson et al, ibid., p.70. As a collector of Geddes etchings himself, he was sent a dedicated copy of Laing's 1875 publication (see below) which is now in the library of the National Gallery of Scotland. On 18 July 1874 Gibson Craig wrote a letter of introduction for Laing to Adela Geddes requesting access to her collection of her husband's etchings (Laing MSS, La.IV.17, fo.3567). The contributor of the inaugural account of Geddes for the *Dictionary of National Biography* was another member of this antiquarian circle in Edinburgh, John Miller Gray (1850–1894), first Keeper of the Scottish National Portrait Gallery. Some of Gray's impressions of Geddes's etchings are in the National Gallery of Scotland. An impression of Geddes's etching of George Chalmers appears among the background bric-a-brac in Fettes Douglas's portrait of Laing in his natural habitat [fig.74]. Sir William Fettes Douglas PRSA (1822–91) also collected Geddes etchings. See Campbell Dodgson, ibid.

[161] David Laing, *Etchings by Sir David Wilkie, RA. Limner to HM for Scotland and by Andrew Geddes ARA with Biographical Sketches*, Edinburgh 1875. See note 5 and the essay by Peter Black.

Andrew Geddes: The Herald of the Etching Revival

[1] Lumsden's collection, including a group of etchings and three of Geddes's copper plates, was acquired by the National Gallery of Scotland in 1949.

[2] The standard catalogue of Geddes's etchings is contained in Campbell Dodgson, *The Etchings of Sir David Wilkie & Andrew Geddes*, London 1936.

[3] E.S. Lumsden, *The Art of Etching*, London 1925, p.263.

[4] The source for Geddes's study with Alexander Nasmyth is James Nasmyth (ed. Samuel Smiles), *Autobiography*. The relationship with Alexander Nasmyth was long and fruitful. The portrait of *Nasmyth* (CD 10) is one of Geddes's finest prints. The artists made at least one sketching trip together and Nasmyth's daughters Elizabeth and Charlotte feature in portraits by Geddes (Elizabeth seated with her husband Daniel Terry, the comedian, in *Dull Reading* (CD 16).

[5] Geddes and Wilkie met at the RA Schools in 1806. There are four entries in Wilkie's Journal for the end of May, beginning of June 1808, where he mentions contact with Geddes, three times in the company of Burnet (Alan Cunningham, *The Life of David Wilkie, with his Journals, Tours and Critical Remarks on Works of Art; and a Selection from his correspondence*, London 1843, vol.1).

[6] *The Works of Robert Burns, with an Account of his Life* edited by James Currie, M.D. London, William Allason; Edinburgh W. Blair 1819. Three of the small plates are signed as drawn by Geddes: *Strathallan's Lament*; *John Anderson My Jo*; *Lament of Mary Queen of Scotts*.

[7] David Laing, *Etchings by Sir David Wilkie, R.A., Limner to H.M. for Scotland, and by Andrew Geddes, A.R.A., with biographical sketches*, Edinburgh 1875, p.7, states that Philipe was 'a well-known printseller and auctioneer, for many years at Edinburgh, but afterwards on a more extensive scale at London'. Reference has been found to a T. Philipe working in Edinburgh as a printseller in 1770 (Scottish Record Office, Clerk Papers, GD/18/4681). That Philipe may

be the same man. Philipe auctioned the best part of David Geddes's collection in London in 1804. For Philipe's involvement with the British Museum, see Antony Griffiths, *Landmarks in Print Collecting*, British Museum Press 1996.

[8] Geddes could conceivably have toyed with the monogram of Abraham Genoels (1640–1723), a Flemish etcher whose work he would have known.

[9] That they are not conceived as reproductions is clear from the transformation of the background of the *Molesworth Phillips* in the 5th state. A curtain and books are brought in to replace the painting of Captain Cook's murder which formed the original setting for the aged Colonel.

[10] See E.S. Lumsden, *The Art of Etching*, London 1925, p.259.

[11] *St Jerome in a Dark Chamber* was sold as lot 106 in Geddes's posthumous sale at Christies, London, 8–14 April 1845.

[12] Rembrandt's *Cottage with a White Paling* (B 232) was lot 228 in Geddes's sale.

[13] Geddes describes it as such in the prospectus for the 1826 publication which is quoted by Laing, 1875, p.27.

Andrew Geddes: Aspects of Technique discussed in the Context of Nineteenth-century British Painting Practice

[1] Quoted in D. and F. Irwin, *Scottish Painters At Home and Abroad 1700–1900*, London 1975, p.202 as note 49; *Art Union*, V, 1843, p.167.

[2] The paintings that were examined are: *George Chalmers* (PG 2037), *John Clerk, Lord Eldin* (PG 625), *Anne Geddes, the Artist's Sister* (NG 2156), *The Artist's Mother* (NG 630), *George Sanders* (NG 416), *Self-portrait in Van Dyck Dress* (PGL 42) and *Anthony Stewart* (PG 430).

[3] In general terms commercially-prepared artists' paint is composed primarily of inert powdered coloured pigment ground in oil. The oil component represents the paint 'medium' or 'vehicle'.

[4] See Leslie Carlyle, 'A critical analysis of artists' handbooks, manuals and treatises on oil painting published in Britain between 1800–1900', unpublished PhD thesis, Courtauld Institute of Art, University of London 1991; Leslie Carlyle and Anna Southall, 'No Short Mechanic Road to Fame. The Implications of Certain Artists' Materials for the Durability of British Painting: 1770–1840' in *Robert Vernon's Gift. British Art for the Nation 1847*, Tate Gallery 1993; *Paint and Purpose. A Study of Technique in British Art*, edited by Stephen Hackney, Rica Jones, Joyce Townsend, Tate Gallery 1999; M. Kirby Talley Jr, '"All Good Pictures Crack" Sir Joshua Reynolds's practice and studio', in *Reynolds*, Royal Academy 1986; Joyce Townsend, *Turner's Painting Techniques*, Tate Gallery 1993.

[5] A notable example of what appears to be bituminous cracking is David Wilkie's *General Sir David Baird Discovering the Body of Sultan Tippoo Sahib after having Captured Seringapatum on the 4th May, 1799* (National Gallery of Scotland NG 2430).

[6] Adela Geddes describing her husband's entrance into the Royal Academy in 1809 wrote in her *Memoir*, p.9: His love and veneration for the old masters, especially Rembrandt was very great; and even at that early period he possessed a few of that master's admirable productions.

[7] This was acknowledged early on in the century as not necessarily an approach to be recommended; Carlyle and Southall, ibid., p.24, note 23; John Opie, *Lectures on Painting delivered* [in 1807] *at the Royal Academy of Arts...*, 1809, p.145, condemned *nostrums for producing fine pictures without the help of science, genius, taste or industry....*

[8] The practice of artists copying Old Master paintings was very common at this time – another expression of the high regard in which they held such works. Andrew Geddes held a sale at 'Messrs Christie and Manson' on 8 April, 1845, which included some of his copies. Those listed include copies after Van Dyck, Veronese, Rembrandt, Correggio and Titian. Talley (1986), ibid., p.56, refers to copies of Raphael, Rubens, Titian and Rembrandt executed by Reynolds, while Carlyle and Southall, ibid., p.23, make reference to Edwin Landseer and William Etty copying works by Rubens and Titian, respectively.

[9] Talley (1986), ibid., p.56, note 22; J. Northcote, *The Life of Sir Joshua Reynolds*, 2 vols., 1818, II, p.22: *Northcote recalled that his investigations were indefatigable – 'I remember once, in particular, a fine picture by Parmegiano, that I bought by his order at a sale, which he rubbed and scoured down to the very pannel on which it had been painted, so that ... nothing remained of the picture.'* Also Talley (1986), ibid., p.57, note 23; Northcote, ibid., II, p.23: *The Redgraves claimed to have known a restorer, formerly a pupil of West, 'who possessed portraits by both Titian and Rubens which he said had belonged to Sir Joshua, and parts of which, to obtain this wished-for secret, had been scraped or rubbed down to the panel, to lay bare the under-paintings or dead colourings.'*

[10] Carlyle, ibid., 1991.

[11] M.K. Talley and K. Groen in 'Thomas Bardwell and his practice of painting: a comparative investigation between described and actual painting technique' in *Studies in Conservation*, 20, 1975, pp.44–108; L.A. Stevenson, 'The Technique of Sir Henry Raeburn examined in the Context of Late Eighteenth-Century British Portraiture', in *Painting Techniques History Materials and Studio Practice*, International Institute for Conservation 1998.

[12] As described by John Gage, 'Magilphs and Mysteries', *Apollo*, 80, no.29 (July 1964), p.38: *When William Sandby published the first history of the Royal Academy, London in 1862, he made a special plea for instruction in the chemistry of colours, citing the physical decay of many pictures by Reynolds, Turner, Etty and the late Wilkie ... None of the later eighteenth century academies seems to have concerned itself with the teaching of technique; this was left to private masters, and in England they were often unable or unwilling to provide instruction. The technical manuals complained of secretiveness and recipes were spread by rumour and hint rather than by any systematic teaching.* Academic art education is also discussed by Rica Jones, 'The Artist's Training and Techniques' in *Manners and Morals: Hogarth and British Painting 1700–1760*, Tate Gallery 1987.

[13] The methods of examination employed in the studio include use of a stereo-binocular microscope, x-radiography and infrared reflectography. Minute samples of paint were removed from the edge or from areas of damage for cross-sectional analysis, which incorporated the use of UV fluorescence microscopy. A number of the cross sections were examined with energy-dispersive x-ray analysis (EDX) carried out with a scanning electron microscope (SEM) by Siobhan Watts, Conservation Scientist, at the Conservation Centre, National Museums and Galleries on Merseyside, Liverpool.

[14] Gas chromatography-mass spectrometry (GC-MS) was carried out by Suzanne Lomax, Conservation Scientist, National Gallery of Art, Washington DC.

[15] Colourmen had been in existence since at least as early as the seventeenth century and there are several known to have traded in Edinburgh. As noted by John Burnet, 'Recollections of My Contemporaries'. The Early Days of Wilkie in *The Art Journal*, 1860, p.237, Wilkie as well as Raeburn and Nasmyth is reputed to have used the Edinburgh firm of Taylor and Norrie. John Dick in 'Raeburn's methods and materials,' in *Raeburn*, Edinburgh 1997, pp.39–45, noted that canvas stamps visible on unlined portraits reveal that Raeburn also used the firm Middleton in London.

[16] Examination of the panel portraits of *George Sanders* and *David Wilkie* reveal just the thin white ground layer (the small *Self-portrait in Van Dyck Dress* panel being an exception with a thicker multi-layered structure) whereas samples taken from *Anne Geddes* and *George Chalmers* reveal what is regarded as an added artist-applied lightly-coloured layer.

[17] Identified visually and by EDX with a scanning electron microscope. For further information on the range of pigments used by artists of this period see H.W. Williams, 'Romney's palette' in *Technical Studies in the Field of the Fine Arts*, VI, 1937, pp.19–23; J. Dick, ibid., 1997; L.A. Stevenson, ibid., 1998; M.K. Talley, ibid., 1986.

[18] J.S. Mills and R. White, *The Organic Chemistry of Museum Objects*, 2nd edition, London 1999, pp.103–4.

[19] L. Carlyle, 'British nineteenth-century oil painting instruction books: a survey of their recommendations for vehicles, varnishes and methods of paint application' in *Cleaning, Retouching and Coatings*, International Institute for Conservation, London 1990, pp.76–80.

[20] As all the canvas paintings examined were lined with a wax-resin adhesive it was expected that there might be some adulteration of those sampled. *George Sanders*, however, is painted on a panel support.

[21] Burnet, ibid., 1860, pp.236–7: *Wilkie's first canvas and colours were purchased in the shop of Taylor and Norrie, of Edinburgh, the colourmen who supplied our two great Scottish painters of portrait and landscape – Raeburn and Nasmyth. The vehicle he then used for a mixture of drying linseed-oil and mastic varnish (megilp); but when in London, engaged upon the picture of 'The Village Festival,' Thomson, the academician, called and advised him to use wax, as Reynolds had done. In his journal for 1810, Wilkie writes, 'Went to buy some wax from Barclay, in the Haymarket, who, on learning who I was, insisted on my acceptance of a large quantity as a present.'* Wax has also been analysed in the works Reynolds and Turner. See Talley, ibid., 1986; Joyce Townsend 1993; Hackney Jones and Townsend, ibid., 1999.

[22] R. White, 'Brown and Black Organic Glazes, Pigments and Paints', in *The National Gallery Technical Bulletin*, vol.10, 1986, p.63.

[23] R. Dossie describes asphaltum in *Handmaid to the Arts*, London 1764, p.129, quoted in Carlyle, ibid., 1991, p.202; 1835 is the year of the earliest known artist's catalogue.

[24] Leslie Carlyle, 'Authenticity and Adulteration: What materials were 19th Century Artist's Really Using?', in *The Conservator*, number 17, 1993, pp.56–60.

[25] George Field 1835, quoted in Carlyle and Southall, ibid., p.21, 1993.

[26] From William Muckley, *A Handbook for Painters and Art Students...*, 2nd edition, 1882, pp.72–3; note 11 in Carlyle and Southall, ibid., 1993, p.23.

[27] From Richard and Samuel Redgrave, *A Century of Painters of the English School*, 1866, pp.594–5: *Wilkie began with simple pigments and vehicles, his 'Pitlessie Fair' painted perhaps with linseed oil still remains in sound condition, as do many others of his early and careful works; even before he went abroad, however, he began to use asphaltum and used asphaltum not only in his darks, but mixed even with his solid lights ... When visitor in the painting school, he asserted Titian could only be so copied. A careful study of the 'Venus and Adonis' from the Dulwich Gallery, was made by one of the most talented students of the day, under their joint direction; and however beautiful at the time of its production, it now shows only a network of dark seams and corrugations. Wilkie's own picture of 'The First Ear-ring' and 'The Peep of Day Boys' in the Vernon Collection are other fast decaying evidences of this dangerous practice.*

[28] Carlyle and Southall ibid., p.24, 1993, note 21; John Scott Taylor, *Modes of Painting Described and Classified...*, 1890, p.33. Documentary sources describe other practitioners using the gelled medium; Carlyle and Southall, ibid., 1993, p.24, note 22; quote from Alexander Gilchrist, *The Life of William Etty*, 1854, p.68: *Megilp was also used on its own. William Etty, for example, recommended its application before and during painting: 'with a large brush rub [megilp] over the canvas or picture you have paint on.'*

This is the best medium ... a vehicle that will keep flesh tints pure'.

[29] Talley, ibid., 1986, p.62: *He [Reynolds] made frequent use of megilp. A notation dated 1767 for his portrait of Miss Hester Cholmondeley reads: 'verniciulo con yeos(?) lake e megilp [73].* This means that he glazed the picture with a yellow lake made by Richard Yeo mixed with megilp. For information on Turner's use of megilp see Townsend, ibid., 1993, pp.49–57; 'Painting Techniques and Materials of Turner and Other British Artists 1775–1875', in *Historical Painting Techniques, Materials and Studio Practice*, ed. A. Wallert, E. Hermans and M. Peek, Leiden 1995, pp.176–85.

[30] One early warning reported as James Barry to Reynolds, 17 May 1769, Gage, ibid., 1964, p.38: *...such people as ours who are floating about after Magilphs and mysteries, and are very little likely to satisfy themselves with that saying of Annibal's (Carracci) 'Buon disegno e colorito di fango'.* For a fuller discussion of how artists are known to have been aware of the shortcomings of their materials see 'The artist's anticipation of change as discussed in British 19th century instruction books on oil painting', L. Carlyle, *Appearance, Opinion and Change – Evaluating the Look of Paintings*, United Kingdom Institute for Conservation, 1990, pp.62–7. Warnings continued well into the latter half of the nineteenth century: J4, Nov. 19, 1875, letter from Holman Hunt, re. Deterioration of colours (from *Pre-Raphaelitism and the Pre Raphaelite Brotherhood*, vol.II, London 1905, chapter XVI, pp.454–5): *He is particularly critical in the use of asphaltum, 'this pernicious Dead Sea pitch'. Many admirable works by Wilkie, Hilton and their contemporaries, have thereby been doomed to complete destruction. In another century no one will know what powers delicacy in manipulation those artists had, for the bitumen, ever dilating and contracting with atmospheric changes, is tearing the paintings to pieces.*

[31] Glue and wax-resin lining procedures, ie. the adhesion of a second canvas to the reverse of the original for added support, both involved excessive heat when practiced in the 19th and early 20th centuries.

[32] Frederick Peter Seguier, *A Critical and Commercial Dictionary of the Works of Painters*, London 1870: *Andrew Geddes is chiefly remembered as a portrait painter ... Like Lawrence, he was fond of introducing a great deal of red and lake in the background of his portraits. In his landscapes he loved to represent broad effects of 'light and shade'.*

[33] Madder was identified in the chair of *George Chalmers*. This pigment fluoresces uniquely orange when viewed under an ultraviolet light source.

[34] Burnet, ibid., 1860, p.237.

[35] For fuller explanation of 'oiling out layers', see Jones, ibid., p.24, 1987; Carlyle, ibid., 1990, pp.76–80; Carlyle, ibid., 1991, p.293.

[36] Such layers are detected using an ultraviolet light source to examine the cross sections. Portraits that revealed evidence of interlayer oil or varnish application are *Anne Geddes*, *Archibald Constable* and *George Chalmers*.

[37] Spike Bucklow, 'The description of craquelure patterns', in *Studies in Conservation*, vol.42, no.3, 1997, p.130.

[38] Recent research has made an attempt at 'cataloguing' crack patterns and using them as a tool for attribution purposes. For a fuller description see Bucklow, ibid., 1997, pp.129–40; 'The description and classification of craquelure', in *Studies in Conservation*, vol.44, no.4, 1999, pp.233–44; 'Micro-cissing' is a term coined to describe a peculiarly British phenomenon – fine cracks on a minute scale identified in paintings of this period: R. Jones, 'Drying Crackle in Early and Mid Eighteenth Century British Painting', in *Appearance, Opinion and Change*, United Kingdom Institute for Conservation, 1990, pp.50–2.

[39] Michael Gallagher, Keeper of Conservation at the National Galleries of Scotland, cleaned the painting. The portrait had been heavily overpainted prior to the recent treatment. This had been applied by a previous restorer in an attempt to conceal the extent of cracking on the surface.

[40] Flexible fabric and rigid panel supports naturally engender different types of natural ageing cracking as they respond differently to changes in temperature and humidity.

Acknowledgements: Grateful thanks are due to Suzanne Lomax, National Gallery of Art, Washington DC; Siobhan Watts, National Galleries and Museum on Merseyside, Liverpool; and also Donald Forbes, Michael Gallagher and Helen Smailes, National Galleries of Scotland.

Exhibition Checklist

Measurements are in centimetres height before width. Undated works follow those with a known or assigned date.

I · ORIGINAL WORKS BY ANDREW GEDDES

OIL PAINTINGS

[1]

A Storm Coming On or *The Approaching Storm*, probably 1810

Oil on canvas, 30.7 × 47.3cm
Scottish Private Collection
Illustrated on page 26

[2]

David Bridges Senior (died 1830), 1812

Oil on oak panel, 55 × 42cm
Scottish Private Collection
Illustrated on page 32

[3]

Euphemia Cargill Macduff, Mrs David Bridges Senior, 1812

Oil on oak panel, 54.5 × 42cm
Scottish Private Collection
Illustrated on page 32

[4]

George Chalmers (1742–1825), 1812

Oil on canvas, 76.2 × 63.5cm
Scottish National Portrait Gallery, Edinburgh
Illustrated on page 28

[5]

Agnes Geddes, The Artist's Mother (died 1828), 1812

Oil on oak panel, 50 × 37.7cm
Scottish Private Collection
Illustrated on page 14

[6]

Self-portrait in Van Dyck Dress, 1812

Oil on mahogany (?) panel, 34 × 28cm
On loan from the Society of Antiquaries of Scotland to the Scottish National Portrait Gallery, Edinburgh
Illustrated on page 27

[7]

Anne Geddes, The Artist's Sister (1785–1843), c.1812

Oil on canvas, 127 × 94.7cm
National Gallery of Scotland, Edinburgh
Illustrated on page 59

[8]

Archibald Skirving (1749–1819), 1812

Oil on canvas, 72.7 × 60cm
National Gallery of Scotland, Edinburgh
Illustrated on page 30

[9]

Anthony Stewart (1773–1846), 1812

Oil on canvas, 61.4 × 46.4cm
Scottish National Portrait Gallery, Edinburgh
Illustrated on page 21

[10]

Archibald Constable (1774–1827), 1813

Oil on mahogany panel, 58.9 × 42cm
Scottish National Portrait Gallery, Edinburgh
Illustrated on page 28

[11]

Agnes Geddes, The Artist's Mother (died 1828), probably 1813

Oil on canvas, 72 × 61cm
National Gallery of Scotland, Edinburgh
Illustrated on page 35

[12]

Charles Knowles Robison (died 1846) Skating on Duddingston Loch, 1813

Oil on panel, 66 × 45cm
Private Collection
Illustrated on page 33

[13]

Captain Robert Skirving of Croys (1757–1843), 1813

Oil on mahogany (?) panel, 66 × 45cm
Scottish National Portrait Gallery, Edinburgh
Illustrated on page 29

[14]
Andrew Plimer (1763–1837), 1815
Oil on mahogany panel, 47.5 × 39.4cm
National Gallery of Scotland, Edinburgh
Illustrated on page 25

[15]
George Sanders (1774–1846), 1816
Oil on mahogany panel, 70 × 49.5cm
National Gallery of Scotland, Edinburgh
Illustrated on page 40

[16]
Sir David Wilkie (1785–1841), 1816
Oil on mahogany panel, 66 × 48.2cm
Scottish National Portrait Gallery, Edinburgh
Illustrated on page 41

[17]
Amelia Penrose Cumming of Altyre,
later Mrs B. Yeaman, c.1817
Oil on mahogany panel, 71 × 50cm
Private Collection
Illustrated on page 43

[18]
Sir Walter Scott (1771–1832), c.1818
Oil on mahogany (?) panel, 55.7 × 41.9cm
Scottish National Portrait Gallery, Edinburgh
Illustrated on page 53

[19]
Self-portrait, 181[?]
Oil on canvas, 73.5 × 61cm
Scottish Private Collection
Illustrated on page 34

[20]
Alexander Nasmyth (1758–1840),
c.1820–5
Oil on canvas, 77.5 × 64.8cm
Royal Scottish Academy, Edinburgh
Illustrated on page 18

[21]
Grace Pratt, Mrs Thomas Chalmers
(1792–1850), c.1821
Oil on canvas, 142.3 × 118cm
(sight measurement)
Private Collection

[22]
Henry Mackenzie (1745–1831),
before 1822
Oil on mahogany panel, 66 × 50.3cm
Scottish Private Collection
Illustrated on page 45

[23]
Archibald Montgomery of Whim
(1771–1845), his wife Maria Rausch,
and their elder children James (born
1811) and Charles (born 1813),
exhibited 1822
Oil on canvas, 73.6 × 94.6cm
Scottish Private Collection
Illustrated on page 61

[24]
Summer, c.1826
Oil on canvas, 81.3 × 64.2cm
National Gallery of Scotland, Edinburgh
Illustrated on page 63

[25]
The Marble Quarries at Carrara,
c.1829
Oil on canvas, 73 × 98cm
(sight measurement from the front)
Scottish Private Collection

[26]
John Gibson (1790–1866), 1830
Oil on canvas, 127 × 100.3cm
Walker Art Gallery, National Museums and
Galleries on Merseyside
Illustrated on page 75

[27]
'Nellie Hepburn'?, 1830
Oil on canvas, 75 × 62cm
Scottish Private Collection
Illustrated on page 70

[28]
Hannah Fry, Mrs Harris Prendergast
(1814–59), 1838
Oil on canvas, 126.5 × 101cm
National Gallery of Scotland, Edinburgh

[29]
Hagar, exhibited 1842
Oil on canvas, 75.5 × 62.7cm
National Gallery of Scotland, Edinburgh
Illustrated on page 79

[30]
'Boy with a Hurdy-Gurdy', 1843
Oil on canvas, 76 × 63.5cm
Walker Art Gallery, National Museums and
Galleries on Merseyside

[31]
John Clerk, Lord Eldin (1757–1832)
Oil on canvas, 41 × 33.4cm
Scottish National Portrait Gallery, Edinburgh
Illustrated on page 17

[32]
Self-portrait
Oil on canvas, 76.2 × 62.9cm
Scottish National Portrait Gallery, Edinburgh
Illustrated on page 58 and front cover

[33]
Jeremiah Greatorex
Oil on canvas, 90.2 × 70.5cm
Glasgow Museums: Art Gallery & Museum,
Kelvingrove
Illustrated on page 60

[34]
Sir John James Steuart of Allanbank
(1779–1849)
Oil on canvas, 127.4 × 102.3cm
Scottish National Portrait Gallery, Edinburgh
Illustrated on page 80

[35]
James Wardrop (1782–1869)
Oil on canvas, 74 × 61cm
Royal College of Surgeons of Edinburgh

[36]
Portrait of Two Women (possibly
Adela Geddes (1791–1881), the Artist's
Wife, and a Friend)
Oil on mahogany (?) panel, 20 × 17cm
National Gallery of Scotland, Edinburgh
Illustrated on page 66

[37]

Portrait of an Unknown Lady with a Paisley Shawl

Oil on canvas, 35.5 × 30.5cm
(sight measurement)
Scottish Private Collection

[38]

View of Edinburgh from St Anthony's Chapel

Oil on mahogany panel, 24.5 × 28cm
Scottish Private Collection

[39]

Landscape in the Manner of Rembrandt

Oil on paper laid on mahogany (?) panel,
20 × 29.6cm
National Gallery of Scotland, Edinburgh
Illustrated on page 83

DRAWINGS

[40]

Professor Alexander Murray (1775–1813), 1812

Pencil on paper, 24.6 × 17.4cm
Scottish National Portrait Gallery, Edinburgh
Illustrated on page 29

[41]

Hugh Murray (1779–1846), 1813

Pencil with chalk highlights on paper,
29.4 × 24.5cm
Scottish National Portrait Gallery, Edinburgh

[42]

The Apostles St Paul, St Peter and St John, 1817

Pencil, watercolour, and bodycolour on paper,
laid down, 23.5 × 29.4cm
National Gallery of Scotland, Edinburgh

[43]

The Sceptre from the Regalia of Scotland, 1818

Indian ink on paper, 44 × 27cm
National Archives of Scotland, Edinburgh
Illustrated on page 50

[44]

Compositional sketch for The Discovery of the Regalia of Scotland, c.1818

Pen, brown ink, and graphite on paper,
22.4 × 33.5cm
The British Museum, London
Illustrated on page 52

[45]

Sir Walter Scott (1771–1832), 1823

Pencil and chalk on paper, 22.2 × 16.9cm
Scottish National Portrait Gallery, Edinburgh

[46]

After Sir Peter Paul Rubens 1577–1640
Compositional study after 'Le Chapeau de Paille', c.1823

Pastel on paper, 12 × 8.7cm
National Gallery of Scotland, Edinburgh
Illustrated on page 62

[47]

Compositional study for 'Summer', c.1823–6

Pastel on paper, 15 × 11cm
National Gallery of Scotland, Edinburgh
Illustrated on page 62

[48]

Portrait study of Lady Gwendoline Talbot (died 1840), c.1829

Black chalk, heightened with red and white
chalk, on buff paper, 28.2 × 21.8cm
National Gallery of Scotland, Edinburgh

[49]

Compositional study for 'The Ladies Talbot' showing the Ladies Gwendoline (died 1840) and Mary Talbot (died 1858) with Pope Pius's Pug Dog, c.1829

Black chalk on buff paper, 32.8 × 25.4cm
National Gallery of Scotland, Edinburgh
Illustrated on page 72

[50]

Studies of Pope Pius's Pug Dog for 'The Ladies Talbot', c.1829

Black chalk on paper, 28.5 × 21.1cm
National Gallery of Scotland, Edinburgh
Illustrated on page 72

[51]

Study of a Turk, c.1830

Pencil on paper, 15.2 × 9.5cm
Scottish Private Collection

[52]

Nevile Reid II (1839–1913), 1843

Black, red, and white chalk on paper,
37 × 28.6cm
Private Collection
Illustrated on page 83

[53]

Sir John Marjoribanks of Lees (1763–1833)

Black chalk, with white heightening, on buff
paper, 25.5 × 20.4cm
National Gallery of Scotland, Edinburgh

[54]

*Study of a Seated Man Asleep
(possibly Daniel Terry, c.1780–1829)*

Black, red, and white chalk on pink paper,
21.1 × 18.1cm
National Gallery of Scotland, Edinburgh

[55]

*Compositional study for 'A Lady
Wearing a White Dress and Resting
her Right Hand on a Pedestal'*

Coloured chalks on paper, 12.4 × 7.8cm
The British Museum, London

[56]

*Study for 'A Man Seated in Profile to
the Left, Red Drapery Behind'*

Black, red, and white chalk on brown paper,
13.2 × 11.3cm
The British Museum, London

[57]

*Cottage Interior: a Seated Woman
with a Child on her Lap, and another
Child Standing at her Side*

Charcoal and black chalk on paper,
26.4 × 20.9cm
The British Museum, London

[58]

*Compositional study for 'A Woman
and Child with a Fiddler in a Cottage
Interior'*

Black chalk, 14.9 × 12.7cm
National Gallery of Scotland, Edinburgh

[59]

*Compositional study for an
unidentified subject picture*

Black chalk, 15.4 × 34.3cm
National Gallery of Scotland, Edinburgh

[60]

*Probably a compositional study for a
fancy picture of 'A Woman Wearing a
White Dress and a Red Shawl'*

Coloured chalks on brown paper, 8.5 × 7.3cm
The British Museum, London

[61]

*Possibly a compositional study for a
fancy picture of 'A Young Woman with
her Head and Left Hand Resting on a
Pillow'*

Black and white chalk on paper, 11.8 × 9.1cm
The British Museum, London

[62]

*A Man in Armour, Wearing a Red
Cloak or Tunic*

Coloured chalks on paper, 10.7 × 8.8cm
The British Museum, London

[63]

*Compositional study for a subject
picture of 'Christ Among the Doctors'*

Black chalk, 14.5 × 21.4cm
National Gallery of Scotland, Edinburgh
Illustrated on page 58

[64]

Halliford on Thames

Black and white chalk on buff paper,
13.4 × 29.1cm
National Gallery of Scotland, Edinburgh

[65]

An English Farm

Black chalk, with white heightening,
on buff paper, 20.1 × 33.7cm
National Gallery of Scotland, Edinburgh

[66]

*A Glade in a Wood with Two Lines of
Trees and a Hill on the Left*

Black, white chalk, and graphite on pink-
brown paper, 20.7 × 27.3cm
The British Museum, London

[67]

Studies of Trees and Parkland

Black and white chalk on blue-grey paper,
21.1 × 35.3cm
National Gallery of Scotland, Edinburgh

[68]

*Study of a Man in Seventeenth-
Century Costume*

Black, red, and white chalk on grey paper,
28.1 × 23.5cm
National Gallery of Scotland, Edinburgh

[69]

After Antoine Watteau 1684–1721
A Man Holding a Guitar

Red chalk, touched with black chalk, on buff
paper, 22.8 × 17.9cm
The British Museum, London

[70]

After Antoine Watteau 1684–1721
Three studies

Black chalk, touched with red, and white
chalk, on buff paper, 23.6 × 26cm
The British Museum, London
Illustrated on page 67

[71]

After Antoine Watteau 1684–1721
Nine studies

Red chalk, touched with black and white
chalk, on paper, 25.7 × 31.5cm
The British Museum, London

II · ETCHINGS AND DRYPOINTS BY ANDREW GEDDES

PRINTS

The prefix CD, followed by a catalogue number and a number referring to the state of the etching, refers to Campbell Dodgson, *The Etchings of Sir David Wilkie and Andrew Geddes: A Catalogue*, published in London, 1936, for the Print Collectors' Club.

[72]

Sir William Allan (1782-1850), 1815, published 1826

Etching touched with drypoint, 22.5 × 15.1cm
CD 1/ii
National Gallery of Scotland, Edinburgh
Illustrated on page 90

[73]

David Bridges Junior (1776-1840), 1816

Drypoint, 24.1 × 15.8cm
CD 3/i
National Gallery of Scotland, Edinburgh

[74]

Henry Broadwood (1793-1878)

Drypoint, 24.5 × 15.6cm
CD 4/iii (printed by Ernest Stephen Lumsden 1883-1948)
National Gallery of Scotland, Edinburgh
Illustrated on page 55

[75]

George Chalmers (1742-1825), 1812

Etching and drypoint, 22.2 × 15.8cm
CD 5/i
The British Museum, London
Illustrated on page 87

[76]

George Chalmers (1742-1825), 1812

Etching and drypoint, 22.2 × 15.8cm
CD 5/ii
The British Museum, London

[77]

After Sir Thomas Lawrence 1769-1830

Lady Henrietta Drummond (1783-1854) and her child

Drypoint, 22.5 × 14.9cm
CD 6/i
National Gallery of Scotland, Edinburgh

[78]

After Sir Thomas Lawrence 1769-1830

Lady Henrietta Drummond (1783-1854) and her Child, published 1826

Drypoint on India paper, 22.5 × 14.9cm
CD 6/iii
National Gallery of Scotland, Edinburgh

[79]

Agnes Geddes, The Artist's Mother (died 1828), 1822, published 1826

Drypoint, 24.3 × 15.3cm
CD 7/vii
National Gallery of Scotland, Edinburgh
Illustrated on page 89 and back cover

[80]

William Martin (1744-1820)

Etching and drypoint, 22.6 × 16.2cm
CD 9/i
National Gallery of Scotland, Edinburgh

[81]

Alexander Nasmyth (1758-1840) c.1825

Drypoint, 19.9 × 13.7cm (trimmed on all sides)
CD 10/ix
The British Museum, London

[82]

Nathaniel Plimer (1757 - after 1822)

Drypoint, 18.6 × 13.2cm
CD 12/iii
The British Museum, London
Illustrated on page 24

[83]

John Sheepshanks (1787-1863) c.1826-8

Etching and drypoint 14.8 × 12.1cm
CD 13/vi
Victoria and Albert Museum, London
Illustrated on page 94

[84]

Archibald Skirving (1749-1819)

Etching, 22.3 × 16.3cm
CD 15/i (second plate)
National Gallery of Scotland, Edinburgh

[85]

Archibald Skirving (1749-1819)

Etching touched with drypoint, 22.3 × 16.3cm
CD 15/v (second plate)
National Gallery of Scotland, Edinburgh

[86]

Andrew Geddes and Archibald Skirving

Archibald Skirving (1749-1819)

Etching, drypoint and aquatint, 22 × 15cm
CD 15/vi (second plate)
Scottish National Portrait Gallery, Edinburgh
Illustrated on page 30

[87]

Dull Reading: with Portraits of Daniel Terry (c.1780-1829) and Elizabeth (Nasmyth) Terry (1793-1862), published 1826

Etching and drypoint, 13.8 × 17.6cm
CD 16/iii
National Gallery of Scotland, Edinburgh
Illustrated on page 90

[88]

Child with an Apple: Portrait of the Artist's Niece Agnes Paul (died 1866), published 1826

Drypoint, 15.9 × 13.4cm
CD 18/v
National Gallery of Scotland, Edinburgh

[89]

Whim, Peebles-shire

Drypoint, 9.8 × 13.2cm
CD 22/ii
National Gallery of Scotland, Edinburgh

[90]

Whim, Peebles-shire, 1922

Drypoint, 9.8 × 13.2cm
CD 22/iii (impression from the cancelled plate)
National Gallery of Scotland, Edinburgh

[91]

The Field of Bannockburn and the Bore Stone, 1826

Etching and drypoint, 12.2 × 16.8cm
CD 23/iii
The British Museum, London
Illustrated on page 92

[92]

Trees in Hyde Park, with a Cow Feeding

Etching, 8.3 × 12.5cm
CD 24/i
National Gallery of Scotland, Edinburgh

[93]

Trees in Hyde Park, with a Cow Feeding, published 1826

Etching with some drypoint, 8.3 × 12.5cm
CD 24/ii
National Gallery of Scotland, Edinburgh

[94]

View in Caen Wood, Hampstead

Etching, 9.9cm × 15.2
CD 25/ii
National Gallery of Scotland, Edinburgh

[95]

View in Richmond Park (?) with a Fountain

Drypoint, 17.6 × 24.2cm
CD 27/ii
National Gallery of Scotland, Edinburgh

[96]

Landscape View from a Hill with Trees and Figures

Drypoint, 14.2 × 17.8cm
CD 28/i
The British Museum, London

[97]

Landscape View from a Hill with Trees and Figures

Drypoint, 14.2 × 17.8cm
CD 28/ii
The British Museum, London

[98]

Halliford on Thames: Stump of a Tree in Centre

Etching, 16.1 × 15.8cm
CD 29/iv (printed by Ernest Stephen Lumsden 1883–1948)
National Gallery of Scotland, Edinburgh

[99]

Halliford on Thames : Long Row of Trees

Drypoint, 15 × 22.8cm
CD 31/i
Victoria and Albert Museum, London

[100]

Peckham Rye, published 1826

Drypoint and aquatint on India paper (laid), 15.3 × 23.1cm
CD 32/v
National Gallery of Scotland, Edinburgh
Illustrated on page 92

[101]

Claude Lorrain's House in Rome, c.1830

Etching and drypoint, 14.5 × 18.2cm
CD 33/ii
Victoria and Albert Museum, London
Illustrated on page 92

[102]

Landscape in the Manner of Rembrandt

Drypoint, 11.6 × 24cm (trimmed)
CD 34/i
The British Museum, London

[103]

Landscape in the Manner of Rembrandt

Drypoint, 11.6 × 24cm (trimmed)
CD 34/ii
The British Museum, London

[104]

Christ Disputing with the Doctors in the Temple after Andrea Schiavone (Andrea Meldolla) (c.1510–1563), published 1826

Etching, drypoint and aquatint, 19.9 × 30.2cm
CD 36/iv
National Gallery of Scotland, Edinburgh
Illustrated on page 86

[105]

Self-portrait as Rembrandt van Rijn (1606–1669)

Etching, 15.6 × 12.3cm
CD 44 (only state, second plate)
National Gallery of Scotland, Edinburgh
Illustrated on page 89

[106]

Nicholas Rockox, after Sir Peter Paul Rubens (1577–1640), 1822; published 1826

Etching and drypoint on India paper (laid), 22.8 × 16.5cm
CD 45/vii
National Gallery of Scotland, Edinburgh

[107]

The Infanta Isabella Clara Eugenia (1566–1633)

Drypoint, 22.5 × 15cm
CD 46/v (printed by Ernest Stephen Lumsden 1883–1948)
National Gallery of Scotland, Edinburgh

[108]

After Sir Anthony van Dyck 1599–1641, before 1826
Philip IV of Spain (1605–1665)

Etching and drypoint on India paper (laid), 18.3 × 12.4cm
CD 47/vii
National Gallery of Scotland, Edinburgh

[109]

Sir Anthony van Dyck (1599–1641)
after a Self-portrait

Etching and drypoint, 15 × 12.3cm
CD 48/ii
The British Museum, London

[110]

Portfolio Etchings by A. Geddes
London, Published by A. Geddes,
58 Brook Street, Grosvenor Square

Perth Museum & Art Gallery, Perth & Kinross
Council

ETCHING PLATES

[111]

Sir William Allan (1782–1850)

Copper etching plate (cancelled),
22.5 × 15.2cm
CD 1
National Gallery of Scotland, Edinburgh

[112]

Agnes Geddes, The Artist's Mother
(died 1828)

Copper etching plate (cancelled),
24.3 × 15.3cm
CD 7
National Gallery of Scotland, Edinburgh

[113]

The Field of Bannockburn and the
Bore Stone

Copper etching plate, 12.3 × 17cm
CD 23
National Gallery of Scotland, Edinburgh

[114]

Halliford on Thames

Copper etching plate (cancelled),
10.2 × 16.2cm
CD 29
National Gallery of Scotland, Edinburgh

III · WORKS BY OTHER
ARTISTS

OIL PAINTINGS

[115]

Sir William Fettes Douglas 1822–1891
David Laing (1793–1878), 1862

Oil on canvas, 25.5 × 63.5cm
Scottish National Portrait Gallery, Edinburgh
Illustrated on page 84

[116]

Attributed to Sir Anthony van Dyck
1599–1641
Portrait of a Young Man

Oil on canvas, laid on wood panel,
77.5 × 56cm
On loan from the Duke of Sutherland to the
National Gallery of Scotland, Edinburgh
Illustrated on page 49

[117]

Studio of Sir Anthony van Dyck
1599–1641
The Infanta Isabella Clara Eugenia
(1566–1633)

Oil on canvas, 143.5 × 114.3cm
Walker Art Gallery, National Museums and
Galleries on Merseyside
Illustrated on page 49

[118]

Frans Hals *c*.1580–1666
Young Man Holding a Skull
(Vanitas), c.1626–8

Oil on canvas, 92.2 × 88cm
National Gallery, London
Illustrated on page 81

MINIATURES

[119]

Nathaniel Plimer 1757 – after 1822
*Self-portrait, c.*1805–10

Watercolour on ivory, height 8.9cm
On loan from a private collection to the
Scottish National Portrait Gallery, Edinburgh

[120]

Adela Plimer, Mrs Andrew Geddes
1791–1881
Self-portrait

Watercolour on ivory, height 5cm
Scottish Private Collection

WORKS ON PAPER

[121]

Alexander Nasmyth 1758–1840
Andrew Geddes Sketching in the Kent
Countryside

Pencil on paper, 15.5 × 24cm
National Gallery of Scotland, Edinburgh
Illustrated on page 26

[122]

John Burnet 1784–1868 after
Rembrandt van Rijn 1606–1669
The Toilet of Bathsheba, 1815

Etching and engraving on India paper (laid),
41.2 × 55.4cm
The British Museum, London
Illustrated on page 38

[123]

William Ward 1766–1826 after
Andrew Geddes
Revd Dr Thomas Chalmers
(1780–1847), 1822

Mezzotint, 50.6 × 35.6cm
Scottish National Portrait Gallery, Edinburgh
Illustrated on page 46

IV · MANUSCRIPTS AND PRINTED BOOKS

MANUSCRIPTS

[124]

A Catalogue of the Books, Paintings and Prints belonging to David Geddes D. Auditor of Excise, 1777–93
Scottish Private Collection

[125]

Book of Disbursements
[David Geddes], 1777–94
Fine Art Library, Edinburgh City Libraries and Information Services

PRINTED BOOKS AND EPHEMERA

[126]

A Catalogue of the Valuable and Choice Collection of Prints and Books of Prints, of the late Mr Colin Macfarquhar, of Edinburgh (Deceased)
(auctioneer, Mr King, Covent Garden, London 11–20 May 1796)
National Gallery of Scotland, Edinburgh

[127]

Catalogue of the Valuable Collection of Prints ... By the Antient and Modern Masters Formed with Superior Taste and Judgment, during a period exceeding Forty Years by David Geddes, Esq. of Edinburgh, dec.
(Auctioneer, T. Philipe, Warwick Street, Golden Square, London 30 April 1804 and five following days).
National Library of Scotland, Edinburgh

[128]

A Catalogue of the valuable and choice Collection of Pictures, the property of the late Mr David Geddes ... which will be sold ... 24th February 1804 ... by Mr William Martin (Edinburgh 1804)
National Library of Scotland, Edinburgh

[129]

Provincial Antiquities and Picturesque Scenery of Scotland with descriptive illustrations by Sir Walter Scott, Bart. (London 1826), vol.1
National Gallery of Scotland, Edinburgh

[130]

Prospectus for David Laing, *Etchings of Sir David Wilkie, R.A., Limner to HM for Scotland and by Andrew Geddes, A.R.A., with Biographical Sketches* (Edinburgh 1875)
National Gallery of Scotland, Edinburgh

[131]

David Laing, *Etchings by Sir David Wilkie, R.A., Limner to HM for Scotland and by Andrew Geddes, A.R.A., with Biographical Sketches* (Edinburgh 1875)
National Gallery of Scotland, Edinburgh

[132]

Ed. Samuel Smiles, James Nasmyth *Autobiography* (London 1883)
National Gallery of Scotland, Edinburgh